SCHOOLING AT HOME

PARENTS, KIDS, AND LEARNING

MOTHERING MAGAZINE

Edited by Anne Pedersen and Peggy O'Mara

John Muir Publications
Santa Fe, New Mexico

Dedicated
To the memory of
John Holt
(1923–1985)

John Muir Publications, P.O. Box 613, Santa Fe, NM 87504

© 1990 by Mothering Magazine
Cover © 1990 by John Muir Publications
All rights reserved. Published 1990
Printed in the United States of America

First edition. First printing

Library of Congress Cataloging-in-Publication Data

Schooling at home: parents, kids, and learning/[revised excerpts from] Mothering magazine: edited by Anne Pedersen and Peggy O'Mara.
    p. cm.
Includes bibliographical references.
ISBN 0-945465-52-1
1. Home schooling. I. Pedersen, Anne, 1949-   . II. O'Mara, Peggy. III. Mothering.
LC40.S36 1990
649'.68—dc20   89-78400
                                                                              CIP

Distributed to the book trade by:
W. W. Norton & Company, Inc.
New York, New York

Cover illustration and overall design: Sally Blakemore
Typographer: Copygraphics, Inc.
Printer: McNaughton & Gunn, Inc.

CONTENTS

PART IV: HOME SCHOOLING STORIES

FOREWORD

Children are the most learning-hungry beings in the world. Their continual questioning is wonderful to behold. The need for open-mindedness, imagination, and order; the need to think, to learn, and to know; to love and be loved; to dance, to sing, and to play—all these and more are basic behavioral needs of the child, at least as important as basic physical needs. It is by the encouragement of these basic behavioral needs that the education and socialization of the child proceeds.

Just as physical needs are genetically inborn, so, too, are basic behavioral needs. But behavioral needs exist initially only as potentialities; to become developed abilities, it is necessary that they be appropriately encouraged. For example, we would never learn to speak unless we received the encouragement that comes from being spoken to, and the way we speak echoes the models we have had. An ability is a trained potentiality or capacity, and learning is the increase in strength of any act through repetition. As we learn, our abilities are strengthened.

The word *education* comes from the Latin *educare*, meaning "to nourish and to cause to grow." The various essays in *Schooling at Home: Parents, Kids, and Learning* are beautifully designed to help parents and other care givers do just that, and to do so in a more authoritative and practical manner than any other work I know of.

The increased popularity of home schooling bears testimony to its importance as something more than a substitute for our often inadequate public and private schools. Home schooling is unsurpassed not only as a method of education and learning but also as a way to promote essential, invigorating bonding between members of a family. For those parents who are dissatisfied with their children's education in conventional schools and for those who would like to provide their children independent study within the framework of those schools, this book will prove a real boon. It offers an exhilarating adventure to all who read it.

—*Ashley Montagu*

Preface

Fifteen years ago, when my first child was a baby, I began exploring the educational options available in my community. The prospects were so disheartening that I considered moving. I was interested in starting an alternative school, but there was not enough support in our area to sustain a school of this nature. About this time, the first issue of John Holt's *Growing Without Schooling* newsletter arrived in the mail. My reaction to reading it was to heave a great sigh of relief. It confirmed my growing suspicion that learning didn't have to be difficult.

During those early years of examining educational options, it seemed to me that I was not so much opposed to the public schools as I was simply *in favor* of learning at home, which was a natural evolution of our family life-style. We were already very much home oriented: I had given birth to our children at home, and we had our own home business. Also, I had learned that I could trust my children. Their perceptions of their experiences were usually accurate, and those experiences did not seem to indicate a desire for formalized learning. As I had been able to trust them to wean themselves, learn to crawl, walk, speak, and use the toilet, it seemed that I could rightly look to them for clues as to when they were ready to learn to read and write.

I was also uncertain as to the effect of formalized learning on their individuality at this young age and was very concerned about being separated from my children when they were young. Five or six years old seemed too young an age for them to leave home for long periods of time. It seemed logical to me that if my children spent thirty hours a week away from home, soon the values of their peers would supplant the values of our home. Certainly, being exposed to other values is necessary at some point, but I felt that if it happened too early in their education my children would be at risk.

I have four children, aged 15, 13, 11, and 7. All of them have been home schooled. With each one I have worried whether he or she was getting a good enough education. In the early years of our home schooling, we registered with the state as a private school and filled out simple paperwork twice a year. We gave our school a name and assigned formal grade levels because this made it easier for the children to answer people's questions about where they went to school and what grade they were in. We even had stationery, a logo, and a motto that read, "Every experience carries its lesson."

We originally intended to use our private school as an umbrella for other home schooling families, but during most years there have been only four students at Sandhill Day School.

Over the years, I've gathered a lot of supplies from a variety of sources. I particularly like to order from textbook companies because they have good photographs and descriptions of the books, and it is possible to order only small quantities of books, teacher's editions, and workbooks. I've also gotten books and supplies from large office and school-supply stores, as well as from local public school book depositories. Sometimes schools give away old books. In addition, universities often have resource libraries for teachers, where individual books and teaching aids can be checked out. College-level correspondence courses may also be appropriate for home schoolers. Some of the better children's magazines have issues and supplements that can be used for lessons as well.

I spend a lot of money on quality art supplies for the children and take them to classes in drama, dance, singing, and art. These classes, along with our busy personal life and the fact that they home school with their siblings, keep them in touch with other people, which is important so that they do not experience a sense of isolation. Home schooling four children at once can challenge the individualized learning characteristic of the home environment, but the age spread in our family is such that the two older children went on to formalized school at a time when I felt that the younger two needed more attention academically.

Having been a teacher myself, I am sympathetic to formal schools and teachers, although I am critical of some modern educational practices. I do not believe that our society allocates enough money to education or appreciates the importance of a low student-to-teacher ratio. Neither do we fully acknowledge that children learn from a living model. Home schooling underscores the diversity present in our population and the variety of educational choices that are possible. When we open ourselves to the dissidents in our society, when we appreciate and understand the home schooling choice, we help to revitalize education in America.

Home schooling represents a great leap of faith. Over the years, I found that I had to continually trust my children to learn what they needed, at their own pace. I had to trust that their early time of imaginative play and creative learning would give them a strong foundation for more abstract study later, rather than put them at a disadvantage. And although I felt strongly that the kind of socialization characteristic of the early years in school is often more harmful to children than helpful, I sometimes wondered if my children were meeting "enough" friends. And it surprised me that what I thought of as a marvelous educational experiment was sometimes a source of embarrassment to the children themselves.

Children do not know of the diversity that exists within our society, and often adults don't seem to, either; they tend to stick to commonly accepted practices, educational or otherwise. However, during the ten years that we have been home schooling, we have experienced a great change in its social acceptability. I have noticed that my youngest child is particularly confident when asked about school. "Oh, I go to home school," she replies. No one flinches anymore. She certainly doesn't. Luckily, we live in a community where alternatives are common, so that while people may sometimes be surprised to hear about home schooling, very few are critical. In fact, every child who has heard of it for the first time has been excited and has gone home, I would guess, to ask his or her parents some challenging questions.

I have often wondered whether or not my children were at grade level in certain subjects. They have not learned to read or do square roots or play instruments at amazing ages. And while their accomplishments and their spirits astound me at times, I now see home schooling as a contributor to, rather than the cause of, those achievements. It has been important for me to temper my enthusiasm for home schooling with my awareness of a need for balance. I have not wanted my children to feel inferior to their peers or to be unnecessarily discouraged because they could not yet differentiate between their lack of rote skills and a lack of ability.

This became clear when my older two children entered the school system. My eldest daughter began high school last year after eight years of home schooling. She had learned easily at home and had been presented with a diversity of material. She passed a test to enter a private school and was advised to take math in summer school to prepare for the first year.

Those initial few months required intense adjustment. There were times when I wanted to do her homework for her. She was adjusting not only to the challenging new subject matter but also to the realities of test taking, the sometimes puzzling school procedures, and a newly school-centered social life. However, after this adjustment period, school became manageable. By the end of the year, she had received high honors, doing particularly well in math.

My eldest son entered a public junior high school at the beginning of eighth grade after attending an alternative school for a few months at the end of seventh grade. Even more than his sister, he was eager for the social life that school represented to him. He had more catching up to do in his subjects, but he, too, surprised me by how quickly he did this. The adjustment to the frenetic school social scene was as difficult as the adjustment to the academics. But then, for both children the "first day of school" came a lot later than for most.

I don't think of home schooling as a "cause" that needs promoting or a "salvation" for children. It has rather been a rich source of bonding and togetherness for our family, and I hope that for my children it will prove to have been a strong foundation for their later learning. The rising interest in home schooling today shows that, as a society, we need to do a better job of educating the whole person. We also need to realize that whether one chooses home schooling or formalized schooling, it is always essential for the parent to be involved in the child's learning. Just as I worried whether my children were getting enough from home schooling, so must other parents, regardless of school setting, wonder this same thing and work to ensure the best education for their children.

Our increasingly complex society demands equally sophisticated technological skills; to be able to respond appropriately requires solid human values. More and more, we need the ability to adapt to the unknown, the ability to maintain personal balance in the midst of complexity, and the readiness to learn new things. Home schooling both preserves the sense of learning as a vital and exciting experience and places that learning in the context of personal and family experience. It provides a model of learning that, more than others available, accurately reflects the diversity of who we are as a people as well as who we are as individuals. Instead of the question "What school do you go to?" home schooling encourages the focus of "What did you learn today?"

The individuals and families included in this book have braved the unknown. They have thought about and experimented with difficult questions of education and have left guideposts for others to follow. *Schooling at Home: Parents, Kids, and Learning* includes articles previously published in *Mothering* magazine as well as some new and updated material. This book represents the educational process in motion. It covers a wide range of new thoughts on education, and as such, is of value to home schoolers as well as to those simply asking questions about learning.

Home schooling reminds us that learning is a much more fluid process than we might have realized; it is a dynamic process that cannot and will not be contained in a room or a book. We learn from the living model of life as it happens. The success of home schooling reminds us that learning is simultaneously more fragile than perhaps we once thought and much easier than we often believe it to be.

—*Peggy O'Mara*

PART I:
THOUGHTS ON LEARNING

How We Learn

Andy LePage

One of the biggest obstacles faced by parents and teachers of young and adolescent children is an erroneous belief about how children learn. Adults have been schooled to think that they alone can impart knowledge to children and that the more knowledge they put across, the better teachers they will be. This belief is far from the truth. Children learn by being immersed in the world, by using all their senses—by experiencing life in their own unique ways.

Children question everything. They make connections as they grow and use their own internal systems to make sense of the world. Surrounded by all that is, they gradually choose where they want to focus their attention. Through an internal process that separates the wheat from the chaff, children intuitively and merrily move away from whatever does not capture their interest toward whatever does. They do this many times daily, without a second thought.

Parents and teachers can learn a lot by immersing themselves in the child's world. When we observe children's behavior, one cardinal lesson becomes clear: More often than not, children can "do it themselves." Well-meaning adults must be willing to gradually let go and let children develop their own resourcefulness. Our job as adults is to offer guidance, answer questions as best we can, provide encouragement, assist in the development of a "can do" attitude, and help children gradually wean from dependency so that they may ultimately become self-sufficient.

In our society, we frequently overprotect our children in their formative years. Holding them down and keeping them from confronting situations that would help them become more mature can have repercussions in later life. By adolescence, many children are not motivated to do even the simplest tasks, such as keeping their room clean

or taking care of personal hygiene, let alone the more challenging
responsibilities of utilizing their time meaningfully, making contribu-
tions to the family's well-being, and making responsible decisions.
The teenage years become especially difficult for parents, teachers,
and the teenagers themselves when the "can do" attitude was not
given full expression in the formative years.

Parents and teachers must learn that their job as care givers and
nurturers is really paradoxical. They must be available, yet always willing to back off and allow children to do things in their own ways and
for themselves. As a culture, we are abysmally poor at backing off.[1]
The early influence of Puritanism may have contributed to our belief
that parenting and teaching consist of handing on prepackaged
truths, neatly tied up and then spoonfed. But this form of nurturing
does not help children discover their own resourcefulness.

When we observe children's behavior, we learn that idle hands are
not the devil's workshop. Children learn much by being internally
absorbed—in daydreaming or in periods of quietness. Unaware of this
fact, we often go to great extremes to keep children "occupied." We
become anxious and decide they need another agenda—ours! The
scene typically goes like this: "What are you doing?" asks the parent.
"Nothing," says the child. "You must be doing *something*," says the
parent.

Underlying such dialogues is a hidden desire to catch the child
doing something "wrong." Yet, how often do we have our hearts and
minds set on catching our children doing something right, something
terrific? The inability to allow for inner absorption can set up patterns
that interfere with the development of trust.

Trusting children to "be"—without necessarily having something to
"do"—is a feeling-oriented rather than content-oriented approach.
This approach invites the deeper levels of communication we need to
have with our children. Without intruding on quiet moments, parents can share with their children the feelings associated with these
moments. One way to do this is by asking such questions as "What do
you like about the music?" "Where is your dolly going on her journey?" "Which rhythm instruments would you like to play with?" "Tell
me what you saw in your dream!" "What were you feeling when you
saw the horse?" These open-ended questions engage children and
their world.

Children also learn by having models who reflect excitement and encouragement. The parental enthusiasm that accompanies and inspires the child's initial attempts at crawling, standing, and then walking can serve as a prototype for that child's future learning experiences. Parents and teachers of the very young can indeed be some of the most encouraging people the child will ever meet.

Because encouragement is usually so high during the early years, young children generally learn quickly and readily. This is not to say that they will walk, for example, before they are ready to: they walk on their own timetable, not on ours. However, when children feel love and positive regard coming from many quarters—parents, aunts, uncles, grandparents, clerks in neighborhood stores—they begin to trust that they *can* walk, and so they soon do. Such experiences lead to a later belief in their own judgments and trust in themselves.

Unfortunately, we have forgotten this early lesson. Parents and teachers tend to address teenagers in an altogether different manner, in a way that does not inspire learning. Imagine saying to a crawling baby, "You'll *never* learn to walk because you're lazy!" or "You can do better!" or "By the time I come home, I want to see you walking!" We cannot fathom addressing our infants in this way, and yet these messages are given repeatedly to our youth in homes and classrooms across the country.

What transforms so many parents and teachers? Why do the encouragers become discouragers? Perhaps they have given up their initial immersion in the child's world and, with it, a certain depth of understanding. Perhaps, as the child grows older, these adults fail to recognize that learning is a process involving facts *and* feelings. Perhaps they fail to back off and let the child learn by trial and error. Such failures can easily rob the adults themselves of their own personal maturity as well as the child of powerful growth experiences.

When we observe children's behavior, we also find that they learn well from the world *as it is*, with all its ups and downs. Parents and teachers need not feel that they "should not" show their down side to children. A facade of a smile is not better than genuine tears: children see through facades.

The 1987 movie *Moonstruck* illustrates this principle. Some emotionally complex, difficult decisions about love and life are laid out at the kitchen table for all the family to see and deal with. Here we find no whitewash, nothing couched in fancy terms—just the guts of what it means to live as fully as possible. In the witnessing, problems get solved, families heal, and life becomes not only worthwhile but quite beautiful. This is learning at a high level.

We wonder about the wisdom of letting young children witness difficult events: a husband and father having an affair, a daughter searching for the right person with whom to share her life, a grown man refusing to change his clinging relationship with his mother. With parental support and dialogue, however, exposure to such real-life situations can be a positive learning experience. People *do* have difficulties and *do* manage to deal with them. Children who have discussed these realities with their parents, and who have been trusted to make decisions and become responsible in their dealings with their friends, enter adolescence with awareness and resourcefulness. They also enter adolescence with the belief that their parents and teachers are able to communicate with them, are able to enter into their world, and are able to discuss drugs, sex, and relationships in an honest and meaningful way.

The optimum learning environment, both at home and at school, contains the following ingredients:

1. *Acceptance*. Children need to know in their bones that they are wanted, that they will be listened to, and that they will be unconditionally welcomed. Distinctions, prejudices, and exclusions do not inspire learning. Inclusive environments encourage inclusive processes.

2. *Touch*. Children need to be touched frequently in meaningful ways. Hugs, pats, kisses, holding, and rocking are universal forms of communication. Meaningful touch is one of the best builders of trust, and if trust has been broken, a loving touch can be one of its prime restorative measures.

3. *Trust*. Children imbued with a "can do" attitude love learning. Similarly, environments that foster belief and trust help a child to thrive. If a child is found to be untruthful, he or she must be gently shown that trust is the way and that truth is never punishable. (However, prearranged consequences for choices that youngsters make regulate their behavior in a positive way.) Children who have been trusted become teenagers who are willing to continue to trust.

4. *Encouragement*. Encouraging parents and teachers find "the good" in children and let them know it is noticed. Encouragers are asset-finders rather than fault-finders, and they look for the positive.

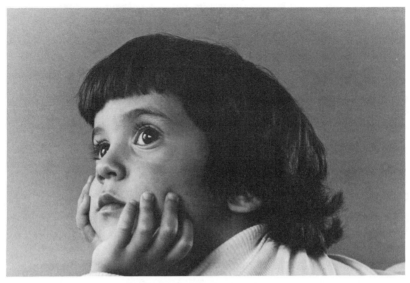

MARILYN NOLT

5. *Play*. Play has been called the very stuff of childhood, but it really is the very stuff of adolescence and adulthood as well. When we develop an attitude of play, we become more congenial, more open to spontaneity, more real in relationships, and more prone to humor. Play has no product; it is merely process. And as a process, it is transformative. Children can teach us how to learn while playing, how to make a game out of everything, and how to engage that part deep inside ourselves that needs to have fun.

6. *Celebration*. Children who have celebrated have experienced wonder in their lives. Moreover, they have delightful anchors in their sea of memories. Celebration can mean anything from a special visit from a distant relative to a Fourth of July party to the rituals around Christmas, Hanukkah, Chinese New Year, birthdays, or Sunday dinner—whatever is worthy of celebrating. These are times for coming together, for letting go, for giving up work (except for the preparations, which can be shared by everyone), for "time off." Folk dancing, religious rituals, circle dancing near a river, singing, eating special foods—these occasions become warm remembrances that make life special.

You may augment this list as you wish. But be sure to note that the ingredients for a learning environment cost almost no money, yet bring great joy and learning to individuals, families, and classrooms. Moreover, they are essential to any and all learning. No family or school setting can make sense without them.

Notes

1. For an excellent discussion on this point, see Jean Liedloff, *The Continuum Concept* (New York: Warner Communications, 1978), 140, 142.

A Decent Learning Situation

Herbert Kohl

At the minimum, a decent learning situation should:

1. Respect the arts as essential to life, treat science and mathematics as arts, and nurture all of these areas in classical and experimental ways;

2. Help young people learn to analyze events in the world (both near home and far away) and to speak capably and intelligently about their opinions;

3. Introduce the magic of literature, focus on the content of a work, and be sensitive to the intent of the author;

4. Help children learn to accept criticism offered in the spirit of love and to offer criticism in the same way;

5. Help young people feel solidarity with all of the peoples, animals, and plants on earth and be willing to act on this feeling;

6. Make it possible for young people to know adults who live the beliefs they teach, no matter how imperfectly;

7. Create a writing environment in which the writer is not afraid to express her or his ideas, opinions, and feelings;

8. Eliminate all grading and testing procedures that do not help children learn what they want to learn;

9. Respect classical learning and children's creativity, bouncing them off each other;

10. Abandon the notion that some students are "better" than others.

The world is imperfect, and it is imbalance and imperfection that make life both a troubled and rewarding ongoing adventure. In helping children learn about the world, we can draw on our connections with the past and on our resolve to struggle against small and large forms of injustice, while having some fun along the way.

MICHAEL WEISBROT

A mural painted on a wall in Chile during the time when Salvador Allende was president proclaims that in a good society "los unicos privilegiados los niños." Loosely interpreted, this says that in a decent world the only privileged people will be the children, who will—every one of them—have all of the resources of society to help them grow and, as adults, pass the same gifts of love on to their children.

I do not believe in isolating children from the pain in the world, which they experience anyway. Education should be a big stew composed of elements from the past, dreams of the future, and confrontations with the pains of the present. It should involve fun and also the hard work of understanding the brilliance and personal importance of creators from all cultures of the world, creators as diverse as Shakespeare, Virginia Woolf, Alexander Pushkin, Wole Soyinka, and Langston Hughes.

Young people should know of the struggles and joys of other people throughout the world and not see themselves in small, protected environments. They should have an opportunity to cry out against apartheid and sing along with the complex and joyous struggle music being created in South Africa; they should hear the love songs of Chilean martyr Victor Jara; they should be fully part of the world and have a vision of a better place for which they are willing to work.

Of course, the setting for this kind of learning must be open and must manifest a love for the spirit of democracy. Such a learning place would respect differences, incorporate debate, encourage dissension, and insist upon analysis of ideas, structures, and strategies. Ideally, it would be a circle of learning, where Plato and Marx would be as present as John Lee Hooker and J. S. Bach, and where students would feel the presence of others who have tried to come to compassionate terms with life. The primary purpose of such learning places is to inspire a love of learning and a fearlessness toward the unfamiliar.

Who are the teachers of this kind of learning? They are people who never presume to know which children can or cannot learn. They are individuals who never give up on a person and never stop learning themselves. Other than feeling connected with the whole world and maintaining, as Che Guevara put it, "great feelings of love," it does not make much difference who you teach or where you teach if you need to teach.

3

Nature and Nurture

Edward T. Clark, Jr.

Kahlil Gibran, in the section "On Children" in his book *The Prophet*, reminds us that children are not possessions but have a unique destiny of their own:

> Your Children are not your children.
> They are the sons and daughters of Life's longing for itself.
> They come through you but not from you,
> And though they are with you yet they belong not to you.
> You may give them your love but not your thoughts,
> For they have their own thoughts.
> You may house their bodies but not their souls,
> For their souls dwell in the house of tomorrow, which you cannot visit, not even in your dreams.

Katharine Kersey, in her book *Sensitive Parenting*, suggests a similar thought. "Children are given to us—on loan—for a very short period of time. They come to us like packets of flower seeds, with no pictures on the cover and no guarantees. We do not know what they will look like, be like, act like, or have the potential to become. Our job, like the gardener's, is to meet their needs as best we can: to give proper nourishment, love, attention, and caring, and to hope for the best."[1]

These concepts take us light years beyond the limitations of the rationalistic, scientific "nature versus nurture" debate that has confused at least two generations of parents, including my own. This debate has recently been refueled. On one side of the question are some geneticists, who seek to reduce personality, character traits, and emotions to particular genes that will someday be able to be engineered according to human preference. On the other side are some behaviorists, who propose that all behavior results from, and is therefore traceable to, specific, identifiable environmental factors.

Each of these perspectives is based on a set of reductionist, materialistic, and mechanistic assumptions about the nature of reality. The impact of these particular assumptions is summarized by Joseph Chilton Pearce in his book *The Magical Child*: "We have a cultural notion that if children were not engineered, if we did not manipulate them, they would grow up as beasts in the field."[2] Because the assumptions we hold effectively shape our behavior, it is important to explore those that have shaped several generations of scientific thinking about childhood.

The first of these assumptions is that everything that is real can be reduced to physical matter and, as such, can be measured empirically. Based on this premise, science has reduced both intelligence and learning to items that can be quantified by IQ tests and Scholastic Aptitude Tests (SAT) scores. At the same time, it has reduced mind to the electrical and chemical interactions of the physical brain.

The second assumption grows out of Newton's premise that the universe is a giant clock in which the whole is equal to, but never more than, the sum of its parts. Based on this mechanistic premise, humans are considered to be no more than wonderfully crafted machines. It follows logically that if we can identify all the parts and discover how each one works, it will someday be possible not only to replicate but also improve on nature's handiwork. The dream of artificial intelligence is based on just such assumptions about the nature of the human organism.

The third assumption is a rational consequence of the first two. Behavior, too, can be reduced to a set of physical, cause-and-effect interactions that follow logical, identifiable, and measurable patterns. Just as any malfunction of a machine can be traced to the malfunction of a specific part, so can inappropriate behavior be traced to a specific malfunction of the child. Thus, we have a long list of "learning disabilities" that, once identified, can be corrected. This has led to an entirely new profession of learning- and behavior-adjustment specialists, who have been trained to "engineer" and "manipulate" children in order to eliminate such perceived problems.

Every parent knows intuitively that these assumptions are false. Unfortunately, in a society that deifies rational pragmatism, times arise when one's own intuition does not seem to offer sufficient evidence on which to base crucial child-rearing decisions.

The nature of living organisms cannot be reduced to, predicated on, or created from their parts. Children represent a potential that can be only anticipated. Call it life, spirit, consciousness, or, as the ancient Hebrews termed it, breath. Refer to it as will, thought, or mind. Regardless of how we define this potential, we must acknowledge that it reflects the mysterious, unknowable elements of existence that are irreducible to quantifiable physical matter.

All children, apart from those who are severely brain-damaged, have a virtually unlimited and unmeasurable potential for what we call intelligence. Howard Gardner of Harvard University has identified seven forms of intelligence, only two of which have been given credence by our educational system. In addition to linguistic and logical-mathematical intelligence, with which we are familiar, Gardner distinguishes the following five forms of intelligence: bodily-kinesthetic, musical, spatial, and two forms of personal intelligence—interpersonal (knowing how to deal with others) and intrapersonal (knowledge of self). No single form of intelligence is given priority over any other, for each is as important as the others. Based on this theory of multiple intelligences, Gardner concludes that every child quite possibly has the potential to be a genius in at least one of these areas.

Thinking and learning are innate processes that are intuitive, whole-brain, integrative, and creative. They are reducible neither to isolated right- and left-hemisphere brain activity, nor to the purely cognitive, rational domain usually associated with thinking and learning. As with all organic processes, they follow a natural developmental pattern that must be honored if a child is to be intellectually and emotionally healthy.

It is usually when children leave home and begin some form of schooling that this developmental process tends to be interrupted. In their eagerness to provide the best education possible, well-meaning parents and teachers encourage children to read, write, and calculate before the organism is developmentally ready. Such a practice is much like force-feeding hothouse plants: they may bloom on demand, but their capacity to sustain growth and survive without an undue amount of attention is limited.

One of the great ironies of educational reform is that although four-year-olds may be our society's most creative problem solvers (try hiding the cookie jar from them), by the time they reach fourth grade, someone has to "teach" them creative problem-solving skills. Current evidence concludes that many educational problems, including

MARILYN NOLT

"learning disabilities," reflect a "brain antagonistic" curriculum—a curriculum in which the content and methodology do not match the appropriate developmental capacities of the child.

   Most of us seldom question the assumptions that form the foundation of our thinking. In a pragmatic world, we dismiss assumptions, philosophy, and theories as irrelevant. We prefer new techniques to new ideas. What we have not yet realized is the essential role that assumptions play in determining our behavior. Assumptions form the foundation upon which our mental models of the world are built. These models, in turn, shape our behavior. In short, the assumptions we hold about the nature of reality and, consequently, about human nature have profound consequences in the way we raise our children. If parents assume that children are inherently wild beasts that must be tamed, they will focus on control in order to shape "good" behavior. On the other hand, if they assume that children are like unmarked flower seeds, with innate potential that is unpredictable and unmeasurable, they will follow the gardener's wisdom of "tuning in" to the plant. As Katharine Kersey reminds us, the gardener "knows that all plants are different, need varying amounts of care and attention, and grow at different rates of speed."[3]

   Our educational system, as currently organized, is based on the old reductionist, mechanistic, materialistic assumptions. While I have yet to find one administrator or teacher who really believes in these outdated postulates, these ideas nevertheless continue to shape our views of learning. It is therefore crucial that parents who intuitively acknowledge a different set of assumptions about the nature of reality think carefully through the implications of these assumptions in parenting their children. After all, the assumptions that we hold probably do more to shape our behavior as parents than any other single factor.

I suspect that all parents, at one time or another, dream that their child could become a genius. We now know that such a dream may not be a fantasy. To paraphrase a familiar aphorism, "If I had believed it, I would have seen it." Or, as Einstein once said, "Imagination is more important than knowledge."

Notes

1. Katharine Kersey, *Sensitive Parenting* (Washington, D.C.: Acropolis Books, Ltd., 1983), 9.

2. Joseph Chilton Pearce, *The Magical Child* (New York: Bantam Books, 1980).

3. Kersey, *Sensitive Parenting.*

4

UTOPIAN SCHOOLS IN THE HERE AND NOW

Thomas Armstrong

Hardly anyone talks about educational utopias anymore. We seem to be too caught up in test scores, basic skills, teacher burnout, school violence, and so-called excellence to be concerned with visions of what our schools really could be at their best.

The early 1970s gave rise to exciting books like George Leonard's *Education and Ecstasy* and John Mann's *Learning to Be*, which painted fantasy pictures of futuristic schools that educated the total spectrum of human capability. In Leonard's book, children used computer-assisted technology to interact with almost every symbol known to human culture. Mann's book described a utopian school where children attended "empathy classes" and simulated trips to Mars. Now, nearly twenty years later, some of these fantasies seem laughably outdated, whereas others are just being realized. In their time, however, these books revealed a freshness of vision and an unabashed impulse to explore the heights of possibility in education, something of which we haven't seen much evidence in the 1980s.

As we move into the 1990s, perhaps we will bring together the idealism of the seventies with the materialism of the eighties and produce utopian schools grounded in the here and now. Already we have many fine examples of schools that seem headed in this direction. Waldorf education, as a whole, is one of the best examples of a true "living out" of utopian principles (and these schools were envisioned sixty years ago!). Individual public and independent schools across the country have likewise created shining examples of schools reaching for the best.

A New Paradigm

Parents and educators in search of a new paradigm for schools can find a wealth of inspiration in Howard Gardner's theory of multiple intelligences. Dr. Gardner, a psychologist and codirector of the Harvard Project on Human Potential, is author of *Frames of Mind*, a veritable handbook for educational utopias. In this book, he suggests that our concept of intelligence—fashioned from years of experience with IQ testing—is far too limited.

According to Gardner, we possess not one but seven distinct forms of intelligence: linguistic, logical-mathematical, spatial, bodily-kinesthetic, musical, interpersonal, and intrapersonal. His theory is different from many other currently popular human-potential approaches in that it is supported by the most up-to-date academic research in neuropsychology, psychological testing, developmental work with young children, and cross-cultural studies, as well as by biographical accounts of exceptional ability among scientists, artists, musicians, and individuals skilled in many other fields.

Gardner argues convincingly that Western society as a whole, and its schools in particular, seem to reinforce linguistic and logical-mathematical forms of intelligence while neglecting other ways of knowing. Teachers love children who are good with words and logic. However, children who show ability in dance, art, music, social relations, intuition, drama, and other areas of self-expression tend not to receive as much recognition. In my own research, I have found that many children with talents in these neglected intelligences are in fact likely to be labeled "learning disabled" if they do not perform adequately on their assigned worksheets and pop quizzes. In order to bring these children back into the mainstream and also empower the millions of culturally diverse children in our country, schools must provide a broad spectrum of classroom methods and activities.

Full-Spectrum Learning Environment

Gardner's model of the seven intelligences provides a solidly grounded structure that can be used in designing a full-spectrum learning environment for children. Because each child possesses all seven kinds of intelligence, a truly integrated curriculum can be developed to address every intelligence in a balanced way. And because, according to my experience, each child has a personal learning style that emphasizes certain intelligences over others, parents and teachers also need to be sensitive to individual differences and give children methods and approaches tailored to their own uniqueness.

Children with strength in a particular intelligence demonstrate the ability to work well with a specific way of processing information within a given symbol system. Primarily linguistic children, for example, learn through words; logical-mathematical children, through concepts; spatial children, through images; bodily-kinesthetic children, through tactile and bodily sensations; musical children, through melody and rhythm; interpersonal children, through social interaction; and intrapersonal children, through self-paced study.

Following are some examples of educational tools that can meet this broad range of learning abilities:

1. *Linguistic intelligence*: Books, tape recorders, typewriters, word processors, label makers, printing sets, storytelling, talking books, writing materials, discussions, debates, and public speaking.

2. *Logical-mathematical intelligence*: Strategy games (chess, checkers, Go), logic puzzles (Rubik's cube), science kits, computer programming software, nature equipment, brain teasers, Cuisenaire rods, and detective games.

3. *Spatial intelligence*: Films, slides, videos, diagrams, charts, maps, art supplies, cameras, telescopes, graphic-design software, three-dimensional building supplies (Legos, D-stix), optical illusions, visualization activities, and drafting materials.

4. *Bodily-kinesthetic intelligence*: Space to move, playgrounds, obstacle courses, hiking trails, swimming pools, gymnasiums, model-building kits, wood-carving sets, modeling clay, animals, sports equipment, carpentry materials, machines, costumes for drama, and video games.

5. *Musical intelligence*: Percussion instruments, metronomes, computerized sound systems, records and tapes, musical instruments (pianos, guitars, saxophones), the human voice, the sounds of nature, and things to strum, tap, pluck, and blow into.

6. *Interpersonal intelligence*: Clubs, committees, after-school programs, social events, cooperative learning, interactive software, group games, discussions, group projects, simulations, competitive and noncompetitive sports, and peer teaching.

7. *Intrapersonal intelligence*: Self-paced instruction, individualized projects, solo games and sports, forts, tree houses, lofts and other spaces into which a child can retreat, diaries and journals, meditation, and self-esteem activities.

Brainstorming for Today's Classroom

The activities listed above are a starting place for parents and teachers interested in brainstorming strategies that can lead to a truly holistic education. One way to begin implementation is to designate seven specific areas for the seven intelligences. For example, each classroom or learning space might include a book nook (linguistic), a math/science lab (logical-mathematical), an art area (spatial), a carpeted open space (bodily-kinesthetic), a listening/performing center (musical), a group discussion table (interpersonal), and a quiet loft (intrapersonal).

Another way of applying Gardner's model is to design seven different ways of teaching a given skill, using the symbol systems of each intelligence. To teach reading, for example, a teacher or parent can link up the word-based symbol system to spatial intelligence by having children learn to read through rebuses (drawings that represent words, such as a picture of a bee to designate the word *be*) or by presenting the alphabet pictorially (a picture of a snake evolving into the letter *s*). Musically, children can learn to read by singing the lyrics to songs with simple vocabularies. Kinesthetically, children might act out written words in little pantomimes or trace letters on each other's backs. Mathematical children might learn reading easily when it is presented logically or through a computer software program. Interpersonally oriented children would probably enjoy leading a reading group or teaching a younger child to read, whereas intrapersonal children might prefer to teach themselves to read by going off to a quiet corner.

Many schools have already implemented the spectrum of intelligences in their classrooms, some without even knowing about Gardner's model. Certainly, Waldorf and Montessori schools integrate the seven intelligences in their own way, and open classrooms have been using "activity areas" for years. The Key School in Indianapolis, Indiana, is one of the first public schools in the nation to officially adopt Gardner's theory in organizing its curriculum.

Gardner's educational model articulates an ideal that many parents and teachers have cherished for years: that there are many ways of learning and knowing. At the same time, it expresses this ideal in a clear way that can be applied directly to any number of learning environments. Emerging from the hardheaded academic rigor of the

JILL FINEBERG

1980s, this model nevertheless embodies principles that progressive and open educators have held dear for decades. Most importantly, it gives those of us who still love to dream about educational utopias a way to bring our lofty visions down to earth, where they can be realized in the lives of children.

Bibliography

Armstrong, Thomas. *In Their Own Way: Discovering and Encouraging Your Child's Personal Learning Style.* Los Angeles: Jeremy P. Tarcher, 1987.

Gardner, Howard. *Frames of Mind: The Theory of Multiple Intelligences.* New York: Basic Books, 1983.

Hendricks, Gay, and James Fadiman. *Transpersonal Education.* Englewood Cliffs, N.J.: Prentice-Hall, 1976.

Houston, Jean. *The Possible Human.* Los Angeles: Jeremy P. Tarcher, 1982.

Leonard, George B. *Education and Ecstasy.* Reprinted as *Education and Ecstasy and the Great School Reform Hoax.* Berkeley: North Atlantic Books, 1987.

Mann, John. *Learning to Be: The Education of Human Potential.* New York: The Free Press, 1972.

Montessori, Maria. *The Secret of Childhood.* New York: Ballantine, 1966.

Nyquist, Ewald B., and Gene R. Hawes. *Open Education: A Sourcebook for Parents and Teachers.* New York: Bantam, 1972.

Richards, Mary C. *Toward Wholeness: Rudolf Steiner Education in America.* Middletown, Conn.: Wesleyan University Press, 1980.

HOME-GROWN KIDS

Raymond Moore and Dorothy Moore

In 1967, when I left my position as graduate research and programs officer for the U.S. Department of Education, I felt frustrated. The "Great Society" millions the country was spending on its public schools seemed only to be creating new problems. The focus was more on dollars than on our children, and those dollars seemed to be confusing the situation more than helping it. After several years of further frustration directing an advanced-study center in Chicago, I, my wife Dorothy, and some colleagues in the education field decided to check the research on some areas of education that had been largely scuttled or ignored. What was the cost of ignoring the work ethic? Was institutionalizing children a sound educational trend? What were the best ages for school entrance? We activated the Hewitt Research Foundation (now replaced in this effort by the Moore Foundation) and went to work.

We sought guidance in our endeavour from top authorities in their fields: John Bowlby of the World Health Organization's early childhood program; Joseph Wepman of the University of Chicago; family psychologist Urie Bronfenbrenner of Cornell; early childhood specialists Sheldon White and Burton White of Harvard; parental attachment researcher Robert Hess of Stanford; learning authority William Rohwer of the University of California at Berkeley, as well as more than a hundred other noted researchers. Although these scholars hardly agreed on all elements of child development, we found an astonishing consensus about the use of caution in institutionalizing children early unless absolutely necessary and in subjecting unready juvenile nervous systems and minds to formal academic constraints. We discovered also, with the particular encouragement of Dr. Marvin Wirz, of the United States Office of Education's Division of the Handicapped, that while there was a plethora of research on these subjects, there was an astonishing indifference to it. Scholars often seem so absorbed in their own narrow specialities that they ignore the work of colleagues in related fields. An example of this tendency is learning specialists who insist on delaying formal education, yet advocate pre-school. Their research appears largely to disregard family psychologists like Urie Bronfenbrenner, who find that putting children of less than junior high school age in school results in excessive peer dependency, as these children often spend more time with their age-mates than they do with their parents.[1]

For such reasons, we initiated a series of multidisciplinary analyses, cross-referencing research on children's senses, brain development, cognition, coordination, and the like. Our investigative teams worked at Stanford University, the University of Colorado Medical School, and the National Center for Educational Statistics. We also utilized a Michigan-based analytical group. We analyzed more than eight thousand studies.[2] These included twenty studies that compared early school entrants with late starters. Additional early-childhood research grew out of experiences in the classroom with children who were misbehaving or not learning because they were simply not ready for the stress of early academics or out-of-home care. This work eventually led to our unexpected interest in home schools.

When we set out to determine the best ages for school entrance, our first concern was *formal learning*. However, we soon became concerned with *socialization* as well, realizing that it, too, involves the senses, cognition, brain development, coordination, and other aspects of the whole child. Our concern was increased when we realized that all fifty states have policies that require little children to attend school before they are ready.[3] Furthermore, they require boys to go to school at the same age as girls, even though it is well known that boys trail their female peers a year or so in general maturity levels at school entrance. Perhaps as a result, studies on sex-role differences find that there are between three and thirteen boys to every girl in learning-failure classes and a ratio of eight to one in programs for emotionally impaired children.[4]

Readiness for Formal Learning
As noted in 1972, when they were first published, our conclusions are actually quite old-fashioned. They seem new to some because they

differ from, and often challenge, conventional practice. We found that no child should be subjected to formal schooling constraints before age twelve. Peer pressures are especially dangerous for children younger than this. Bronfenbrenner warns of the dangers of peer association before fifth or sixth grade (about age twelve); William Rohwer of the University of California at Berkeley insists we could save millions of youngsters from academic failure if we would delay formal academics until junior high school.[5] Whereas Piaget told us that the average child reaches formal cognitive operations (adult-type perceptions and judgment) between ages fifteen and twenty, Texas school counselor David Quine reports that his research with University of Oklahoma professors Jack Henner and Ed Merrick finds that children who have the advantage of family life during their early years reach cognitive maturity between eight and twelve.[6]

Despite early excitement for school—on the part of parents as well as children—most early entrants (ages four, five, and six) are tired of school before third or fourth grade, the minimal levels where they should be starting. David Elkind, professor of child studies at Tufts University and author of *The Hurried Child*, calls them "burned out."[7] These children would have been far better off whenever possible waiting until age eight, ten, or later to start formal studies, either at home or at school in the third, fourth, or fifth grade.[8] Children who delay school entrance and then, when enrolled, are placed in the same grade as their age-mates quickly pass early entrants in achievement, behavior, and sociability. When early care is needed, it should be informal, warm, and responsive, in a setting similar to that of a good home, with a low adult-child ratio and sound values.

Vision, hearing, and other senses—as well as brain, cognitive, and coordination development—are not ready for normal academic sanctions until at least ages eight to ten or twelve. In these days of early schooling, most children's eyes are permanently damaged before age twelve. Neither the maturity of their delicate nervous systems, nor the "balancing" or "lateralizing" of the hemispheres of their young brains, nor yet the insulation of their nerve pathways provide a basis for thoughtful learning before at least age eight. We call the age range of eight to twelve, when these abilities tend to mature, the "integrated maturity level," or IML.[9]

The IML is a crucial consideration. Some children mature more rapidly in vision, others in hearing, still others in cognition. The sum

total of these abilities should be allowed plenty of time to develop. No
parents know, short of these ages, that their child's learning faculties
have matured.

Our findings on the IML coincide with the well-established findings of Piaget and others, namely, that children cannot normally handle cause-and-effect reasoning in any consistent way at today's school
entrance ages, whether they are bright or not.[10] In support of this
point and of Rohwer's contentions, Hasler Whitney, a distinguished
mathematician with Princeton's Institute for Advanced Studies, cites
L. P. Benezet's historic study that suggests that math should not be
forced on children before the seventh grade.[11]

Socialization

We were forced unexpectedly to concede, at the suggestion of Bronfenbrenner and others, that not only are children better taught at
home than at school during their first ten or twelve years but they are
also far better socialized. Stanford's Albert Bandura observes that the
tendency toward dependency on peers rather than family for basic
values has in recent years moved down to preschools.[12] Contrary to
popular belief, children normally are best socialized by parents, not
other kids; in fact, adds Bronfenbrenner, the more children in a
group, the fewer meaningful human contacts they have.

We found that socialization is not neutral. It is either positive or
negative. Positive, or altruistic and principled, sociability is firmly
linked with the family in both quantity and quality of self-confidence,
self-respect, and self-worth. This is, in turn, dependent largely on the
values and experiences provided by the family at least until the child
can reason consistently. In other words, the child who works, eats,
plays, has his rest, and is read to daily more with his parents than with
his peers senses that he or she is a part of the family corporation—
and, as such, is needed, wanted, and depended upon. Such a child is
more often a thinker than a mere repeater of other children's
thoughts. He or she is independent and self-directed in values and
skills, and largely avoids peer dependency. This child's attitude is, "To
heaven with me."

Negative, narcissistic, me-first sociability is born from more peer-
group association and fewer meaningful parental contacts and responsibility experiences in the home during the first eight to twelve years
of life. Early peer influence generally brings an indifference to family

values that defies parental correction. Children who do not yet
understand the *why* of parental demands replace their parents with
their peers as role models simply because they are with them more.
Kids do what comes naturally: they adapt to the ways of their age-
mates because everyone's doing it and, following suit, give parents the
backs of their hands. According to Bronfenbrenner, they often lose
self-respect, optimism, respect for parents, and even trust in their
peers.[13] They have few values to pass on to the next generation, and
their general attitude is, "To hell with you."

Of the more than seven hundred doctoral candidates and other
researchers whom the Moore Foundation has helped in some way in
their studies of home education, many have been interested in some
aspect of socialization. John W. Taylor's national sample-based study
of self-concept found that 77.7 percent of all home schoolers scored in
the top quarter of scores recorded.[14] Additionally, he found that excellence in home education has little to do with the educational level of
the parents.

Home schools have proven to be a viable alternative for parents who have any reasonable doubts about the influence of schools on their children. Virtually all states have changed their laws or policies through legislative or court actions in the past twenty years. All states who have compared home schools with conventional schools (Alaska, Oregon, Tennessee, Washington) have found the home to excel significantly. In a Moore Foundation study of fifty families (most of lower socioeconomic standing and less than average educational backgrounds) who were taken to court because of some aspect of their home schooling, standardized testing of the children involved found that they averaged 80.1 percent on tests, or 30.1 percent above the average or "mean" score of 50 percent.

Although many parents don't know it, they are usually top teachers for children at least through ages ten or twelve and often through high school. A Smithsonian Institution study of twenty-three world-class geniuses found they had three things in common: warm, loving, educationally responsive parents, as well as contact with other nurturing adults; scant involvement with children outside the family; and a great deal of creative freedom, under parental guidance, to explore their own interests.[15] These ingredients for genius are a mixture of head, hands, and heart. Blended in balance in the home, with the parents' sound example, they can help develop great characters and personalities.

The following is a blueprint for home study that we have devised based on our research findings. It unites study, work, and service. Friends call it "the Moore formula."

First, don't subject your children to formal, scheduled study before age eight, ten, or twelve, whether they can read or not. No sound evidence exists for rushing children into formal study at home or at school before these ages.

Read, sing, and play with your children from their first few months of life. If you read to them several times a day, they will learn to read in their own time, be it as early as three or as late as twelve. Late readers are no more likely to be retarded or disabled than early ones. Indeed, they often become the best readers of all—with undamaged vision, acute auditory perception, more adultlike reasoning (cognition) levels, and more mature brain structure.

If your children are early readers, let them read from fifteen to twenty minutes at a time, reminding them to look out in the distance periodically to accommodate their need for faraway focusing. As they grow older, they can use crayons or chalk for writing on big pieces of paper (paper sacks are useful here) or blackboards. In this way they will gradually develop the finer muscle coordination required for using pencils and pens or for detailed drawing and sewing.

When your children seem ready, let them "practice" spelling, phonics, and number work, but don't put any study pressure on them until they are at least eight to twelve years old. Girls are usually ahead of boys in readiness for academic work. Even when your children seem ready for formal studies, a few minutes a day may be all that is necessary for drill in spelling, writing, and arithmetic. Just as important, and perhaps more so, is to identify what motivates them, what their interests are, and what makes them "tick" best.

Whatever those interests (and they may range from bugs to baking, astronomy to politics), open the door wide to knowledge. Don't give your children mostly textbooks or workbooks: let them do original reading about what interests them, and watch them grow! A child's motivation is more productive than the fanciest teaching. Also, expose them to standardized tests or manuals so that they lose any fear of testing.

Instead of toys, give your children kitchen implements, shop or desk tools, encyclopedias, magazines, and books. Don't be shocked at their interests, even if they involve motorcycles! A child can learn a lot from a Harley or a Honda: for example, the chemistry and physics of how an internal combustion engine works; economics; math; the history and sociology of transportation; and manual skills, to be later used either at local repair shops or in his or her own business.

Constructive, skill-building, entrepreneurial work builds children's self-confidence, creativity, and self-control, and it does so quickly. It is the most dramatic and consistent cure there is for behaviour and personality problems. If you give children the authority to manage your home to the extent that they can accept responsibility, they mature rapidly and naturally.

Begin small. Start your children working when they start walking. Teach them that freedom and authority go with responsibility, and give them responsibilities in your home as fast as they can accept them. No cash allowances! Let them earn their way, helping you make (and perhaps sell) cookies and bread, grow vegetables, or baby-sit. Teach them to comparison shop. Decisions about buying apples or peaches, or shredded wheat as opposed to sugar pops, offer on-the-spot lessons in nutrition and math. Put your children on your checking account and let them pay your utility bills. Such activities offer great hands-on math lessons and will quickly teach your children the importance of learning and common sense.

As work experience balances study, so service experiences balance the materialism that often affects entrepreneurship. Children who are too young to be allowed to visit in pediatric wards are almost always welcomed in nursing homes. School-age children can do chores for the aged or sick, such as weeding gardens, shoveling snow, putting out garbage for pickup, cleaning houses, or washing cars. This is the Golden Rule in practice. Our own children once had a secret society (SOS, for "Service over Self") that specialized in *secret* good deeds for the old, poor, sick, or handicapped—like washing cars, repairing rocking chairs, pulling weeds, or painting fences. Great fun, although they sometimes had to tell the police in advance, lest they be arrested for trespassing when they "stole" an item to repair it!

Properly done, home education offers significant promise of great children. It deserves the benefits of the best research and professional concern. It also demands patient inquiry and thoughtful study of available materials. But rest assured: if you are loving and responsive and can read, write, count, and speak clearly, you are ipso facto a master teacher.

Notes

1. Urie Bronfenbrenner et al., *Two Worlds of Childhood: US and USSR.* (New York, Simon and Shuster, 1970).

2. See *Better Late Than Early* (Readers Digest Press, 1975, 1977; updated 1982 and 1989 and sixth printing by the Moore Foundation, Box 1, Camas, WA 98607); *School Can Wait* (Brigham Young University, 1979, 1981; updated 1982, 1986, and 1989 and sixth printing by Moore Foundation).

3. P. D. Forgione and R. S. Moore, "The Rationales for Early Childhood Policy Making" (prepared for the U.S. Office of Economic Opportunity at Stanford University, 1973-75).

4. Anne K. Soderman, Commentary, "Schooling All Four-Year-Olds: An Idea Full of Promise, Fraught with Pitfalls." *Education Week* (4 Mar. 1984).

5. W. D. Rohwer, Jr., "Prime Time for Education: Early Childhood or Adolescence?" *Harvard Education Review* 41 (1971): 316-341.

6. David Quine, "The Intellectual Development of Home-Taught Children" (an unpublished exploratory study, 2006 Flat Creek Place, Richardson, TX 75080).

7. David Elkind, *The Hurried Child* (Reading, Mass.: Addison-Wesley, 1981).

8. Raymond S. Moore et al., *School Can Wait* (Brigham Young University Press, 1981), and *Better Late Than Early* (Readers Digest Press, 1975), both revised and available through Moore Foundation, Box 1, Camas, WA 98607.

9. *Better Late Than Early*, 7, 34-35.

10. Jean Piaget, "The Stages of the Intellectual Development of the Child," *Bulletin of the Menninger Clinic* 26 (1962): 3; and John L. Phillips, *The Origins of Intellect: Piaget's Theory* (San Francisco: H. W. Freeman & Co., 1969).

11. New York Times Bureau, "Math Crisis Predicted in U.S. Classrooms," *The Denver Post* (Sunday, 15 June 1986).

12. Albert Bandura and Aletha C. Huston, "Identification as a Process of Incidental Learning," *Journal of Abnormal and Social Psychology* 63 (1961): 311-318. Albert Bandura, Dorothea Ross, and Sheila A. Ross, "Transmission of Aggression Through Limitation of Aggressive Models," *Journal of Abnormal Psychology and Social Psychiatry* 62 (1961): 575-582. Albert Bandura and Richard H. Walters, *Social Learning and Personality Development* (New York: Holt, Rinehart & Winston, 1963).

13. Bronfenbrenner, *Two Worlds of Childhood*.

14. John W. Taylor, "Self-Concept in Home Schooling Children" (Ph.D. dissertation, Andrews University, 1986).

15. Harold McCurdy, "The Childhood Pattern of Genius," *Horizon* 2 (1960): 33-38.

AN INTERVIEW WITH JOHN HOLT

The late John Holt (1923-1985) wrote about education for many years. His books How Children Learn, How Children Fail, *and* What Do I Do Monday *are standard fare in higher-education curricula, while* Never Too Late *and* Teach Your Own *established him as a major spokesperson for home schooling in this country today.* Growing Without Schooling (GWS), *the bimonthly newsletter that he established, contains letters from home schooling parents, teaching ideas, legal information, and book reviews; it also has its own mail-order bookstore. Holt Associates, the organization that publishes* GWS, *is a clearinghouse for home schooling and education information nationwide.*

In 1981, Marlene Anne Bumgarmer, a contributing editor of Mothering, *interviewed John Holt. Following are her impressions of their meeting:*

> *The reality of John was even better than the expressions he puts on paper. Watching this quiet man with my children was an experience I will never forget. I think he is a little uncomfortable with us grown-up folks—perhaps we play too many games for him to understand each of us in such a short time—but there is no doubt that the smaller people see in him a kindred soul. He does not talk down to them, but directly at them, looking them in the eyes. And they respond, because they know that this is a person who understands their uniqueness, their integrity, and their capability.*

Q: *What is your philosophy of learning?*
JH: That basically the human animal is a learning animal. We like to learn, we need to learn, we are good at it, we don't need to be shown how or be made to do it. What kills the process is people interfering with it or trying to regulate it or control it.

Q: *Why home schooling?*
JH: That's a big question. The great advantages are intimacy, control of your time, flexibility of schedule, and the ability to respond to the

needs and the inclinations of the child. If the child is feeling kind of tired or out of sorts, or a little bit sick, or kind of droopy in spirits, OK, we take it easy and things go along very calmly and easily. When the child is full of energy and rambunctious, then we tackle big projects, we try tough stuff, we look at hard books. I think schools could do much more than they do with this kind of flexibility, but in fact they don't. I want to make it clear that I don't see home schooling as some kind of answer to the badness of schools. I think that the home is the proper base for the exploration of the world that we call learning or education. Home would be the best base no matter how good the schools were. The proper relationship of the schools to home is the relationship of the library to home or the skating rink to home. It is a supplementary resource.

But the school is an artificial institution, and the home is a very natural one. There are lots of societies without schools, but never any without homes. Home is the center of the circle from which you move out in all directions, so there is no conceivable improvement in schools that would change my mind about that.

Q: *What does one DO at a home school?*
JH: That's what GWS is about, of course. What one can do depends a lot on one's own life. A lot of families have small businesses, or subsistence farms or crafts, or various kinds of activities that the parents are involved in that the children are also very involved in. The children just partake of the life of the adults wherever they are, and then questions are answered as they come up. Other people may live at home and work somewhere else; they may have a more conventional kind of existence.

I don't believe in formal fixed curricula, but it may very well be that when parents and children start off, they're both a little nervous. They're both kind of wondering what they should be doing. If it makes people feel happier to have a little schedule and to work with a correspondence school for a year or so, kind of as a security blanket, there's nothing wrong with that. It's a starting place.

My advice is always to let the interests and the inclinations of the children determine what happens and to give children access to as much of the parents' lives and the world around them as possible, so that children have the widest possible range of things to look at and think about. See which things interest them most, and help them to go down that particular road.

How that's done depends very much on the family's circumstances and interests and the particular interests of the children. Some kids are bookish; some children like to build things; some are more mathematical or computerish or artistic or musical or whatever. The mix is never going to be exactly the same.

Q: *Does home schooling require that the parents spend a great deal of structured time with their children in a formal learning situation?*
JH: Home schooling doesn't require that parents spend a great deal of structured time. I think as parents get into it, they tend to spend less time. How much time they spend with their kids depends a little on the circumstances in their own lives. Sometimes they spend a lot of time together just because it's fun. Other times that's harder for them to do. The children, though they may enjoy a lot of their parents' company during the day, don't need it once they get past the age of seven or eight.

Q: *Is the parent without a background in education or experience as a teacher at a disadvantage in a home schooling situation?*
JH: I'd say they have a very great advantage. I wouldn't say that a person was disqualified from home schooling because they had a training in education, but I would have to say that practically everything they taught you at that school of education is just plain wrong. You have to unlearn it all. I never had any of that educational training. The most exclusive, selective, demanding private schools in this country do not hire people who have education degrees. If you look through their faculties—people with degrees in history, mathematics, English, French, whatever—you will not see people with degrees in education. I think for the most prestigious private schools, you could almost set it down as a fact that to have a teacher's certificate, to have had that kind of training, would disqualify you.

Q: *What if, in addition to the lack of education background of any sort, the parents are not, for example, talented enough or knowledgeable enough to teach physics or math?*
JH: Your children don't have to learn physics or math from you. There are plenty of people to learn from; there are plenty of books;

there are plenty of extension courses. GWS has information on that. There are plenty of other people to answer your questions. You don't have to get it all from Mom and Pop. There are people who have had only high schooling, or may not even have finished that, who are now teaching their children at home and doing a very good job of it.

Q: *What about the child's social life?*
JH: As for friends, you're not going to lock your kids in the house. I think the socializing aspects of school are ten times as likely to be harmful as helpful. The human virtues—kindness, patience, generosity, et cetera—are learned by children in intimate relationships, maybe groups of two or three. By and large, human beings tend to behave worse in large groups, as you find in school. There they learn something quite different: popularity, conformity, bullying, teasing—things like that. They can make friends after school hours, during vacations, at the library, in church.

Q: *What about the opportunity for youths to meet members of other backgrounds, other socioeconomic classes?*
JH: Most of the schools that I know anything about are tracked. There is a college track and a business track and a vocational track. Studies have shown over the years that these tracks correlate perfectly with economic class. I think I know enough about most high schools in this country to say there is very little mingling of people from different backgrounds or different religious groups. The rich kids hang out with the rich kids, the jocks hang out with the jocks, the pointy heads hang out with the pointy heads, the greasers hang out with the greasers. Maybe there are some exceptions to that . . . but the idea of school as a social melting pot where people of all kinds of backgrounds get together—pure mythology, folks.

Q: *What is the legal status of home schooling in various states? Which states seem to be the most receptive? How can one go about finding out the legal status of home schooling in one's own home state or school district? Is it advisable to deal at the state or local level?*
JH: In the first place, what really makes the difference is not what the state laws say but how the local school superintendents react. There isn't any state in which the school district can't cooperate if they want to, and there isn't any state in which the school district can't make a

lot of trouble for you if that's what they want. I think, on the whole, probably the best states are the ones that have easy regulations about private schools. California is one. I think New Mexico is another. I know New Jersey is another. Most of the southern states have pretty lenient school regulations.

As for legal status of home schooling in one's own state, it's easy enough to find out what the state law is. That you can find in any library. You can find out by writing a state legislator, who can send you a copy. Or, as I said, it's not a hard thing to look up. Again, you could find out the private school regulations. I think it's a good idea to deal with elected representatives on this because it calls their attention to something that they need to know more about. It makes them aware of you.

As for the kind of reaction you may get from your school district, I have sometimes suggested to people that they attend a couple of school board meetings just to see how the people behave, how the meetings are run, the way that the board and the superintendent deal with questions and how they talk to people. Also, it may be possible to have a friend who lives out of the district write a probing letter saying something like: "I'm moving into your part of the state, and I've been teaching my children at home in another state, and I want to continue this activity. I've been doing it with the support of the schools, and I know people are doing this in Wisconsin (or California, or whatever the state may be), and I'm curious to know what position your district would take on this issue."

How you proceed thereafter depends a lot on what kind of response you get. I think the best of all possible arrangements is a friendly agreement with the local school board, because then you have the school to use as a resource, and that's very nice. But if that can't be arranged, then you have to find other ways.

Q: *Such as?*
JH: Well, I think there are two things that it helps to make clear to local school officials. One is that it is possible for them to say, "OK." A lot of them, to my great surprise, don't understand that. Many of them believe you have to send your kids to school—that if you don't send your kids to school it's a crime, and they have to try to put you in jail. And if they don't try to put *you* in jail, someone's going to put *them* in jail. It's a real primitive kind of notion, and you have to make it clear to them that it's not true. Many court decisions have supported this; there are provisions in the state law that may support it; and aside from anything else, in all fifty states the school districts have the right to define "attendance" in any way they want.

Attendance means taking part in an educational program approved by the school. If the school wants to send you on a field trip, it can. If it wants to tell you to study at home, it can do that, too. A lot of school folks don't know that they have that right, and so it's important to make it clear that they do.

The other thing that it's important to convey to the school is that you're not trying to start some great big public crusade. School people are very frightened and nervous, much more so than they need to be. They're all in a panic. And they say things like, "If one family does it, they're all going to do it." Not true. There just are not that many home schoolers. Not yet, at any rate, and probably not for some time to come.

Q: *I see here a role for GWS, because it's such a good source of information.*
JH: Yes, it's a kind of miniature law review on this subject. There really is no other publication that has as complete a review as we do.

We get our information from the folks who read us. People tell us and send us clippings. When we read about a court case in a newspaper story, we write to the court or the district and the state and try to get a copy of the whole decision. This is a thing people can also do themselves. It's better to read the whole text of the decision than it is just to read the citations in those legal summary books, because when you read a summary, you're reading somebody's condensation of the judge's report. Where we think there are landmark rulings, like *Perchemlides,*[1] we make the whole ruling available to people. It's one of the things we've been doing.

Q: *Can you develop your home schooling just by designating your home as a private school?*
JH: Yes. But even that isn't a guarantee that some real gung-ho fanatic may not come after you and try to make trouble, take you to court, et cetera. There isn't any 100 percent trouble-free way of doing this. But I think there are many states in which that private school thing is quite easy. There are other states—Wisconsin has recently passed a law, New Hampshire has recently passed one—in which there are state regulations about home schooling and a set procedure you have to go through.

And, of course, a lot depends on the state administrators who are running the show. New Hampshire had been a difficult state. Some New Hampshire families are now able to teach their kids at home under the new procedures, but the state has also turned down a couple of other families, and it remains to be seen how that's going to go. Apparently the Wisconsin state authorities are really quite friendly.

Q: *What do you advise as to how to go about home schooling—as a private school, as a correspondent with an alternative school, through a recognized correspondence school, per se, or as a home schooler within the public school system?*
JH: I think the best arrangement, if you can make it, is a friendly agreement with the local public school system, for the reason that it does make all those school facilities available to you. And it gets you out of what I would call the "combat phase." And I believe in getting out of it if we can.

That's not always possible, however. And what is then the best step depends a little on state law. Where the private school route is possible, it's a good one—probably the best one, and probably the safest. In states where that's harder to do, the business of registering with a distant private school is very useful, but again, it's not foolproof. There's no guarantee that a local school district may not try to take you to court about that.

If we're dealing with a school superintendent and board who are nervous about what the law may do to *them* if they let you teach your own kids at home, all they need to be reassured is some kind of official arrangement. And they may be perfectly content with a distant private school. But if they're really trying to make trouble for you, to discourage you and to discourage other families, it's not quite as easy.

I've just had a letter from a family in Ohio, who registered their kids with the Clonlara School in Ann Arbor, Michigan, and then got a threatening letter from the local school superintendent, "letting you know that we're coming in three days to take your kids away." So they backed down temporarily, but I suggested to them that they write a letter to the superintendent and send copies to the school board, the local juvenile court, the local criminal court, the county district attorney, their elected representatives in the state department of education, and local newspaper editors, saying basically, "There is nothing in the Ohio statutes that prevents me from enrolling my children in an out-of-state school. Lots of Ohio people do it. And there is nothing in the Ohio statutes that prevents that school from instituting any kind of program that has my support. And, therefore, there is nothing in the laws that says that among these options, there is not the option of telling a child that that child can study in my home. It would be absurd to say that the law of Ohio says that the Clonlara School can send my child anywhere in the world except Ohio. It's absolute nonsense."

Send that letter out, and add, "If there is anything in the law that contradicts what I've said, please inform me. Unless I hear from you to the contrary, I will assume that my understanding of the law is correct and that you agree." Send this out and see what kind of responses you get. This is going to make it clear to some people that your legal rights are strong in the case. Incidentally, it's very important when sending letters to people in matters like this to send copies to a lot of other people, and not blind copies, but say down there at the bottom of the page, "cc" with a list of all the people.

I remember in the Sessions case,[2] the Sessions were asking a lot of questions of the school district on these matters, and basically the school district didn't answer. And the judge, in ruling in favor of the Sessions family, made a very strong point that the Sessions had tried, in good faith, to find out what the regulations were and the schools had not fulfilled their obligations and had not told them. This was one of the factors that weighed in favor of the family.

Q: *How does one deal with nosy neighbors?*
JH: Well, it's not always easy. It's nice if you actually have the neighbors' support. The very best thing would be to get their support from the beginning. Some people have been able to do that, but on the whole, home schooling looks like a pretty unconventional thing to many people; so if you have hostile neighbors, there's still this very real possibility that they will report you.

One family told the neighbors that they were sending their children to a private school, and that was better because private schools have kind of eccentric schedules, and you can say the teacher's having a conference or a field trip. But your kids really can't be running around on the streets. They can't be highly visible during school hours, because this just bugs people.

Q: *What is your philosophy about teaching reading?*
JH: I think the teaching of reading is mostly what prevents reading. Different children learn in different ways. I think reading aloud is fun, but I would never read aloud to a kid *so that* the kid would learn to read. You read aloud because it's fun and companionable. You hold a child, sitting next to you or on your lap, and read this story that you're having fun with, and if it isn't a cozy, happy, warm, friendly, loving experience, then you shouldn't do it. It isn't going to do any good.

I think children are attracted to the adult world. It's nice to have children's books, but far too many of them have too much in the way of pictures. I also tend to feel that children, inside their small bodies, are heroic-scale people and that when they look into a book they want, and need, to see something other than themselves looking out. They need stories of real danger, adventure, heroism, not just talk about what it's like to go with Mommy to the supermarket, or whatever it may be.

I don't think there's any way to make reading interesting to children in a family in which it isn't interesting to adults. When children see books with pages and pages and pages of print, as they do in a family where the adults read, it becomes pretty clear that if you're going to find out what's in those books, you're going to have to read that print. One other thing. I was reading recently about a mother who made her own child's toys, and it reminded me once again that when I was little nobody ever thought that children had to be *taught* colors and shapes. Nobody ever taught me colors and shapes. I figured it out, just as I figured out thousands of other things, by seeing what people did around me, hearing what they said about what they did, and maybe asking a question if I wanted to confirm one of my hunches.

Every year we get more and more deeply mired in the fundamentally false idea that learning is, must be, and can only be the result of teaching—in short, that ideas never get into children's heads unless adults put them there. No more harmful and mistaken idea was ever invented. The fact, as all parents of young children can easily observe, is that children create learning out of experience, and they do it in almost exactly the same way that the people we call "scientists" do it: by observing, wondering, theorizing, and experimenting (which may include asking questions) to test their theories.

The idea that, unless taught, a child might actually grow up not knowing squares from triangles or red from blue is so absurd that I hardly know what to say about it. But it is an astonishingly widespread idea. The worst thing about it is that after a while kids come to believe it themselves.

Q: *What is your philosophy about math?*
JH: My approach to math is to say, "What do we adults use numbers for? We use them to measure things." And we measure things so that having measured them, we can do things with them or make certain judgments about them. And so I say, let children do with numbers what we do with numbers. I'm a great believer in many kinds of measuring instruments: tapes (centimeter tape, inch tapes, rolls of tapes); rulers; scales; thermometers; barometers; metronomes; electric metronomes with lights flashing on and off, which you can make go faster and slower; stop watches; and other objects that measure time.

Another thing is money. Kids are fascinated by money. I say family finances ought to be out on the table, in charts on the wall: income, expenses, food, taxes, insurance, health care, how much this costs, how much it cost last year. This is interesting, for God's sake. I think that, like typing, double-entry bookkeeping and basic accounting are actually fascinating skills, and, really, if you're talking about basics, these are basics.

The fundamental idea of double-entry bookkeeping—that is, the distinction between your income and expenses and assets and liabilities—is one of the really beautiful inventions of the human mind. It's fabulous the way it works, and I think families should do their finances as if they were little teeny corporations, with income and expenses and assets and liabilities and depreciation.

Some kids may get to the point where they want to be the family treasurer and keep the family books and balance the checkbook. This is all really "big adult stuff." Let the child write out the checks that pay the bills. Why not? This is inherently interesting, so let's at least make this part of our life—like every other part—accessible to children.

The best way to meet numbers is in real life, as with everything else. There they are embedded in the context of reality. What schooling does is to try to take everything *out* of the context of reality, and it's a terrible mistake. You know, there are numbers in building, there are numbers in construction, there are numbers in business, there are numbers in photography, there are numbers in music, there are fractions in cooking. So wherever numbers are in real life, then let's go and meet them and work with them.

Q: *What subject matter do you see as essential?*
JH: None.

Q: *What about the parent who works outside of the home?*
JH: One question that often comes up is, "How am I going to teach my kids six hours a day?" And I respond to that by saying, "Who's teaching your kids six hours a day?" I was a good student in supposedly the best schools, and it was a rare day that I got five minutes of teaching—that's five minutes of somebody's serious attention to my personal needs, interests, concerns, difficulties, problems. Like most other kids in school, I learned that if you don't understand what's going on, for heaven's sake, keep your mouth shut. What happens when children become ill or have an injury? Home teachers come in

for three to five hours a week. It has been found that this is perfectly sufficient. These children don't fall behind. No child needs, or should stand, six hours of teaching a day, even if a parent were of a mind to give it. It would drive them up the wall.

Q: *How are home schoolers evaluated when they go to enroll at the university level?*
JH: Just like anyone else. You know, there are these tests you can take—the college boards, the SAT, and so forth. Actually, home schoolers do exceptionally well on these things. They're more motivated to learn what areas will be covered and prepare for them.

Q: *Does it sometimes happen that a home schooling student will express a desire to return to traditional schooling? How do parents handle this?*
JH: Various ways. Sometimes parents have to decide (we're the grown-ups) that we don't want them to go back to that school and then stick with it. But other times, if the children want to go, then that means they're immune to the manipulation the schools can do with the children who don't have a choice about whether they have to be there or not. The school loses some of its power when the children know they can quit if they want.

Notes

1. *Perchemlides et al. v. Donald Frizzle* (1978). A Massachusetts case in favor of a home schooling family. The ruling was that home schooling was a legal alternative. This case became a model for others.

2. *State of Iowa v. Robert and Linda Sessions* (1978). A home schooling case decided in favor of parents.

The History of Alternative Education

Ron Miller

A mericans have had a stormy relationship with public education ever since Horace Mann and his colleagues established the modern school system in the 1830s. On the one hand, we have taken enormous pride in their ideal of "common" schooling, an ambitious innovation that has sought to educate children of all social classes, all ethnic groups, and all levels of academic ability. On the other hand, we have placed far too much confidence in the school's ability to overcome social conflict. Public schooling, by its very nature, is bound to reflect the divisions and prejudices of society, and therefore some segment of the public will inevitably be dissatisfied with the schools at any given time.

Some people have become so thoroughly discouraged with mainstream education that they have given up trying to reform the schools and have, instead, set up alternatives. The majority of these attempts reflect the religious diversity of American culture. In a more specific sense, however, the term "alternative" refers to a smaller, more radical group of critics: parents and educators who are uncomfortable with the materialistic, competitive, nationalistic, and individualistic industrial-age values that permeate public education. Since the dawn of the Industrial Revolution early in the nineteenth century, alternative educators have established a variety of schools that are vastly different, in goals and structure, from the typical public institution. Rather than merely training students to take their place in modern industrial society, these educators have sought to nurture the complete and integrated development of the child's unfolding personality.

Although alternative education has taken many forms, these forms all share a few key characteristics. Children are treated as individuals with personal temperaments, interests, and abilities. Grading, standardized testing, and classification schemes (such as IQ) are minimized or totally eliminated. Human relationships, between adult and child as well as within the school community, are nonauthoritarian. Intellectual and vocational skills are highly valued, but not at the expense of the emotional, artistic, social, physical, and spiritual development of the personality.

The history of alternative education is filled with a colorful assortment of idealistic, rebellious, and, sometimes, eccentric figures. One of the founding fathers of the alternative tradition was the romantic philosopher Jean-Jacques Rousseau (1712-1778). He was among the first to decry the artificial, materialistic values of the so-called Enlightenment in Europe, which preceded the Industrial Revolution. In *Emile* (1762), Rousseau argued that education, rather than ruthlessly instilling intellectual and social discipline, should seek a harmony between the organic needs of child development and the demands of social life. He observed that young children do not learn or reason in the same way as adults, and he urged educators to respect—rather than suppress—"the first impulses of nature."

Rousseau himself did not found a school, but the Swiss humanitarian Johann Heinrich Pestalozzi (1746-1827) applied many of Rousseau's ideas at his boarding schools for paupers and orphans. In one of the most concise statements of holistic education, Pestalozzi said, "God's nature which is in you is held sacred in this House. We do not hem it in; we try to develop it. Nor do we impose on you our own natures. It is far from our intention to make of you men such as we are. It is equally far from our intention to make of you such men as are the majority of men in our time. Under our guidance you should become men such as your natures—the divine and sacred in your nature—require you to be."[1] The essential starting point of alternative, holistic education is this trust in the organic, or perhaps divine, human spirit—and the desire to nurture it despite the narrow worldview of an industrial society.

In 1808, Joseph Neef (1770-1854), an associate of Pestalozzi's and an emigrant to the United States, criticized the traditional method of educating through rote memorization and harsh discipline. Neef encouraged his students to question and reason for themselves. As he put it, "My pupils shall never believe what I tell them because I tell it [to] them, but because their own senses and understandings convince them that it is true."[2] He saw himself not as an authority figure but as his students' "friend and guide." He took his classes on extensive field trips—an extraordinary innovation in his time. Neef's schools were so far in advance of accepted educational practice that they repeatedly attracted public criticism and eventually failed.

America's first homegrown rebellion against the industrial age was the transcendentalist movement of the 1830s and 1840s. Inspired by European romanticism and the religious humanism of the Unitarian sage William Ellery Channing, this group of young men and women—many of whom were accomplished scholars—yearned for emotional and spiritual wholeness. A. Bronson Alcott (1799-1888), father of author Louisa May Alcott, fully articulated and practiced a transcendentalist approach to education. Believing, like Pestalozzi, that all people carry within themselves something of the divine, he asserted that the educator "should look to the child to see what is to be done, rather than to his book or his system. The Child is the Book."[3]

Indeed, Alcott was a sensitive observer of child development. A century before Piaget, he kept detailed journals describing the activities of his infant daughters. What he saw in them and in his students led to a holistic approach. He wrote, "The animal nature, the affections, the conscience, and the intellect present their united claims for distinct and systematic attention. The whole being of the child asks for expansion and guidance. The child is essentially an active being."[4]

Consequently, Alcott argued that education should not seek to fit people for "specific employment, by the installation of a given amount of knowledge" but should strive to nurture "the complete development of human nature."[5] For Alcott, this meant primarily moral and spiritual development. Unfortunately, Bronson Alcott, apparently a rather dreamy idealist, managed to alienate almost every community in which he taught (rural Connecticut, Philadelphia, and Boston). Parents—who wanted their children drilled in basic skills and taught to obey authority—were shocked that their children enjoyed Alcott's company enough to go home with him after school, dismayed when he encouraged them to question and discuss passages from the Bible, and angered when he admitted a black girl into his school and refused their demand to dismiss her.

Progressive Education

Between the 1840s and 1910, the industrial age took hold of American culture. These were the years of Manifest Destiny, the Civil War, and the Gilded Age. Society turned increasingly to science, technology, professionalism, and bureaucracy. The public schools became established institutions, and few educational alternatives were available.

Toward the end of the nineteenth century, however, an energetic reformer named Francis W. Parker (1837-1902) began to raise significant questions about the course American education had taken. Although he worked within the public school system—as superintendent of schools in Quincy, Massachusetts, and later as head of a teacher training institute in Chicago—his writings accused public education of encouraging the competition, materialism, and greed of the Gilded Age. He attacked the educator's use of punishments, grades, and prizes and asserted that "real, genuine educative work, real search for truth and its ethical application, needs no other stimulus."[6] Parker argued that if young people were given a challenging environment where they could actively explore and discover, they would by nature seek to learn. He shared the view that the child has within himself or herself "divine power and divine possibilities"—an inner urge to grow, discover, and learn—which should not be tampered with or corrupted by adult prejudices. "No human being can find the truth for another," he said.[7]

Although many of Parker's ideas were radical, mainstream educators were willing to listen, for in the 1890s, middle-class Americans began to address the social and human costs of the industrial age in a movement that came to be known as progressivism. Searching for new directions, a number of educators were influenced by Parker, who subsequently became known as the father of "progressive education."

In 1896, the new University of Chicago launched a laboratory school to experiment with novel approaches to learning. Its director, a brilliant young philosophy professor named John Dewey (1859-1952), had worked with Parker as well as with the pioneering social worker Jane Addams. Over the next two decades, Dewey produced several classic works in educational thought: *The School and Society* (1899), *The Child and the Curriculum* (1902), and, most notably, *Democracy and Education* (1916), as well as many important articles and lectures. Like Parker, he argued that the truest, most meaningful learning occurs through purposeful activity rather than passive reading, memorizing, and reciting. He called for schools to become experimental communities where children can learn about society's needs and

ROB KOENIG

occupations by actively participating in constructive group projects. Dewey's name has become synonymous with progressive education in the twentieth century.

Conservative critics, charging that Dewey's emphasis is "anti-intellectual," have disregarded two essential points: that Dewey himself was an accomplished intellectual who valued the wisdom of the classic works of civilization; and that Dewey supported book learning not as an end in itself but rather in alliance with an active and sensitive social conscience. To Dewey and other liberal progressives, it was becoming clear that industrial society was creating a serious split between well-educated professionals and managers on the one hand and a poorly educated working class on the other. This division threatened the loss of a democratic community of shared concerns and mutual respect. While more conservative progressives sought to institute a two-tier educational system to separate academic from vocational students, Dewey argued forcefully for preserving the common school tradition in America.

Dewey was not, strictly speaking, an advocate of alternative education. He apparently never lost faith in the belief that an education conducted according to experimental, scientific, and rational principles could transcend the economic, religious, and ideological divisions of American culture. But when the First World War utterly failed to "make the world safe for democracy" (a crusade supported by the Progressives, including Dewey), a more truly alternative "progressive education" movement emerged.

These educators rejected institutional reform in favor of the pursuit of personal wholeness and happiness. Deliberately "child centered," they adopted many of the educational ideas of Parker and Dewey along with an invigorating dose of Freudian and Jungian psychology. And in seeking to educate "the whole child," they emphasized self-expression through the arts. Margaret Naumburg, founder of the progressive Walden School in New York, wrote, "The real job of education ought to be to develop what is still buried or less evolved in our natures. . . . About 90 percent of what we really are is pushed out of sight by the time we're seven years old! The standards of education and society force back below the surface the most living and essential parts of our nature."[8]

The Progressive Education Association, founded in 1919, was the best organized and most ambitious attempt of its time to support a truly alternative system of education. Its journal, *Progressive Education*, was an important forum for "the new education." However, in turning their backs on social reform, this group of predominantly upper-middle-class people failed to connect their alternative, holistic education with alternatives to the competitive, materialistic industrial society. A group of Dewey's more politically oriented followers, the social reconstructionists, accused the child-centered movement of being "romantic" and called for educators to actively work against the materialism and individualism of modern American society. An articulate spokesperson for this group, George Counts, wrote a powerful little book entitled *Dare the School Build a New Social Order?*

European Influences

Two educational movements from Europe have enjoyed a great deal of success and are the leading alternative movements in contemporary American education: the Montessori and Waldorf schools. Maria

Montessori (1870-1952), the first woman in Italy to become a medical doctor, began her career by treating "mentally deficient" children. She decided that a primary cause of their difficulties was an unstimulating environment, and she developed an impressive array of learning materials that would answer to children's developmental needs. This "didactic apparatus" became the core of the Montessori school environment.

Trusting in the spontaneous, organic unfolding of "sensitive periods" that cause an intense interest in exploring the world, Montessori's approach encourages children to work at their own pace, either individually or in groups, while developing uncommon levels of concentration and self-direction. Montessori's methods support the young child's natural inclination to learn sensorially, by manipulating concrete materials, and teach young children the generally abstract three Rs in this way.

Montessori schools have become highly popular, largely because the children's academic achievement and self-discipline are so apparent. The Montessori approach is not usually considered socially or culturally radical. Yet in her writings, Maria Montessori passionately proclaimed the child to be a "spiritual embryo"—a mysteriously self-forming being whose inner needs must not be thwarted by the self-interest of adults. As she said, "Our care of the child should be governed not by the desire to 'make him learn things,' but by the endeavor always to keep burning within him that light which is called the intelligence."[9] Montessori argued that humankind will achieve true peace only when the child's developmental needs are fully and lovingly met—that is, when the child's needs become society's highest priority.

Waldorf education, founded in 1919 by Austrian philosopher Rudolf Steiner (1861-1925), reflects Steiner's spiritual-scientific research known as anthroposophy, or the knowledge of man. Seeing human life as essentially the spiritual journey of our personal souls, Steiner designed the Waldorf approach to nurture the intuition, imagination, and spiritual capacities of the child. Drawing upon the creative arts and legends that tap into archetypal levels, the Waldorf curriculum aims to keep alive the deepest sensitivities of human nature. Steiner asserted that true education is not the inculcation of socially approved facts and skills into a passive student, but is "an Art—the Art of awakening what is actually there within the human being."[10]

This art of education seeks to engender a healthy social community and virtually eliminates competition. Waldorf teachers, trained to pay close attention to their interactions with the children, move up grade by grade with their students and spend eight years developing a close, loving, trusting relationship with them. Waldorf educators believe that young children are not developmentally ready for academic learning. They oppose the competitive, high-pressure demands of early-childhood education and believe that premature intellectual endeavors drain the child of physical resources needed for future well-being. Thus, they disagree even with Montessori's concrete and seemingly natural approach to teaching the three Rs in preschool.

Yet, this is not to say that Waldorf students lag in academic achievement; on the contrary, older students delve deeply into the humanities and sciences—far more deeply than most public school students. It appears that when the soul is given the nurturing it requires, academic learning occurs easily and spontaneously. Both the Montessori and Waldorf school movements provide alternatives to the materialistic worldview of the industrial age.

The End of the Industrial Age?

"Alternative education" as a distinct movement arose from the culturally unsettling 1960s. The social unrest—the civil rights and women's movements, environmentalism, campus uprisings, and resistance to the Vietnam War—resulted in what I call "the education crisis," which peaked between 1967 and 1972. During this time, the institutions of the industrial age came under the most intense and penetrating criticism yet, visibly shaking the American people's faith in common schooling. Open classrooms, based on the innovative British "integrated day" approach, appeared in many public school districts. And "public schools of choice"—giving parents the opportunity to choose among different educational methods—emerged as a decentralized option.

Educational critics such as Paul Goodman, A. S. Neill, John Holt, Jonathan Kozol, Herbert Kohl, James Herndon, George Dennison, and others launched a passionate and morally charged argument against the public schools. They accused traditional education of stifling the aspirations and creative energies of youth, of losing the individual in a maze of bureaucratic roles, and of perpetuating a brutal competition for social success without regard for the needs of human development. These critics inspired a substantial following of parents and alternative educators, who established "free" schools and cooperatives and ultimately contributed to the rise of the home schooling movement.

So far, these approaches, like their predecessors, have failed to catch on with the majority of the public. As Ira Shor has pointed out, mainstream American culture fought back against the tide of social and educational reform.[11] The 1970s and 1980s have seen a reaffirmation of competitive individualism and nationalism, accompanied by a return to "basics" in education. Nevertheless, much of the criticism raised in the 1960s has provoked changes in today's world: blind nationalism is being challenged by the realization that all humankind must share and protect this fragile earth; the human potential movement and a new interest in spiritual fulfillment are inspiring us to take a hard look at the materialism and competitiveness of the past century; and we are discovering (or rediscovering) aspects of our humanness that are far deeper and more nourishing than academic and professional success. Today, humankind is embarking on a renewed quest for meaning that may thoroughly transform the values of the industrial age and, consequently, our ideas about the aims of education.

Notes

1. Kate Silber, *Pestalozzi: The Man and His Work*, 2d ed. (London: Routledge and Kegan Paul, 1965), 116.

2. Joseph Neef, *Sketch of a Plan and Method of Education* (1808; reprint, New York: Arno/New York Times, 1969), 77.

3. Odell Shepard, ed., *The Journals of Bronson Alcott* (Boston: Little, Brown, 1938), 12.

4. Walter Harding, ed., *Essays on Education by Amos Bronson Alcott* (Gainesville, Fla.: Scholars' Facsimilies & Reprints, 1960), 4.

5. Dorothy McCuskey, *Bronson Alcott, Teacher* (1940; reprint, New York: Arno/New York Times, 1969), 163.

6. Francis W. Parker, *Talks on Pedagogics* (1894; reprint, New York: Arno/New York Times, 1969), 371.

THE HISTORY OF ALTERNATIVE EDUCATION **53**

7. Ibid., 24, 227, 288, 353.

8. Margaret Naumburg, *The Child and the World* (New York: Harcourt, Brace and Co., 1928), 311.

9. Maria Montessori, *Spontaneous Activity in Education*, trans. F. Simonds (1917; reprint, New York: Schocken, 1965), 240.

10. Rudolf Steiner, *The Younger Generation* (Spring Valley, N.Y.: Anthroposophic Press, 1967), 23.

11. Ira Shor, *Culture Wars: School and Society in the Conservative Restoration 1969-1984* (London: Routledge and Kegan Paul, 1986).

PART II:
LEGAL ISSUES

Home Schooling, A Legal View

Michael S. Shepherd

Criticism of the public schools and alienation of parents from those schools are among the most fundamental reasons why home schooling has gained increasing public support over the past decade. Gallup Polls generally show a steady decline in confidence in the public schools between 1969 and 1978.[1] Discipline concerns, busing for purposes of racial integration, and declining test scores have been cited as important alienating factors.

Although the Supreme Court, in *Pierce v. Society of Sisters* (1925), upheld the right of parents to use private schools to educate their children, many parents who were alienated from the public schools during the 1970s and 1980s could not afford to pay for a traditional private school while paying taxes to support the public schools.[2] The impressions of the late home education advocate John Holt[3] as well as the survey results of doctoral research[4] indicate that very few home schooling families are affluent. Thus, today's home schooling movement may be partially explained as an attempt by families of modest means to provide the kind of education they feel their children need, which they are convinced the public schools do not provide.

As the home schooling movement gains momentum, so do the legal controversies and debates surrounding it. During the 1970s and 1980s, these have focused on the general questions of academic quality, health, socialization, and religious conviction. Court-mediated arguments for and against home schooling center around an open question: Who is responsible for setting genuine standards—the parents or the state?

In the area of academics, home-tutoring advocates consistently argue that the quality of home instruction is superior to that of traditional classroom instruction. Standardized test results are cited frequently in court cases[5] and in comparative studies[6] as evidence of academic quality. The fact that students with home instruction perform well on standardized tests whereas public school students often do poorly on those same tests has been used to discredit arguments favoring a need for state control of home schools.[7] Also frequently cited are the personal success records of individual home-tutored students who have been admitted to such major universities as the University of California at Berkeley[8] and Harvard.[9]

In some home schooling court cases, however, prosecutors have argued that the very process of home education fails to allow adequate access to certified teachers, proper materials, or acceptable curriculum, and thus it fails to meet state requirements. In these cases, prosecutors are often unable to successfully argue that the educational results are inadequate.

Partisans of home teaching list famous people in America who were taught wholly, or for a large share of the time, at home.[10] Woodrow Wilson, Franklin Roosevelt, George Washington, and Abraham Lincoln were all home-taught; Andrew and Jamie Wyeth did not attend school outside their artistic home; John Quincy Adams went directly from home to Harvard; and Frank Vandiver, a distinguished Civil War historian and until recently president of Texas A & M University, studied at home.

Some attorneys assert that "an important part of the educational effectiveness of home instruction is the proved tutorial method that it embodies."[11] The tutorial method, argues developmental psychologist and home schooling promoter Raymond Moore, is superior to group instruction because this method gives children a greater opportunity to obtain answers to their questions.[12] The classroom teacher, no matter how good he or she may be, simply does not have the time that a parent has for individual concern and attention.[13] Moore further holds that tutoring makes much more efficient use of time; he insists that a child can learn more in two hours or less by being tutored than in a whole day of classroom group instruction. A former school teacher who began home schooling her children states that the "hurry-up or busy-work" atmosphere of group instruction is eliminated by home tutoring.[14]

Advocates hold that home schooling provides children with time to explore and discover things on their own, something that may be lacking in a structured classroom curriculum.[15] Holt argues that children are naturally curious learners, but that formal schooling tends to stifle this innate inclination. Creative, aggressive learners like junior playwright Ishmael Wallace of Ithaca, New York, appear to thrive in a more relaxed, informal home setting with limited structure and plenty of time to read freely.[16] Alternative school promoter Hal Bennet contends that individualized learning, with its benefits of free exploration, is more meaningful for the child.[17] The only true education is that in which individuals are motivated to learn for themselves, claims Holt, and the only true teachers are those who encourage the individual to pursue his or her interests.[18]

According to Moore, the academic benefits of home instruction are that "parents... have enough concern for their children to take on the task of systematically teaching them"; that "parents provide the partiality that young children need but schools cannot allow"; that "children thrive on routines that involve a few children who share the same family values"; that "a child in the home school daily experiences from 10 to 100 times as many personal adult-to-child responses as he or she would in a formal school," and that "such responses—along with adult examples—mean an educational power far more than books" can convey.[19]

Many administrators and judges who criticize the academic quality of home instruction focus on the issue of teacher certification. Certified teachers are viewed as essential to the process of instruction by the National Association of School Boards.[20] However, court cases have established that noncertified teachers (parents) often have been successful in teaching their children at home using correspondence materials.

In one case, the state attempted to prove that a correspondence school education was an "inferior education." The parents, a mother with a high school education and a father with a tenth grade education, used a curriculum purchased from the Calvert School of Baltimore, which had begun its correspondence program in the early 1900s and was accredited by the state of Maryland. The state could not prove that the home schooled children were receiving an inferior education. In fact, according to a newspaper report, "Lee Joyce Richmond, Associate Professor of Education at Johns Hopkins University, who tested the children, said Terry, Jr., a fifth grader, was reading at a 10th grade level and his sister, a second grader, was reading at a fifth grade level."[21] It was the judgment of the court that the correspondence course was justified by its academic results and that the parents, although "uncertified teachers," were indeed competent.

Other arguments for and against home schooling focus on the physical and emotional health of the child. Some parents believe that certain disciplinary measures taken in the public school are not conducive to their children's well-being. Several parents have recorded an improvement in their children's dispositions when they have been taken out of the classroom for health reasons.[22] Letters addressed to John Holt by parents who have removed their children from the public school for health purposes include the following statements: "The changes that have occurred...since we took him out of school have been unbelievable. Gone are the fits of temper that erupted every day around 4:00 p.m., gone are the headaches, the lines of tension around his mouth, and gone is his depression...."; and "Let me tell you what happened to our son after we removed him from a local public school's first grade last November. He stopped wetting his bed, he stopped suffering from daily stomach upsets and headaches, and he has not had a cold for six months, although he averaged one cold a month while attending school."[23]

In addition to the debates regarding academic quality and children's health, the social environment of the school as a place to learn has received a good deal of attention. Socialization, defined by educators as contact with other children, is a major issue in the debate over the legitimacy of home schooling. School personnel and psychologists argue the need for social contact with peers as a compelling reason for school attendance.[24] School officials often state that children need to be out in the "real world," as represented by the school.[25]

Home schoolers of the 1970s and 1980s reject the socialization argument. Moore distinguishes between "positive socialization," based on a stable family life, and "negative socialization," a me-first attitude, peer dependency, and the rejection of family values. Schools tend to provide too much negative socialization, he claims; and with preschooling, unhealthy forms of peer dependency come at even earlier ages.[26]

A survey of home schooling parents reveals general agreement with this view of socialization: "This [socialization] is one of the major reasons that many home schoolers want to take their children out of school. As one home schooling mother said, 'We want our children to be peer-independent. These parents want their children to be family

MICHAEL WEISBROT

socialized and have their family be the center of the children's social world, at least until they are old enough to be on their own socially. This attitude does not preclude children from associating with other children; most parents do encourage social encounters, either with other home schooling families or with neighborhood children. . . . Most home schooling parents see home school as a means of protecting their young from the rivalry, ridicule, competition, and conflicting moral values they believe are associated with much of the socialization that takes place in schools."[27]

The socialization issue is directly related to the strengthening of family life. Attorney Brendon Stocklin-Enright points out that home schooling, as opposed to compulsory attendance, strengthens the bonds of family life by requiring parents to devote more time and energy to their children.[28] Holt accuses the schools of simply getting children out of the way of adults.[29]

Of course, parents who do not want their children "out of the way" may have difficulty adjusting their schedules to teach them at home, and may encounter criticism from unsympathetic neighbors. Dean Merrill describes the situation thus: "Home schooling, in the end, amounts to a trade-off of sorts: family closeness is gained at the expense of the varied experiences of school. Controlling the input means the mother (or someone) must streamline her schedule and say no to competing activities. The flexible scheduling is a bonus, but neighbors and friends are likely to misunderstand."[30] Nevertheless, a number of energetic parents are not deterred by the challenge. They enjoy being parents, watching their children learn, and even learning with them.[31]

A variety of practical social activities takes place in home schools. According to Moore, "True homework is work at home—chores and industries done with parents."[32] He lists more than two hundred cottage industries conducted by home schooling families—from agriculture to bicycle repair. Peter Yarema, a public school teacher, describes the activities of his own children as they are taught at home: "The education here is broader than they could ever get in the classroom. Molly, who's eight, sews on all the buttons in this family. Kathy's made an apron. If Char [Mrs. Yarema] asks her to make muffins for lunch, she can do it. All three kids use ledger sheets with their allowances so they know exactly where their money is going. You'd have a much harder time getting around to these things if your kids are gone two-thirds of the day."[33]

Some courts have been reluctant to accept socialization as a justification for compelling students to attend school. In fact, this argument was ruled out as a legitimate consideration in a 1979 case in Amherst, Massachusetts.[34] Greater emphasis is now being placed on academic success than on social equivalency.[35]

Religious conviction is another area of controversy. Home schooling has become a logical activity for parents who do not want to compromise their cultural or spiritual beliefs. One case has involved children whose parents refused to send them to school because the school did not teach Native American heritage or culture. Because it was determined that the parents provided no appropriate alternative to public schooling, the children were declared "neglected."[36] Another parent's complaint that the public school curriculum ignored and belittled a student's Native American heritage was deemed an insufficient defense for an attendance law violation.[37]

Looking at the Bible as a direct source of guidance in education, Blair Adams and Joel Stein have authored a series of books in which they criticize state control of education and justify private nonaccredited schools and home schools.[38] Emphasizing the advantage of home schooling for religious parents, Dean Merrill says, "Parents get to instill their values and spiritual commitments directly, without countermanding."[39]

Parents often argue that religious teaching is a parental responsibility and that home schooling is therefore a constitutional right. Acknowledging that the First Amendment to the United States Constitution guarantees "the free exercise" of religion, devout Amish Americans have been successful in claiming that the free exercise of religion includes their exemption from compulsory high school.[40] One such Michigan family has won the right to teach younger children at home.[41] However, religious convictions do not always supersede state law. The results have been mixed, with some judges ruling with the parents and others with the school authorities.

The controversies surrounding home schooling form a classic case of individual rights pitted against the modern regulatory state. While parents seem willing to try anything they think may help their children, state officials who may disagree with those parents also claim to be acting solely in the interest of these same children. Since it appears impossible for Americans to agree on the role the state should play in regulating private education, a case-by-case approach may be the best way to judge the quality of education provided by parents. Certainly, broad policies, such as certification and accreditation requirements, in no sense automatically guarantee educational quality.

Since academic and social success for students is more important than the means of education, it might be wise (and less expensive) for states to allow parents whose children are progressing well at home to pursue this private alternative of home schooling. It is increasingly evident that the academic promise of home instruction, as well as its protective aspects, will encourage more parents to try it. The future of education may require a greater decentralization as well as an appreciation of individual diversity rather than a reliance on state-imposed uniformity.

Notes

1. Stanley M. Elam, ed., *A Decade of Gallup Polls of Attitudes toward Education, 1969-1978* (Bloomington, Ind.: Phi Delta Kappa, 1978), 1.

2. Gerrit H. Wourmhoudt, "Supreme Court Decisions," in *The Twelve-Year Sentence*, ed. William F. Rickenbacker (La Salle, Ill.: Open Court Publishing, 1974), 65.

3. John Holt, *Teach Your Own* (New York: Delacorte Press, 1981).

4. Gunnar Gustavsen, *Selected Characteristics of Home Schools and Parents Who Operate Them* (Ann Arbor: University Microfilms International, 1981); and Norma Jean Freeman Linden, *An Investigation of Alternative Education: Home Schooling* (Ph.D. diss., East Texas University, 1983).

5. Patricia Lines, "Private Education Alternatives and State Regulation," *Jour. of Law and Ed.* 12 (Apr. 1983): 189-234.

6. Raymond Moore, "Home Schooling: An Idea Whose Time Has Returned," *Human Events* 44 (15 Sept. 1984): 824-827.

7. Blair Adams and Joel Stein, *Who Owns the Children?* (Grand Junction, Colo.: Truth Forum, 1983).

8. Wendy Priesnitz, "Schooling at Home," *Orbit* 11 (June 1980): 3-5.

9. "Harvard Freshman," *Houston Post* (29 Apr. 1983).

10. Moore, "Home Schooling," 824-827; and Kirk McCord, Speech at Home School Book Fair in Richardson, Texas (27 Apr. 1985).

11. John Whitehead and Wendell Bird, *Home Education and Constitutional Liberties* (Westchester, Ill.: Crossway Publishers, 1984).

12. Moore, "Home Schooling," 824-827.

13. Dean Merrill, "Schooling at Mother's Knee? Can it Compete?" *Christianity Today* 27 (2 Sept. 1983):16-21.

14. Ibid., 19.

15. Holt, *Teach Your Own.*

16. Nancy Wallace, *Better Than School? One Family's Declaration of Independence* (New York: Larson Publishing, 1983).

17. Hal Bennet, *No More Public School* (New York: Random House, 1972).

18. John Holt, *Instead of Education: Ways to Help People Do Things Better* (New York: E. P. Dutton, 1976).

19. Raymond Moore, *Teachers College Record* (Winter 1982), 372.

20. Ed Nagel and Tom Shannon, "Should Parents Be Allowed to Educate Their Kids at Home?" *Instructor* 89 (Oct. 1979): 30.

21. Marianne Kryzanowicz, "Home Teachers Acquitted," Annapolis, Maryland, *Evening Capital* (28 Apr. 1984), 68A.

22. Moore, *Teachers College Record*, 372.

23. Holt, *Teach Your Own*, 30-31.

24. J. J. Harris and R. E. Fields, "Outlaw Generation: A Legal Analysis of the Home Instruction Movement," *Education Horizons* 61 (Fall 1982): 26-31.

25. Holt, *Teach Your Own*; and Rick Harmon, "Some Parents Think Schools Don't Offer Enough Flexibility," Montgomery, Alabama, *Journal and Advertiser* (14 Oct. 1984).

26. Moore, "Home Schooling," 824-827.

27. David D. Williams, Larry Arnoldsen, and Peter Reynolds, "Understanding Home Education: Case Studies of Home Schools" (Apr. 1984), 5. Conference Paper for the American Educational Research Association in New Orleans.

28. Brendon Stocklin-Enright, "The Constitutionality of Home Education: The Role of the Parent, the State and the Child," *Willamette Law Review* 18 (1982): 563.

29. Holt, *Instead of Education*.

30. Merrill, "Schooling at Mother's Knee," 21.

31. Williams et al., "Understanding Home Education," 7.

32. Moore, "Home Schooling," 122.

33. Merrill, "Schooling at Mother's Knee," 20-21.

34. Perchemlides v. Frizzle, No. 16641 Massachusetts Superior Court (1979). Transcript of decision in letter to author from Rockland Independent School District, Massachusetts.

35. James W. Tobak and Perry A. Zirkel, "Home Instruction: An Analysis of Statutes and Case Law," *University of Dayton Law Review* 8 (Fall 1982): 1-60.

36. In re McMillan, 226 S. E. 2d 693 N.C. Ct. App. (1976).

37. In re Baum, 401 NYS 2d 514 N.Y. App. Div.

38. Adams and Stein, *Who Owns the Children?*

39. Merrill, "Schooling at Mother's Knee," 19.

40. Wisconsin v. Yoder, 406 U.S. 205 (1972).

41. Michigan v. Nobel, 57th Dist. Ct., Allegan Cty., Mich. (cited in *Teach Your Own* by John Holt, 290-294).

9

HOME SCHOOLING IN THE UNITED STATES AND CANADA

Susanne Miller and Ross Campbell

Following is a list of basic home school regulations, condensed from the Home School Legal Defense Association's *Statute Chart of the Fifty States* and Holt Associates' *Growing Without Schooling*. The regulations are current as of August 1989, but they are open to legislative changes and new judicial interpretations.

Alabama allows home schooling in the form of private tutoring or attendance at a church or church-affiliated school. Both the parent and the church school administrator must sign an enrollment form to file with the local superintendent. Certification is required only of private tutors, and testing is not required.

Alaska allows for home tutoring, enrollment in an approved correspondence course, instruction in a private school (home school may qualify), and "educational experiences" approved in advance by the local board. Only tutors must be certified, and testing is required in grades 4, 6, and 8.

Arizona home schoolers must file an annual home school affidavit. No certification is required, but parents must pass a proficiency exam in basic skills. The child must take an annual standardized test of the parents' choice, and results must be filed with the county superintendent.

Arkansas home schoolers must give the local superintendent annual notification of their intent to home school, and they must submit results of annual tests chosen by them from the state board's list and administered by the board's designee. A child with unsatisfactory results (eight months below grade level) may repeat the test or enroll in school. Certification is not required.

California home schools are allowed to (1) operate as private schools by filing an annual private school affidavit; (2) have instruction provided by a certified private tutor; (3) be enrolled in an independent study program at home, using the public school curriculum; or (4) enroll in a private school satellite program and take "independent study" through that school. Certification is necessary only if the home school operates as a private tutor. No testing is required.

Colorado recognizes that home-based education is a legitimate alternative to classroom attendance for the instruction of children and that any regulation of nonpublic, home-based educational programs should be sufficiently flexible to accommodate a variety of circumstances. Parents must give notice fourteen days before starting home schooling and annually thereafter. Only tutors must be certified and testing is required for grades 3, 5, 7, 9, and 11. If the child scores below the thirteenth percentile, he or she will have a chance to be retested using an alternative version of the same test chosen by the parent.

Connecticut home schoolers must receive school board approval based on "equivalent instruction." Neither certification nor testing is required.

Delaware home schoolers must get approval based on evidence (including annual test results) of "regular and thorough" instruction. They may alternately qualify as a private school, in which case a private school certificate is evidence of instruction. Certification is not required, and testing is not required of private school students.

District of Columbia home schools must be approved by the board of education as private schools offering "substantially equivalent" instruction. Neither certification nor testing is required, but the teacher's qualifications must be approved.

Florida home schoolers must notify the county superintendent of their plans to home school. Certification is not required. The child may be evaluated by a standardized or state test, a certified teacher, or other means agreed to by the superintendent. A home school may be placed on a one-year probation if the results are unsatisfactory.

Georgia home schoolers must submit to the local superintendent a declaration of intent to home school and annual progress reports. Parents must have a high school diploma or General Equivalency Diploma (GED), or employ a tutor with a bachelor's degree. Testing is required every three years.

Hawaii recognizes an appropriate alternative educational program approved by the superintendent, notification of intent to home school submitted to the principal of the public school, or an employed tutor. Certification is not required. A bachelor's degree only is required for the tutor. An annual report of child's progress must be submitted to local principal. In grades 3, 6, 8, and 10, children must participate in the statewide testing program.

Idaho home schoolers must submit their curriculum for approval by the local board as "comparable instruction." Some boards have required parents to be certified. Testing is not required.

Illinois home schools may operate as private schools and may voluntarily submit to the local district a "statement of assurance" regarding curriculum breadth and attendance. Neither certification nor testing is required.

Indiana requires home schools, as private schools, to provide "equivalent instruction," but the state board is not allowed to define "equivalent" or to approve home schools. Neither certification nor testing is required.

Iowa allows home instruction only if it is approved by the state as "equivalent instruction" and is provided by a certified teacher. Parents may request from the state board a religious exemption from the certification requirement. Testing is not required.

Kansas home schools must register with the state board as private schools. The instructor must be competent although not necessarily certified, and testing is not required.

Kentucky home schools may qualify as private, parochial, or church schools; children enrolled in these are exempt from attendance in public schools. Neither certification nor testing is required.

Louisiana home schoolers must request approval in their first year, and the local school board must approve the request if the parent certifies that the home curriculum will be "at least equal" to the public school curriculum. Annual renewed approval is dependent on satisfactory test results and/or progress as verified by a certified teacher. Parent certification is not required.

Maine home schoolers must obtain approval through the commissioner of education. The regulations for approving home schools are the "Rules for Equivalent Instruction through Home Instruction," adopted by the Maine Department of Education in August 1988. Certification is not required, and testing is optional.

Maryland home schoolers must submit for the local superintendent's approval a schedule and curriculum plan through the parents or a correspondence school. No certification or testing is required.

Massachusetts home schoolers must attend a state-approved nonpublic school or be "otherwise instructed in a manner approved in advance" by the local superintendent or school committee. Neither certification nor testing is required.

Michigan home schools must obtain state approval as private schools providing "comparable instruction" by certified teachers. Testing is not required.

Minnesota home schoolers must submit to the local superintendent annual instructional calendars and progress reports. Certification is not required. Annual testing, given at a location agreed to by the local superintendent, is required. Children scoring below the thirtieth percentile must be evaluated for learning problems.

Mississippi home schoolers may submit to the county recorder of deeds an annual declaration of enrollment and intent to home school.

They must keep records of instruction and evaluation, along with samples of the child's work. Neither certification nor testing is required.

Montana home schoolers must give the county superintendent annual notification of their intent to home school and must provide a "basic educational program" as defined by the board of public education for public schools. Neither certification nor testing is required.

Nebraska home schools may "elect not to meet state accreditation or approval requirements" and instead file a religious objection to the requirements and give the local superintendent annual notice of their intent. Certification is not required, but parents must submit their qualifications to the local superintendent or take a competency exam. Achievement tests are required "for evidence that such schools are offering" basic skills.

Nevada home schoolers must submit for approval by the local board evidence of "equivalent instruction." The parent must either be qualified for certification, consult with a certified teacher, enroll the child in an approved correspondence course, or receive a waiver of this requirement. The Stanford Achievement Test is given in grades 1, 2, 4, 5, 7, and 8.

New Hampshire home schoolers must receive prior approval of their home-education program from the local superintendent. Disapproval may be appealed to the state board. Neither certification nor testing is required, but parent qualifications and evaluation methods are considered in the approval process.

New Jersey home schoolers must provide the local superintendent with satisfactory evidence of "equivalent instruction." Neither certification nor testing is required.

New Mexico home schoolers must notify the district superintendent annually of their intent to home school. Certification is not required, but the parent must have a bachelor's degree or ask the state superintendent to waive this requirement. Annual testing, given according to the local superintendent's procedures, is required.

New York home schoolers are required to send a notice of intent annually to their local school superintendent. The school then provides forms on which parents must submit their curriculum for the year. Quarterly progress reports must be filed. No certification is required. Standardized testing must be done in certain years, and narrative evaluations must be substituted in all other years. Students must score above the thirty-third percentile or show one year's progress; otherwise, the home school program is placed on probation.

North Carolina home schoolers must submit a notice of intent to the state director of nonpublic education, operate for a nine-month school term, keep attendance and immunization records, and administer annual standardized tests. The results do not need to be submitted, but they must be made available upon request by the state. Home schooling parents in North Carolina must have a high school diploma or GED.

North Dakota home school parents must file an annual statement of intent with the county superintendent of schools and maintain an annual record of courses. Parents who are not certified teachers are required either to be supervised by a certified teacher for one hour per week or to pass the state teacher's examination. Annual testing is required. If the child scores below the thirtieth percentile, he or she must be professionally evaluated for a potential learning problem.

Ohio local superintendents have the authority to determine whether a home schooled child is receiving satisfactory instruction by a "qualified" but not necessarily certified person. Disapproval can be appealed to the local juvenile court. The lack of standards for this authority has been labeled "too vague" by the court of appeals. Parents with a bachelor's degree may opt to establish a noncharted school by giving notice to the state department of education and covering public school subjects. Testing is not required.

Oklahoma home schools are recognized as private schools and are unregulated. Neither certification nor testing is required.

Oregon home schoolers must provide the local superintendent with annual notification of their intent to home school. Certification is not required. An annual approved test, chosen by the parent, must be given by a "neutral person," and scores must be above the fifteenth percentile. Disapproval based on test results can be appealed to the state superintendent.

Pennsylvania home school parents are required to file an affidavit by August 1 of each school year or prior to beginning to home school if beginning after the start of the school year. The affidavit must contain information about the students, assurance that subjects are taught in English, an "outline of proposed education objectives by subject area," and evidence of immunization. The parent/supervisor must annually maintain and provide the superintendent with certain documentation, including a portfolio of records and materials and "an annual written evaluation of the student's educational progress" by either a licensed psychologist or certified teacher. The parent/supervisor must have a high school diploma or its equivalent. Standardized tests must be administered to students for grades 3, 5, and 8.

Rhode Island home schoolers must have their program approved by the local school committee or by the state department of education on appeal. Neither certification nor testing is required.

South Carolina home schoolers must have their home-instruction program approved by the local board, or by the state board on appeal, as "substantially equivalent" to public instruction. Parents must have a high school diploma or GED and either have a bachelor's degree or pass a basic-skills exam geared for a junior in college. All students must participate in the new statewide basic skills assessment program. The test must be administered by a "certified school district employee."

South Dakota home schoolers need superintendent approval of their program as "competent alternative instruction." Certification is not required. The child must take an annual standardized test, which may be monitored by the district.

Tennessee home schoolers must give the local superintendent annual notice of their intent to home school. Parents teaching grades K through 8 must have a high school diploma or GED, and those teaching grades 9 through 12 must have a college degree or an exemption from this requirement. Testing is required in grades 2, 5, 7, and 9, and must be given by an approved testing service.

Texas home schools may operate as private schools, providing they use a written curriculum including the basic school subjects. Neither certification nor testing is required.

Utah home schoolers must obtain from the district board an approved attendance exemption based on evidence of curriculum breadth, instructor competence, and academic progress. Neither certification nor testing is required.

Vermont home schoolers must submit an annual notice of enrollment, including a curriculum description. Parent certification is not required. Evaluation options include test results, reports by teachers, and samples of the child's work.

Virginia home schoolers must submit to the local superintendent annual notice of their intent to home school, along with a curriculum description. Parents not using an approved correspondence course must either have a bachelor's degree or otherwise satisfy the local board. The parent must submit to the local superintendent annual progress reports or test results with scores above the fortieth percentile.

Washington home schoolers must file an annual declaration of intent to home school. The parent must be supervised by a certified teacher or be deemed "sufficiently qualified" by the superintendent. A standardized test or evaluation by a certified teacher is required annually. A home school may also operate as a private school extension.

West Virginia home schoolers must notify the county superintendent of their intent to home school. The parent must have a high school diploma and formal education at least four years beyond the oldest pupil or achieve a passing score on the National Teacher's Exam. Annual standardized testing is required, and parents of children scoring below the fortieth percentile must initiate a remedial program.

Wisconsin home schoolers must submit an annual statement of enrollment indicating compliance with basic-skills curriculum and attendance requirements. Neither certification nor testing is required.

Wyoming home schoolers must submit an annual curriculum plan in order to show that they provide a basic educational program. Neither certification nor testing is required.

Alberta: The local superintendent of schools is responsible for considering written applications for certification of "efficient instruction." Efficiency includes: a program consistent with the Alberta program of studies; the Alberta Correspondence School; or an approved private correspondence school; instruction by competent persons; and education progress evaluated thorugh the use of examinations or other methods of assessment appropriate to the home instruction program.

Alberta educational policy encourages parents and school boards to enter into contractual arrangements, enabling students to avail themselves of school board services. A Home Schooling Advisory Bulletin, outlining current policy, is available to parents and other interested persons.

British Columbia: New legislation recognizes the right of parents to exercise choice as much as possible in the type of schooling they wish to provide for their children. Parents may educate children at home or elsewhere, in accordance with Division 4 of the School Act, and must provide that child with an educational program, or "organized set of learning activities."

The principal shall offer to the home school learner or the parents, free of charge, evaluation and assessment services and the loan of educational resource materials that are authorized and recommended by the minister. The school has no authority to approve or supervise the education program of a home school learner unless so requested by the parent.

Manitoba: Formal permission and program approval are required from the Department of Education to teach children at home. Application is made directly to the department. Supervision and evaluation are carried out by a field representative in charge of home education.

Parents can borrow texts from their local school; the school is then reimbursed with funds from a textbook grant.

New Brunswick: The parent must apply to the minister of education in writing, requesting permission to teach the child at home. The minister may grant permission if it is determined that the program offered is adequate. If it is determined that the child is not receiving "efficient instruction" at home, the matter becomes an attendance case under the jurisdiction of the local school board.

Newfoundland: Requests to home school are made, following enrollment, to the district superintendent. In cases where parents refuse to enroll their children at school, or in cases where exemption requests have been denied by the superintendent, the Department of Education must be informed by the superintendent. A guide for exemption from attendance for home instruction has been prepared by the school attendance consultant.

Nova Scotia: An inspector or supervisor of schools must certify that a child is receiving instruction equivalent to that which he or she would receive in school, and a teacher must certify that the child has passed an examination in a grade of work suitable to his or her age and previous instruction. Parents or guardians can meet with the local inspector of schools to discuss their plans and receive curriculum guides outlining the provincial public school program. Satisfactory progress is measured by examinations conducted by a staff member of the school board serving the area in which the child resides.

Ontario: The Education Act states: "A child is excused from attendance at school if he is receiving satisfactory instruction at home or elsewhere." (Section 20.2) A working ministry definition of "satisfactory instruction" includes production of a written plan or curriculum, evidence that it is being followed (by way of written work), regular visits by board of education representatives, and standardized testing.

Prince Edward Island: Application must be made to the minister of education for permission to be exempted from public school attendance. When this permission is given, the child's progress must be monitored by a certified teacher and periodic progress reports forwarded to the Department of Education.

Quebec: The statutory requirement to attend school is met if the student "receives effective instruction at home." Home schoolers should write a letter to the person in charge of student services stating intentions and reasons. Request "La scolarisation à domicile: le droit des parents et le droit de la commission scolaire" (Home Instruction: The Obligation of Parents and the Obligation of the School Board).

Saskatchewan: Home schooling is allowed if "the pupil is under a program of instruction approved by the director or superintendent at home or elsewhere." (Education Act, Section 156(a)) A proposed program of instruction should be submitted to the local board of education for consideration by the director or superintendent.

Yukon: Compulsory education does not apply to a child who has reached a standard of education equal to or higher than that to be attained in the school or is being instructed in a manner and to a standard satisfactory to the superintendent.

10

PUBLIC SUPPORT FOR HOME SCHOOLING?

Myron Lieberman

Although home schooling is not appropriate for everyone, it is beneficial for a significant number of children. For reasons to be discussed, home schooling may be a viable option for a substantially larger number of students in the 1990s than it has been in past years. If this should happen, the issues involved in home schooling will become even more important than they are today.

The broad policy issue raised by home schooling is, under what conditions should it be allowed? Not so long ago, the main issue was whether it should be permitted at all. As a practical matter, this issue has been resolved in favor of allowing it under certain conditions; virtually every state currently allows home schooling. Nevertheless, the conditions that must be satisfied before one can teach one's children at home vary widely among the states. In some, conditions severely restrict home schooling; in others, conditions are easy to meet.

Insofar as public support for home schooling is concerned, the statutory distinction between "compulsory school attendance" and "compulsory education" is especially important. Some states require "compulsory school attendance." In these states, the legality of home schooling depends on whether the home qualifies as a "school." In other states, the statutes require "compulsory education." In such states, the legality of home schooling depends on the statutory definition of "education."

Although interpretation and administration of both kinds of statutes can reduce the practical differences between them, this distinction may be extremely important in the future. The reason for this relates to differences between education vouchers and tuition tax credits. Both are ways governments can assist nonpublic education, but their implications for the home school can be quite different. A

voucher is a government credit to be used to defray the cost of education. Usually, but not necessarily, vouchers are used to pay for private
school tuition. If a school charges more than the redeemable value of
the voucher, the parents have to pay the additional amounts required.
In some situations, denominational organizations or various scholarship funds may absorb the additional costs, but vouchers are likely to
cover less than full tuition at most private schools. In effect, an educational voucher system would operate like food stamps or Medicare
benefits: the government credit would be used to defray the charges of
a private provider.

As usually formulated, voucher legislation provides parents with a
credit that can be used to pay the costs of attending a school. In this
situation, only "schools" are eligible to accept and redeem vouchers.
From a home schooling perspective, the critical issue is whether a
home school qualifies as a school eligible to accept and redeem
vouchers. If state law required "compulsory school attendance," home
schools might be eligible to accept and redeem vouchers; if the law
required "compulsory education," home schools would not be eligible
for the benefits associated with status as a "school."

However, states could (and a few do) provide tax deductions or tax
credits for educational expenses. Although such statutes are commonly referred to as "tuition tax credits," the latter phrase is a mis-
nomer for two reasons. First, the statutes may provide a deduction
instead of a tax credit. Second, the deduction or tax credit may not be
available solely, or even primarily, for tuition. Instead, the tax benefits
may be available for transportation, textbooks, and other expenses of
schooling. In this case, the statutes might provide tax deductions or
credits whether or not the expenses incurred were based on attendance at a formal school.

Either vouchers or educational tax credits could be helpful to home
schoolers. Either or both could provide financial support for home
schooling, depending on the specifics of the legislation enacted. If tax
benefits for educational expenses become available, we can expect
some conflict between home schoolers and tax officials over educational expenses. Home schoolers will tend to adopt an expansive view
of such expenses; tax officials are more likely to adopt a restrictive
view. For example, home schoolers may seek tax deductions or credits
for rooms in the home that are modified or equipped to facilitate
learning; tax officials may not be willing to accept such an outcome.

Perhaps the most reliable supposition is that the states will differ on the issue, as they do on most others involved in home schooling.

In one possible favorable scenario, the home qualifies as a "school." Subsequently, the state enacts a voucher plan, whereby parents receive vouchers that can be redeemed by public or private schools, just as food stamps are redeemed for cash by grocery stores. In this case, the parents receive the voucher as parents, but redeem it for cash as a school. In less favorable scenarios, home schools are not eligible for vouchers, either because education at home is not allowed or because the home does not meet the requirements of a school. These are merely some of the possible ways that home schooling might or might not be affected by legislation on educational vouchers or tuition tax credits.

At present, home schoolers are more concerned about being left alone by government than about the possibility of government subsidies for home schooling. Nonetheless, as home schooling continues to receive greater legislative and judicial protection, home schoolers are likely to pursue new objectives that include some public support. After all, if one's home qualifies legally as a school, the temptation to seek the state subsidies that go with this status may be irresistible. As a matter of fact, home schooling might provide a feasible way to strengthen the kind of family structures most conducive to healthy child development. Our society is rapidly becoming age segregated, with adverse effects upon children. Increasingly, children grow up isolated from constructive relationships or relationships of any kind with adults. If parents can educate their children effectively at home, home schooling might be perceived as a desirable family as well as educational policy.

Regardless of its actual or potential benefits, any expansion of home schooling faces formidable political opposition. The opposition consists largely of public school organizations, chiefly the teacher unions. Like unions generally, the teacher unions seek a monopoly over the services offered by union members. Home schooling poses two major dangers to this objective. First, insofar as children are educated at home, fewer teachers are needed; insofar as few teachers are needed, union political influence and bargaining power are reduced. Second, any success of home schooling is highly embarrassing to the entire public school establishment: if children learn as much or more at home than they learn at school, the justification for public school expenditures becomes suspect indeed.

Understandably, public school organizations do not and cannot assert these self-serving reasons. Instead, they allege that children can't learn as much at home as in school, that they will be retarded socially, and that they will be subject to indoctrination, including indoctrination in undemocratic ideologies. The fact is, however, that these undesirable outcomes have not materialized, at least to the extent that they justify a ban on home schooling.

On the contrary, perhaps the most remarkable aspect of these claims is the absence of systematic evidence to support them. For example, consider the criticism that children educated at home would be retarded socially. In fact, this does not appear to be the case. Home schooling does not imply pervasive isolation from other adults and children. For one thing, home schoolers frequently use the public schools in various ways. They utilize school libraries and textbooks provided by the school districts. In addition, they often participate in field trips and extracurricular activities or utilize health services sponsored by the public schools. Inasmuch as these benefits are often provided statutorily to pupils—not to schools or parents—home schoolers are entitled to them on an equal basis.

More importantly, home schooling appears to provide pupils with more interaction with adults than normally takes place in schools. The increased interaction with adults, usually parents, seems to compensate for the decrease in interactions with other children. Regardless of the explanation, the evidence does not support the criticism that home schooling results in retarded social development. Interestingly enough, leaders of home school organizations contend that they have never lost a case that depended upon comparisons of home schooling to formal schooling. Of course, even if this is presently a valid claim, it may not be soon if the number of children educated at home continues to increase. The parents who have overcome the obstacles to home schooling thus far tend to be the most dedicated to home schooling; if and when parents not quite so dedicated try to educate their children at home, the superior showing of children educated at home may decline.

Regardless of the educational outcomes, we can expect more litigation over home schooling, especially on church-state and regulatory issues. For example, if the home qualifies as a school, should public support be prohibited if the home includes any religious symbols or

JILL FINEBERG

objects? Clearly, conventional approaches to separation of church and state may be difficult to apply under home schooling. On the one hand, public agencies are constitutionally obligated to avoid entanglement with religious organizations; on the other hand, such avoidance will or could be difficult in home schooling situations.

In practice, problems such as the foregoing may lead school authorities to abandon a regulatory approach to home schooling. Instead of regulation, states and school districts may rely more upon testing educational achievement; as long as pupils educated at home perform reasonably well on such tests, regulatory approaches may be suspended or relegated to a secondary role. To the extent that this happens, home schooling can make an important contribution to education generally.

By emphasizing their willingness to have the results justify home schooling, home schoolers raise several basic issues. Clearly, there is reason to question the expertise of the teaching profession and the vast sums spent for public education if children educated at home perform as well or better on various tests of educational achievement. Public schools will not be able to avoid these issues on the grounds that achievement tests do not measure all the important objectives of public education. Whatever the objectives are, public and private schools will have to provide some evidence to support their claims of superiority or essentiality.

What is the future of home schooling? As the previous discussion suggests, home schooling will be affected by several issues whose outcome is still very much in doubt. Nevertheless, a quantum increase in the number of home schoolers is a distinct possibility, even though home schoolers are not a large political group in any state.

Technological developments, especially in communication systems, are likely to have two major effects conducive to home schooling. First, the number of parents who work at home is likely to increase dramatically. Indeed, some predictions along this line go so far as to question the viability of cities that are based upon huge office buildings serving thousands of commuters. Given the savings in time, the fact that many workers will not be tied to regular schedules, and the increase in part-time employment, the number of parents choosing to educate their children at home also may increase substantially.

Second, improvements in technology are virtually certain to lead to improvements in the quality of home schooling. For example, future home schoolers will have access to more and better instructional materials than are available in schools today. One bold prediction is that by the year 2000, families will be able to access the entire Library of Congress at a reasonable cost. However, the most critical improvements will be in interactive systems, not simply in access to more information.

An upsurge in home schooling would be a paradoxical turn of events. With the Industrial Revolution, men left the household to work outside the farm or home. With the feminist revolution, more and more women are leaving the home. Now, technological changes already under way have the potential to reduce the separation of home and work. To the extent that this does happen, it will also reverse the trend to educate children away from home in a separate institution called "school."

Broadly speaking, two kinds of problems impede this reversal. One is the statutory environment of public education, especially in conjunction with the public education lobby's active opposition to any legislation that weakens its monopoly. The other is the pervasive tendency to equate education with formal education, that is, attendance at a formal school. Although formidable, these problems are not insurmountable. In my opinion, the emergence of one or two break-through states could trigger a major surge in private education, including home schooling.

To cite just one possibility, New Hampshire law already allows local governments to rebate property taxes for a broad variety of purposes. It is anticipated that in 1990 one or more local governments in New Hampshire will provide a rebate of property taxes for educational expenses. In effect, the law will provide an educational tax credit as a local option. Undoubtedly, the rebate for private school expenses will be challenged in the courts; the implications of it for home schooling are not clear and may not be for some time.

Nevertheless, inasmuch as the rebate legislation is already on the statute books and will be used to reduce the tax burdens of parents who enroll their children in private schools, the New Hampshire situation bears close scrutiny in the immediate future. If the tax credit is applicable to the expenses of home schooling, it is likely to result in more children being educated at home. If the credit is not available to home schoolers, it may encourage some parents who are educating their children at home to enroll them in private schools. In any case, major efforts to enact educational tax credits or vouchers are also already under way in Delaware and Louisiana. Their success or failure could have a major impact on home schooling, as well as on the prospects for private schools in the 1990s.

HOME STUDY AND THE PUBLIC SCHOOLS

Geeta Dardick

Imagine that you want to teach your children at home. Rather than opposing your decision, your local public school officials reply, "Great. That's fine by us. We'll put you in our home study program."

The school's personnel then give you access to books, computers, video supplies, and sports equipment. A friendly home study teacher offers to share useful educational techniques and suggests creative learning materials. Even though your children are now officially categorized as home study pupils, with permission from the classroom teacher at their grade level they can still return to school for interesting courses and field trips. They also have the option of interacting with children their age during educational events sponsored by the home study program. Alternatively, if they wish, they can have no contact with their peers at all. The choice is up to them and you.

Imagine further that this public school home study program is legal, supportive, and open to all elementary students and their parents. It even provides participating families a small stipend for purchasing special materials not available from the school's home study resource center. The only requirement for participation in the program is that the children *learn. How* they learn is left to the discretion of the parents and children involved in the program.

Good news: This home study program isn't imaginary. It has been functioning for the past ten years at the Twin Ridges Elementary School District in North San Juan, California (a small town in the Sierra foothills located halfway between Sacramento and Reno). The long-term acceptance of the Twin Ridges home study program by the parents, teachers, and school board proves that public school home study is neither revolutionary nor threatening. Rather, it is a sound educational practice that many other public schools would welcome if they understood it.

My daughter, Samantha, spent sixth, seventh, and eighth grades on the school's home study program. Before the school adopted its home schooling option, my husband, Sam, and I had spent many years attempting to create a learning environment within the public school that met our expectations for Samantha's education. Like many parents, we started out with the assumption that we had to send our children to school away from home, then tried valiantly to change the public school to fit our image of a good education. We worked diligently as teacher's aides and classroom volunteers, and Sam served three years as a school board member. We typified "concerned, involved parents" whose goal was a creative and challenging public school curriculum.

But despite all our efforts, we were never totally satisfied with the education Samantha received in the public school classroom. So in 1978, when the school principal introduced a plan for an alternative education program called "independent study," Sam, who was then president of the school board, encouraged its passage by a unanimous vote.

Apparently, we weren't the only family ready for an alternative. By 1982, 15 percent of the student body attended school at home. The program attracted families with gifted students whose needs weren't being met in the classroom, as well as those families who disapproved of the social climate at public school. Other families chose home study because it allowed them to incorporate religion into their children's curriculum, while still others used the program because they lived in remote areas and were unable to transport their children to school.

Sam, Samantha, and I joined the program in 1980 so that the three of us could explore the potentials of a home education. For us, home schooling became a twenty-four-hour process in which Samantha was virtually let loose to pursue whatever learning she wished, while Sam and I acted as informal facilitators. The home study teacher required that Samantha keep up with the California state curriculum for her grade level, but that proved no problem. By learning at home, she went far beyond the basics, evolving from a slow learner into an exceptional student.

One factor that helped make our home study experience so enjoyable was the positive link with the public school. Our school did its

utmost to make us feel at ease. During her seventh and eighth grade
years, Samantha received permission from her classroom teacher, Pete
Milano, to join her classmates at school one full day a week just to
maintain the social contacts that were of paramount importance to
her. She also attended all skiing trips and the annual San Francisco
field trip.

Currently a Regents Scholar at the University of California at
Santa Cruz, Samantha feels that her home study years offered her the
best of both worlds. "It gave me the opportunity to experience education in ways unavailable in the public school classroom," she says. "I
didn't have to wait for other kids. If something interested me I could
study it as long as I wanted to—at my own direction, not at someone
else's. Yet, by being in a public school program, when I finished my
three years on home study, I still knew what everyone else knew, just
more. I never was allowed to fall behind, because the school made sure
I stayed at grade level. So I just got far ahead."

The home study program at Twin Ridges currently has sixty-five
students in it. It is administrated by the superintendent, Paul
Alderete, and two home study teachers, Carol Nimick and Betsy
Abrams. Says Paul Alderete, "We are working closer with the parents
than ever before to help them plan their home study curricula. If a
home study student wants to focus exclusively on horses, that's fine,
but we help the child and parents figure out exactly how they can
build math, science, history, reading, and writing into their horse-
based curriculum."

Alderete calls home study an important option for educating children. "In our district, we don't have a singular philosophy that there
is only one way to educate kids," he says. "We prefer a multifaceted
approach, and our home study program serves as an opportunity for
parents to be very involved with their kids' educations. It creates great
family contacts, and it proves that there is more than one way to
receive an education."

When a family signs up for home study, parents and children meet
with the home study teachers to plan their individualized curriculum
for the year. Parents can buy new supplies using the hundred-dollar
materials allotment the school provides each home study pupil. They
can also borrow equipment from the sizable resource library of home
study materials that have been accumulated by previous students during the past ten years.

The most that Carol Nimick or Betsy Abrams work with any home study student is three hours per week. The only required interaction is a once-a-month meeting, conducted at home or at school. Traveling students correspond with the home study teachers by mail on a monthly basis. "Our role is very simple," says Carol Nimick. "We support the parents, who are the primary teachers."

If asked, Nimick and Abrams will help parents create their daily lesson plans. They also offer workshops for parents to improve their teaching techniques, as well as special classes and field trips for home study students. "None of these workshops or trips are mandatory," explains Nimick. "We hold them for children who feel the need to socialize."

Because most public elementary schools do not offer home study programs, Twin Ridges Elementary School has opened its doors to home study students living outside the district. "One-half of my students come from other school districts in California," says Ms. Nimick. "We also have a waiting list, but we have closed off the program at sixty-five students in order to keep our quality high."

At one time, twenty-five students from nearby Nevada City Elementary School District were enrolled in the Twin Ridges program. After a few years, the Nevada City School Board realized the benefits of home study and started a program within its own district. Other nearby districts also have brought in home study curricula in response to the popularity of the Twin Ridges experiment.

But why shouldn't every elementary school have its own home study program? If you are interested in trying to implement a similar program in your school district, here are a dozen basic arguments for home study that you can present to your local school board:

1. Home study programs increase the school budget by including students who are not present at school and who previously may have been considered truant. (At Twin Ridges, the school district currently receives approximately $5,000 in average daily attendance payments for each student enrolled in the home study program. This amounts to over $300,000 per year. After paying two teacher salaries plus all of the program's other expenses, this still gives additional revenues to the school.)

2. Home study programs improve school overcrowding problems.

3. Home study broadens curricula and alternatives offered by public schools.

4. Home study strengthens family ties and lets parents and children learn together.

5. Home study involves parents with the schools.

6. Home study lowers the dropout rate.

7. Home study turns the entire community into an educational resource.

8. Home study allows parents to act as private tutors for students who are behind in certain subject areas.

9. Home study increases the motivation of students with special interests.

10. In home study, advanced students can move ahead at their own pace.

11. Home study eliminates some discipline problems.

12. When tested, home study students do as well or better than the students in the classroom. (Statistics on testing are available from Twin Ridges Elementary.)

It seems logical that what is legal and workable within one public school system can exist in other school districts in the United States; it is simply a matter of educating the educators. Parents need to convince the school administrators that home study is an idea that benefits both schools and children. Remember, many administrators and teachers are parents as well—and all of them were once children. Be optimistic, and don't underestimate your school's ability to respond to new educational programs.

PART III:
WAYS OF LEARNING IN THE HOME

METHODOLOGIES AND CURRICULA

Patrick Farenga

Home schoolers have a broad selection of curriculum methods and materials from which to choose. These range from programs that tell how and when to complete each lesson to flexible, process-oriented curricula, designed by individual families for themselves, that emphasize self-regulation and learning in the real world. In discussing the differences, advantages, and disadvantages of various curricula and their methods, it helps to remember what our own school experiences were like, to envision what school experience is likely for our children, and to imagine the best learning situation we can create right now in our children's lives. To facilitate this, we can speak of three main home schooling methods: the fixed curriculum, the units of study curriculum, and the "unschooling" curriculum. ("Unschooling" is a word coined by the late educator John Holt to differentiate home schools from regular schools and to imply that the one need not be a copy of the other.)

According to the dictionary, a curriculum is simply a "series of studies required for graduation."[1] Many schools boast of the "rigor," the "breadth," the "individualization," or the "uniqueness" of their particular curricula and methods; and this diversity among schools demonstrates that there are as many ways to design and implement curricula as there are people willing to create and buy them. Despite the high-tech names and terms of certain curriculum methods, or, in current parlance, "instruction delivery systems," curriculum making is an art, not a science. We know that if knowledge has a body, it is surely a fluid one, changing constantly as we investigate ourselves and our world. The so-called "body of knowledge" a curriculum represents is not the fluid, real-world body, but rather a "body" instantly frozen once decision makers decide what it should be.

Ultimately, it is your local school administrators who decide "what should be taught, to which persons, and under what rules of learning."[2] These decisions are based on the perceived educational needs of the local community, as determined by the elected and appointed education authorities and influenced by state and district curriculum guidelines. Various curriculum methods are proposed to the authorities, or they seek out or even create ones they want, and then they choose which they will use.

Home schoolers follow the same process school administrators do when they select or design a curriculum for their school year, but with an eye to their own children's educational needs, not those of the general population. Before spending money or presenting your own curriculum to your school authorities, remember that no state has a prescribed curriculum for home schoolers. You must, however, cover the same subjects your local school does. To satisfy compulsory school requirements, you must also be able to prove that an education is taking place; how that education takes place is not within the school board's jurisdiction. In 1923, the United States Supreme Court wrote in *Pierce v. Society of Sisters*, "The fundamental theory of liberty upon which all governments in this Union repose excludes any general power of the state to standardize its children by forcing them to accept instruction from public teachers only."[3]

Potential home schoolers need not fear legal reprisal for attempting to do something different from typical schoolwork with their children. In fact, home schooling parents are provided with an opportunity to exploit what educators and curriculum specialists say is the best form of instruction: the one-to-one tutorial.[4]

Most of us know and have experienced the fixed curriculum known as a "general education": "science, mathematics, language, history/ social science, physical education, and visual and performing arts."[5] Most of us have been graded as deficient, average, or excellent in one or more of these areas because we did or did not measure up to the expected *learner outcome* of the curriculum.[6] This curriculum is based on the idea that there are certain things we all need to know by certain ages, and that if we don't know them we are deficient in our knowledge and need remedial instruction to get us "back on track."

As noted above, administrators subjectively select what "knowledge" is to be included in the fixed curriculum. This body of knowledge is usually presented in outline form as broad subjects for each grade, such as "first-grade mathematics," with a subset of objectives; for instance, (a) be able to count to twenty; (b) use cardinal and ordinal number facts. Home schooling parents should be able to get a copy of the curriculum requirements for their child's grade level from their local school so they can see exactly what is expected of children in their community. You can also get samples and outlines of curricula from curriculum manufacturers and from various other school services.[7]

The main advantage of the fixed curriculum is its ease of execution and evaluation for teachers and administrators. It paces the whole group to an easy-to-measure standard. This is especially useful for instructing large groups of children, where the teacher is expected to lead or direct class activities and give direction, instruction, and evaluation on a predetermined schedule. It allows for a simple method of tracking each student, based mainly on a series of graded tests, and provides a compact paper trail of the child's school achievements. In short, it reduces a child's personality, interests, motivations, social skills, and physical and mental abilities to alpha-numeric data. This reductionist view is then fed into numerous other schools' record-keeping systems and becomes the foundation for a student's "credentials." Once the teacher feels that a specific part of the curriculum has been mastered by the majority of the class, or when the curriculum calls for a particular objective to be completed by a certain date, instructor and class move on to the next curriculum step. The students who lag behind are presumed to do remedial work, perhaps with a bit of individual tutoring, to catch up.

The main problem with this method is that it is paced to the group and not to the individual. Too many children get lost and left behind with fixed-curriculum methods, and too many children get bored by the rigidity. One mother wrote about her encounter with the fixed curriculum when her son went to kindergarten: "the lock-step of the system became apparent when they studied numbers 1-5 in November, even though his teacher admitted all but two children knew 1-5 before entering kindergarten, and those two she didn't expect to learn 1-5 all year! So Nathan was bored."[8] Even among children (and, I must add, university students) who do well on tests based on fixed curricula, achievement is often more a result of short-term cramming of learning objectives for regurgitation than an accumulation of useful, long-term working knowledge.

In response, educators are changing their view of curriculum development to account for individual learning styles. A highly regarded curriculum concept and system, *master learning*, makes a case for breaking down each educational objective into a series of smaller goals. *Units of study*—also called *learning modules* or *teaching-learning units (TLUs)* depending on the system you use—are created to break down each *learning objective* into individual steps to be mastered, one unit at a time. The student does not move on until a particular unit is mastered. Mastery is achieved through the taking of tests (called *diagnostic progress testing*) supplemented by *feedback with correction* procedures for each unit.

The unit approach takes the basic concept of the fixed curriculum, namely, that we can determine a set amount of knowledge to be learned in a particular pattern over a number of years by all students, and splits this knowledge into small groups of units. This approach attempts to make up for the deficiencies of teaching large groups by including study modules to be used individually. This allows children of the same age but of a different academic levels to be in the same classroom at the same time.

To account for individual learning styles, modular curriculum makers advise that several different versions of the same module/unit be available to the learner to allow for different learning approaches to the objective. However, maintaining and updating modules proves to be a big administrative burden for a teacher in a large class, which is the major reason this method has not been successful in our schools.[9]

A parent using the unit approach with one or more children at home has a more manageable task. Home schoolers can take further advantage of this method by tailoring particular units of study to a child's existing interests rather than following predetermined modular learning. Thus, for a socially aware teen who doesn't especially care for mathematics, a parent can create a unit of study as follows:

Learning objective for this unit: to be able to identify and calculate mean, median, and mode.

1. Read *How to Lie With Statistics* by Darrel Huff (Norton, 1982).

2. Correctly find the mean, median, and mode within the following sets.

3. Note uses and misuses of mean, median, and mode in graphs and statistics of current news media.

In school, a typical unit lasts two weeks,[10] but home schoolers can

make them last as long or as short as necessary. In contrast to the fixed curriculum, the unit approach emphasizes the teacher as facilitator and individual tutor rather than as leader and lecturer of learning.

Both the unit and fixed-curriculum approaches are well suited to families who don't disagree with school methods, but who do disagree with school curriculum content. By shifting desirable content, such as more religious studies or more music lessons, into the curriculum or modules, these families can achieve their goals in a language and method the schools readily grasp.

The basic concept behind school and the school curriculum is to prepare children to be useful citizens by teaching them the skills they will need to know as adults. Accordingly, the real world is broken down into subjects—reading, writing, arithmetic—and these subjects are broken down into learning objectives, such as being able to distinguish uppercase from lowercase letters. These learning objectives are then subdivided to teach essential skills needed to obtain the learning objective, such as learning the alphabet. Many more units of study can be created in order to atomize any subject.

However, this categorizing of the world into a "body of knowledge," which is then subdivided into subjects, skills, and expected learner outcomes, is highly questionable. John Holt refused to become an academic for this very reason; in a letter to his first editor, who was encouraging him to get a Ph.D. in education, Holt wrote, "I am truly exploring, and an explorer does not know, when he starts into a bit of unknown country, what he is going to find there. But this is not how most of what passes for educational research is done, or how research proposals are written up."[11]

As to the "body of knowledge" espoused by our school officials, Holt wrote to another educator the following thoughts, which evolved while Holt was walking in snow:

> Physics, chemistry, biology, and the like, are not separate hunks of something called the Body of Knowledge, but different ways in which living men look at the whole of the world and the human experience around them. There is no physics out there in front of us, only snow, but the physicist asks himself a certain kind of question about it, or looks at it in a certain way, while someone else might think about it quite differently. Chemists might examine snow to see whether there was any dissolved matter in it. A biologist might look at it to see whether any microscopic life forms were attached to it, and so on. Perhaps the trouble with the traditional Body of Knowledge is that it makes knowledge dead where it should be alive, and that it divides it up into parts where it should be a whole. This is part of what I am trying to say. The other thing I would like to say is that there is nothing in books but print. There is no knowledge in books; the knowledge only comes when I have the print and, *in my mind*, changed or added to my view of how things are. We like to say that we get knowledge from books; it would be more accurate to say we *make* knowledge out of books.[12]

Before children go to school they are usually able to walk, talk, and socialize (unless they have been cruelly neglected or physically damaged), and some even know the rudiments of reading, writing, painting, drawing, and physical education. Children learn these skills by being with their parents, siblings, friends, and relatives, who use these skills: in short, they learn them from others in the real world, not in specially planned buildings and rooms with professionals ready to fill the children up with "knowledge." Recognizing that "instruction delivery systems" based on theoretical assumptions about groups of children learning in school have little bearing on their child's pre-school learning experiences, home schoolers can decide to forgo school methods and continue with their proven *instruction delivery system*, complete with its own *diagnostic progress testing* and built-in *feed-*

back with correction procedures; that is, the real world of family and local community.

By obtaining a copy of your school's curriculum, you will see that much of what is required is already being done by your child. Susan Richman, an author and home schooler from Pennsylvania, writes:

> I presented a Home Education Plan for Jesse at my initial meeting with the superintendent and his assistant. It included a short statement on our philosophy of education and a conventional subject matter breakdown—language arts (listening, talking, reading, writing), mathematics, social studies, science, art, music, and physical education and health, and also a section on evaluation procedures. I had already looked over the district's curriculum outlines for kindergarten and first grade and felt *very* confident that what we were doing informally at home easily met *all* grade level requirements, and in fact went much farther. Under each subject heading, I simply described, in normal language, not educational jargon, our basic approach in the area and listed specific interests and activities that Jesse had been involved with over the past year, indicating that we planned to continue in the same manner in the upcoming year.
>
> When I wrote these lists, I began to be amazed at how thorough, how *good*, we looked on paper. Why, it even looked like it might have been *planned*! (Reminded me again that our learning is *never* chaotic or without form, but just naturally creates its own form and order. . .) This type of curriculum write-up was almost a delight to do, since I was simply sharing some of the experiences of a favorite little person, and I could avoid the drudgery of trying to come up with dry behavioral objectives, goals, future teaching strategies, etc. And no superintendent could say, as one in western Pennsylvania did when shown a home schooling plan, "Pshaw! Idealism! It will never work!" for our plan wasn't describing what we vaguely hoped *might* happen, but what actually had *already* happened. It was fact and couldn't be argued with.[13]

How does one find form in the unplanned or present records that demonstrate mastery of a curriculum to which no one is forced to adhere? Home schooler Karen Cox writes about how her family's home schooling method is structured so as not to interfere with her family life and also so that it answers the need for written records for school officials to check against her proposed curriculum:

> I buy old-fashioned big blue lesson-plan books, one for each child. . . . On the columns I put headings which, unlike traditional headings, I have found to be very flexible, workable categories. The headings (some of which extend over two or three columns) are:
>
> 1. *Reading/Writing/Graphic Thinking*. On a typical day, the entries in a six-year-old's book might be * *The Lion, the Witch, and the Wardrobe* (the asterisk indicating it had been read to the child) and "Pencil sketches of horse and barn."

2. *Logical Thinking/Math*. Example entries: "Simple addition: oral problems set and answered. Practical application: adding pennies needed to buy stamp."

3. *Knowledge of Physical and Social World*. This one is easy and the possibilities are practically infinite. In this category can be included everything that might fall under the headings of biology, botany, zoology, career education, environmental studies, community studies, geography, geology, dramatic play, etc.

4. *Musical Thinking*. In this category are included everything from "Listening" and the name of the record to "Group Singing," with or without names of some of the songs we sang together in the car. It can, of course, include notations about piano lessons, dance classes, concerts attended, etc., but it's not just for formal lessons.

The categories are not, of course, what make the activities. They are simply baskets into which we can toss such activities. Lots of people feel better when they can see the full baskets, never mind what's in them.

Let me make it clear that I do not think that keeping such records makes me better at the business of growing with my children. Nor does it make any difference to what the children actually do with their time. These records are kept after the fact, not before. They simply record what we do. The children are not aware of the categories and feel, rightly, that I keep them for my own sake. It makes no difference to them that riding horses with a friend has been included under "Knowledge of Physical and Social World." Nor do they care that cutting the muffin recipe in half has been recorded as "Fractions—Divisions/Practical Application: Recipe adjustment and preparation of adjusted recipe."

It soon becomes obvious that there are far too many wonderful things happening each day to ever write them all down. But getting everything down is not the point either. For many of my friends, these records have had the value of proving to them that their children were, indeed, learning. Even though they weren't doing a set number of workbook pages each day and keeping a journal, they were learning and growing. In fact, it would be seen (pointed to on paper for faint-hearted relatives) that the children were actually doing a great deal more than would have been possible in a classroom.

The point is this: The structure of learning is not in the curriculum guidelines, nor in the teacher's plan book, nor in the workbook. The structure is in the world. As the children learn about their world, they are understanding its order, in the only way that makes sense to them. And the first time an adult *believes* that, whether they've used a big blue plan book or not, the sun breaks through.[14]

The "unschooling curriculum" is really just a term to satisfy educational authorities; in practice it simply means doing what you've always done with your child. No state education authority can possibly know what your child will need to know ten years from now, but your child can tell you what he or she needs to know right now, and you can help him learn it. This does not mean you have to become a professional child watcher, child entertainer, or child teacher. You don't have to spend days and nights worrying about your child's progress on the curriculum; you don't have to split the world into narrow subjects, turning every single *instructional opportunity* into training for the real world. *Correction feedback procedures* are immediate for home schoolers. Their children let them know pretty quickly if a method is working, and if it isn't, the parents are free to drop it for now and move onto something else or try again with different media or concepts. They don't need to get anyone's approval beforehand. Home schoolers can account for any departures from the original curriculum much more easily than a classroom teacher can.

John Holt described the unschooling method this way:

> What children need is not new and better curricula but *access* to more and more of the real world; plenty of time and space to think over their experiences, and to use fantasy and play to make meaning out of them; and advice, road maps, guidebooks, to make it easier for them to get where they want to go (not where we think they ought to go), and to find out what they want to find out. Finding ways to do all this is not easy. The modern world is dangerous, confusing, not meant for children, not generally kind or welcoming to them. We have much to learn about how to make the world more accessible to them, and how to give them more freedom and competence in exploring it. But this is a very different thing from designing nice little curricula.[15]

Developing trust regarding our children's abilities to learn is difficult, but if we observe them closely and provide only as much help as they ask for, we can see how industrious and intelligent they really are.

Trusting ourselves as our children's teachers is difficult to do as well, though we have all been "teaching" them (more or less by using an unschooling curriculum) from the moment they were born. The temptation to simply turn our homes into schools is great: purchasing an expert's plans for our children's learning is perceived by most adults as easier and more effective than relying on ourselves to watch and aid our children in learning without daily expert advice. This method may be fine for a while, but there is a strong chance that your children are one day going to protest: "Why is our home so much like school? What's the difference? I might as well be in school if I have to do the same old stuff in the same old way!" Home schooling doesn't need to be perceived as an attempt at making an alternative school. It can be a refreshing alternative to school, a whole new approach to education.

A lot of the choices you make with curriculum will depend on your particular family and school circumstances, but there is absolutely no need to duplicate school methods in your own house. Curriculum design is an art. With home schooling, you have the opportunity to help your children sculpt their own distinctive work.

Notes

1. *Webster's New World Dictionary* (New York: Simon & Schuster, 1984).

2. *Encyclopedia of School Administration* (Phoenix: Oryx Press, 1988), 83.

3. John Holt, *Teach Your Own* (New York: Delacorte Press, 1981), 278.

4. Gagne, Briggs, Wager, *Principles of Instructional Design* (Orlando: Holt, Rinehart, Winston, 1988), 83-84.

5. *Encyclopedia of School Administration* (Phoenix: Oryx Press, 1988), 83.

6. Words in italics can easily be substituted for plain English to prove to school officials you know what's what in their lingo.

7. For instance, write for the "Typical Course of Study, K-12," Worldbook-Childcraft International, Educational Services Dept., Merchandise Mart Plaza, Chicago, IL 60654. This pamphlet is available for $0.25 from them.

8. *Growing Without Schooling* 31 (Boston: Holt Associates, 1989): 10.

9. *Principles*, 309.

10. Ibid., 304.

11. Excerpted with permission from the forthcoming book *A Life Worth Living: The Collected Letters of John Holt*, Susannah Sheffer, ed. (Columbus: University of Ohio Press, 1989).

12. Ibid.

13. *Growing Without Schooling* 34: 5.

14. *Growing Without Schooling* 23: 1-2.

15. Holt, *Teach Your Own*, 168-169.

Teaching Difficult Subjects

Patrick Farenga

> *"Education is not the filling of a bucket,*
> *but the lighting of a fire."*
> —W. B. Yeats

When we are stumped by a question from our children, we can respond in the same ways a school teacher can (1) give the correct answer; (2) obfuscate the questioner with some phony answer; (3) simply avoid the question (and diminish its importance) by saying something like, "It isn't in my field"; (4) or say, "I don't know."

Some parents and teachers feel it is their duty to provide a role model for their children with no chinks in the armor. They steadfastly avoid saying "I don't know," as if all future credibility will be destroyed by such an admittance. But there is no evidence that this is healthy or desirable for child, parent, or teacher. A recent article in the *Boston Globe* entitled "When Children Discover Your Flaws" quotes several professionals on this subject. David Elkind, a professor of child studies at Tufts University and author of *The Hurried Child*, notes that "it is healthy for your child to hear that adults can make mistakes, healthier, still, to hear adults admit to them. When you don't, your child will be watching for the next error and keeping an internal assessment. A pattern of this, over years, can lead to a lack of trust. . . . The parent who can't admit to a child that he is wrong, has a problem." Developmental psychologist Robert Selman says, "Parents who maintain their own self-esteem but acknowledge their imperfections have more secure children."[1]

If you maintain an attitude about home schooling that emphasizes the learning process rather than the teaching process, you allow yourself to learn alongside your children and provide them with a model of how adults behave when confronted, as we often are, with situations we need to know more about. A home schooling father, Robert Smith of Georgia, writes:

> A child can use "I don't know" as an answer. It merely means he has to seek out someone else for the answer. "I don't know" furnishes the child with a fresh start. Of course, it is good to be able to add some helpful advice on where the answer might be found. My son Michael (now 17) has asked me questions and I have said, "I don't know," but I added that we can look in the encyclopedia and see what it has on the subject and start from there. If that didn't produce an acceptable answer I sent him to the library to find out what they have.[2]

Museums and local libraries can be primary resources for many home schoolers. They can be a great ally when your child asks, "Why is the sky blue?" or other questions that puzzle you just as much. Rather than fudge a response like, "I think it has something to do with the light rays from the sun," you can respond, "I'm not sure. I seem to remember it has something to do with the way light enters our atmosphere. Let's write that one down and research it when we go to the library [or science museum, or when we talk to grandpa, who knows a lot about the sky and weather]." Children's museums, science museums, and art museums often provide hands-on exhibits, informal classes and lectures, and ongoing programs that you and your children can volunteer for and learn from.

What if museums and libraries are not near or don't exist in your area? Don't worry. Since the goal of school is allegedly to prepare children for the real world, you always have plenty of primary learning material at hand: the world around you. A teaching-learning metaphor that comes to mind from Mr. Smith's description above is that of the general contractor, who oversees all aspects of a construction project but subcontracts specific parts of the job to individuals who specialize in certain areas of construction. Likewise, home schoolers are able to help their children learn what they need to know by offering their help in areas in which they are knowledgeable and finding people, materials, or learning situations for those areas they don't feel comfortable with.

As the general contractor for your children's education, you have a multitude of resources available to you. Besides searching through home schooling publications, which frequently feature advertising from companies and individuals offering all sorts of tutorial services and specialized curricula, one should think very hard about friends, relations, neighbors, and business associates who have expertise in areas your children want to explore. The advantage of this approach is that a barter arrangement can often be worked out, such as, "If you take time to talk with my child about how airplanes fly [or about what biologists do, how to program a computer, and so on] I'll exchange it for an hour of child care [make you dinner, tune your car, whatever]."

Another way to approach unfamiliar subjects is to find textbooks, workbooks, primary texts, and other materials that pertain to an area of study with which you are unfamiliar and, as Mr. Smith indicates, learn it alongside your children, instead of on your own with the intention of later teaching them. You can also provide these materials to your children and let them learn alone. Children will certainly learn the material if they have asked questions about it. To cite but one example, a great many children have picked up computer skills on their own simply by having one in the house, while the parents remain "computer illiterate." The self-esteem and confidence your children will gain from researching and learning something on their own is one of the great pleasures of scholarship—a pleasure too often relegated to the last years of formal schooling. If your children know how to check a book out of the library, it is a safe bet they can learn how to obtain other information from there as well. This is not to say, however, that you should ignore your children, not answer their questions and requests for help, or give them more responsibility than they can handle.

If you are so inclined you can ask for, and you should receive, the curriculum and textbooks your children would use for their grade levels in your local public school. You can then make use of the method many teachers employ when they find themselves over their heads in certain subjects: simply stay one chapter ahead of the students. But if following a textbook step-by-step isn't your idea of learning, this method will be of limited value. Also, your children may leapfrog through a textbook and actually get to be a few chapters ahead of you!

The main places for finding traditional teachers and tutors are, of course, your local schools, colleges, and universities. A teacher or a graduate student can agree to tutor your child in their area of expertise on a fee-for-service basis or in exchange for using the information and experience they gain from working with your child in their own research and publications. Elementary school teachers often need sec-

ond incomes, and working with a student who wants one-to-one
tutorials would be most enlightening, even enjoyable, for teachers
who must spend most of their day doing "classroom management."

Sometimes money becomes an obstacle in learning more advanced
subject matter. For instance, a child may want to learn more about
biology by dissecting a frog and examining it under a microscope.
Upon discovering the costs of such a project, the parent may try to
work something out with the local school so the child can participate
in the standard biology class. Friendly school districts will often make
such arrangements; indifferent or hostile schools probably will not.

If your school falls into the latter category, you may be put off by the
costs of buying the educational equipment that your children may
need for certain courses, such as chemistry, physics, or language
studies. Don't be. To paraphrase John Holt on this matter, the vast
majority of educational equipment your child will need to perform lab
work equivalent to that of the schools is relatively inexpensive.[3] Most
of the big, expensive equipment in a high school lab is rarely utilized;
it is the individual pieces of equipment that are used repeatedly. This
equipment can be purchased through the mail or at a mall from a
variety of sources, and you can probably adequately equip your home
lab for under two hundred dollars.[4]

"Two hundred dollars for lab equipment!" you scream. It seems like
a lot for something your child may use only for several months, but
you never know. It could be what starts your child on the path to
becoming a scientist. After all, we regularly purchase materials for our
children that cost over a hundred dollars—such as Nintendo, sport-
ing goods, camping equipment, musical instruments, and
computers—without knowing if our children will become computer
programmers, professional athletes, naturalists, or musicians. Why
not purchase the equipment they need for their studies? Unless
damaged, laboratory and other equipment can be sold and reused by
other home schoolers or junior scientists in your area. Local home
schooling groups often arrange swaps of such equipment (as well as
textbooks, curricula, and the like), just as neighbors swap children's
clothes as new children are born or older children outgrow them.

Other local resources you can use to help answer your children's
questions and also expose them to more of the real world at a time
their age-mates are in school follow:

MICHAEL WEISBROT

1. *Elderly people.* You can visit the elderly in your neighborhood or in retirement areas. Make inquiries or post signs asking for older people to meet with your children to share their expertise or information about subjects in which your children are interested but in which you are not well-versed. This can be particularly enlightening for your child if he or she poses questions like, "How did people live without telephones and TV?" or "How did people commute to work before cars?" History has much more meaning and value when one realizes that live people, not just textbooks, are repositories of our cultural heritage. You may even find a few retired teachers or professors who would happily share their work with a child who is interested in their fields.

2. *The Yellow Pages.* If your child is interested, for example, in publishing or architecture, a tactful phone call to a local business asking to visit so you and your child can see what it is publishers and architects do can result in a valuable field trip. If your child is old enough and impresses the businessmen with his or her enthusiasm for the work being done at these places, you might be able to arrange an apprenticeship situation.

3. *New and used bookstores.* An obvious resource, but one we often overlook. Sometimes the clerks in these stores are quite knowledgeable about certain subjects and can direct you to good books on subjects with which you are unfamiliar. If they don't have a book, they can frequently order it for you.

4. *Reference works.* In your local library, such reference books as *Books in Print* and *The Reader's Guide to Periodical Literature* can direct you to many sources of information. Browsing through these books will give you a sense of just how many different ways there are to approach a topic and also a sense of what a real astronomer, writer, or biologist might read. Even though your local library might not carry, for example, *Sky and Telescope* magazine, it can be ordered or obtained from another branch. At the least, you can get the magazine address from these references and write directly to the publisher, requesting an issue, subscription, or reprints of a particular article. Very often the most up-to-date information in a particular area appears first in professional journals, so you and your children will not only get the information you need, but also the feeling of being at the cutting-edge of such fields.

The notion that only people skilled in teaching can effectively teach is a thoroughly modern one and really doesn't have much basis in practical experience—even in school. John Holt wrote:

> The schools, in teaching the poor (and the rich, too) that no one can teach a child anything except a "trained" teacher, have done them (and all of us) a great and crippling injury and wrong. A number of poor countries have had mass literacy programs, often called Each One Teach One, in which as fast as people learn to read they begin to teach others. They have found that anyone who can read, even if only fifty or a hundred words, and even if he only learned them recently, can teach those words to anyone else who wants to learn them. Every now and then, in this country, a school, often a city school for poor kids, lets older children, fifth or sixth graders, teach first graders to read. Most of them do a better job than the regular teachers. Quite often, older children who themselves are not very good readers turn out to be the best teachers of all. . . .
>
> People who make careers out of helping others—sometimes at some sacrifice, often not—usually don't like to hear that those others might get along fine, might even get along better, without their help.[5]

"Paired learning" is educator's jargon for the Each One Teach One concept. So if you or your children know other children who have experience or knowledge in an area in which you are deficient, and they wouldn't mind tutoring your child for a half an hour per week, or whatever it takes for your child to learn the subject, don't be afraid or ashamed of using them. This method was the primary method that teachers in one-room schools used with great success, and many of our modern-day classrooms have fallen back on this time-honored method.

There is no proof that more teaching credentials and courses make one a better teacher; there is, however, ample proof that the more one works with children, the better one becomes at it. In states that are suffering teacher shortages, schools are willing to use people with no teaching credentials and provide them with "provisional" or "alternative" certification. This means they can teach immediately, usually supplementing this work with standard "classroom management" courses during their evenings. This program has been successfully used in several states, usually drawing on people in business who wish to teach. Interviews with such "teaching interns" in Texas showed that except for the incredible amount of paperwork involved in the job, they generally felt the program prepared them for their new task.

"One thing I've learned is the importance of rapport between teacher and students," says Roger Brewer, an intern teaching bilingual classes to fourth, fifth, and sixth graders. "It's definitely not just [a matter of] being smart and knowing the material."[6]

A very important study by British researchers Dr. Barbara Tizard and Martin Hughes used radio microphones to record and analyze interactions between four-year-old children and their mothers and teachers. The book that resulted from this study, *Young Children Learning*, should be read by any parents who doubt their own abilities to help their children learn or doubt their children's abilities to learn from them. While the study concentrated on four-year-olds, its implications are quite important for older children and for parents who want their children to avoid the continuing pressure to attend "early learning classes," followed by "preschool," followed by "kindergarten." The study concluded that the home "is a far richer source of intellectual growth than a nursery class."[7]

> Our analysis of the conversations at home led us to an enhanced respect for intellectual activities of four-year-olds. Children are by no means passive absorbers. On the contrary, their own intellectual efforts are an essential part of the learning process. Even with the most attentive mothers this process was not always easy. In all the homes many questions went unanswered, much was left implicit, misunderstandings were often undetected by the mothers, full explanations were rarely given, and many explanations were definitely misleading. Armed with only their curiosity, logic, and persistence, the children tack-

> led the task of making sense of a world they imperfectly understood....Our
> study suggests that the kind of dialogue that seems to help the child is not that
> currently favored by many teachers in which the adult poses a series of ques-
> tions. It is rather one in which the adult listens to the child's questions and
> comments, helps to clarify her ideas, and feeds her the information she asks for.[8]

John Holt put these conclusions another way when he wrote to a mother who was full of doubts about her abilities to teach her child: "I hope you will not doubt your competence to help your children learn anything they want to learn, or indeed their competence to learn many things without your help."[9]

There are other types of questions with which children stump parents, and these are often philosophical in nature. For instance, when my wife was five she asked her mother, "Why are all the important things in life, like God and love, invisible?" Such questions are opportunities for us to reflect and think of the appropriate response, based more on our own personal religious, philosophical, and moral upbringing than on any textbook learning. We ought to deal with these questions seriously, though they "are from the mouths of babes."

Current learning theory, based principally on the theories of Jean Piaget, claims that children are incapable of logical thought until age seven.[10] This theory gives adults a way out of answering such questions by claiming, "You won't understand why until you are older." But *Young Children Learning* and other important books[11] shed considerable light upon the probing intellectual questions young children ask before age seven and give us ample evidence that we ought not to dismiss such questions out of hand, even though they are not part of any schoolwork.

John Holt spent the latter part of his life as an education reformer arguing that while we may *want* to study something with a teacher or use school facilities, there is no *need* for us to do so—at any age. A large number of the most important scientific and social discoveries of the last hundred years have occurred off campus, often from people with undergraduate degrees or no degree at all. A few such people (all of whom did not have college degrees) are President Harry S. Truman, writer Mark Twain, Walt Disney, and philosopher/inventor Buckminster Fuller.

Thomas Edison's many inventions and discoveries all took place outside of the university, and he had only three months of formal education; he was removed from school because his teacher referred to him as "addled" and discplined him with a leather strap. "Mrs. Edison thought of learning as 'exploring' and set about to make it as much fun for her son as she could. It wasn't long before she couldn't keep up the pace Alva was setting. She bought him books full of experiments, which he tested enthusiastically in an attempt to prove the author wrong. As he grew and one experiment led to another, he invented the telephone transmitter, stock ticker, mimeograph, phonographs, and perfected the electric lightbulb."[12]

Nicola Tesla, inventor of, among many things, the Tesla coil, radio transmitters, and the alternating current, did so independently in his lab in Manhattan.[13] A man in Michigan named Ovshinsky "stood solid-state physics on its ear by inventing a theory by which non-crystalline substances could be used to do things which, according to orthodox theory, only crystalline materials could do. . . . *Ovshinsky never finished high school.* There are probably more cases like [Ovshinsky] than we know, and there would be a great many more except for compulsory schooling laws. It's a Catch-22 to say, first, that all children have to spend all that time in schools, and then to say that all kinds of things can only be learned in schools. How do we know? Where have we given people a chance to learn them some-where else?"[14]

By home schooling, you are providing that "somewhere else" for your child. You are explorers of new territory in the land of learning, and you need not be fearful. Instead, be confident that you and your children are adequately equipped for the mission.

Notes

1. "When Children Discover Your Flaws," *Boston Globe* (4 Sept. 1989).

2. *Growing Without Schooling* 19 (Boston: Holt Associates, 1989): 9.

3. John Holt, *Teach Your Own* (New York: Delacorte Press, 1981), 61.

4. One source of science equipment is Edmund Scientific Co., 101 Gloucester Pike, Barrington, NJ 08007. Their $1 catalog is jam-packed with do-it-yourself science equipment. For budding inventors, the Jerryco catalog (send $0.50 to 601 Linden Place, Evanston, IL 60202) is packed with industrial and military surplus items at incredibly low prices.

5. *Growing Without Schooling* 2: 1.

6. "Short of schoolteachers, Texas eyes new sources," *Christian Science Monitor* (11 Mar. 1986), 3.

7. Martin Hughes and Barbara Tizard, *Young Children Learning* (Cambridge: Harvard University Press, 1984). A key part of the *Young Children Learning* study examined the oft-made charge that working-class children score lower than middle-class children on IQ tests and tests of language development. The educational consensus of the reasons for these low scores is that "working-class children have deficient language skills; that these are due to deficiencies in the language environment of the homes; and that their inadequate language skills are the main cause of their poor performance at school" (pp. 135-136). *Young Children Learning* and the work of American linguist William Labov show that these children do indeed grow up in a rich verbal culture and the "cause of the children's low educational achievement must be sought not in their homes but in the schools—for example, in the low expectations or low standards of the teachers" (p. 136).

8. *Young Children Learning* (Harvard University Press, Cambridge, 1984), 253-254.

9. Holt, *Teach Your Own*, 62.

10. Hughes and Tizard, *Young Children Learning*, 19.

11. *Philosophy and the Young Child* (Cambridge: Harvard University Press, 1980) and *Dialogues with Children* (Cambridge: Harvard University Press, 1984), both by Gareth Matthews, provide striking examples of serious logical thinking by children under and over seven and useful ideas for explaining difficult concepts to children.

12. Malcolm Plant, *Famous Homeschoolers* (Farmingdale, N.J.: Unschoolers Network, 1986).

13. George Trinkaus, *Tesla: The Lost Inventions* (Claremont, Calif.: High Voltage Press, 1988).

14. Holt, *Teach Your Own*, 61-62.

THE COMPUTER AS A CONVIVIAL TOOL

Aaron Falbel

What is the effect of the computer on the mind of the child? Does the computer enhance thinking skills or does it promote heartless, mechanical, instrumental reason? In short, is the computer good for children or bad for them?

It is understandable that these questions should be of great concern to home schooling parents, who are confronted with the growing presence of computers in the workplace and in schools, as well as in the home; a critical outlook is a healthy one. But the problem with asking questions regarding the effect of the computer is that such questions presume that the computer itself can somehow directly affect thinking and learning—that the computer, solely by virtue of its being a computer, can change the way people think and learn. It is all too easy for the technical object, because it is new and not well understood, to loom too large and eclipse our finer critical sensibilities. Seymour Papert, educational theorist and author of the book *Mindstorms*, calls this type of reasoning, where one gives undue centrality to a technical object, "technocentric thinking."

In an essay that appeared in *Educational Researcher*, Papert asks us to consider other "obviously absurd" technocentric questions:

> Does wood produce good houses? If I built a house out of wood and it fell down, would this show that wood does not produce good houses? Do hammers and saws produce good furniture? These betray themselves as technocentric questions by ignoring people and elements that only people can introduce: skill, design, aesthetics. . . . Everyone realizes that it is carpenters who use wood, hammers, and saws to produce houses and furniture, and the quality of the product depends on the quality of their work.[1]

It ought to be equally obvious that *people*, not computers, are the actors when it comes to thinking and learning. People use computers to do things. If we are to say anything meaningful about the thinking and learning involved, then we should look at what people are doing with computers and not what "the computer" is allegedly doing to them. For, in reality, there is no such thing as "the computer" in general—only specific uses of computers in specific contexts.

The fact that this is not obvious and that technocentric questions abound in discussions concerning children and computers is due to a certain basic fallacy in many people's thinking about education generally. This fallacy equates education with schooling or instruction: a designed process or technical act that is *performed on* the learner. With such a definition of education, it is not hard to see how questions regarding the effect of the computer enter the picture.

But education—real education—is not something performed on someone, nor is it something one *gets*. It is something one does for oneself. I generally prefer to use the word *learning* instead of *education*. *Learning* has an active feel to it, whereas *education* carries with it a sense of passivity. Certainly a major reason many families choose home schooling in the first place is because they oppose viewing education in this way, that is, as a service that is "received" or "delivered."

With a passive view of education, we open the door to technocentrism when we speak of the computer as an "educational tool." It should not be an *educational* tool, but just a tool. Like other tools, it allows us to do some things that we couldn't do before or, more usually, to do some things that we could do before better.

It is somewhat vacuous to distinguish the computer by calling it "a tool for learning." In a sense, *all* tools are learning tools: we learn when we do things and tools can help us do things better. Unfortunately, most of the time when people describe the computer as a *learning tool*, what they really mean is that they see it as a *teaching tool*: something you learn *from* as opposed to something you learn *with*, or, even worse, something that they think will *make* people learn.

Much has been written about the question of the "value-neutrality" of technology, that is, whether tools and machines somehow "embody" certain values that are in turn imposed upon their users. But to ascribe values to tools is also a form of technocentrism, for it is not the tools themselves but the *use* of tools that we should be evaluating, and such uses are certainly not value-free. Sherry Turkle, who has written a highly detailed and sensitive account of people's interaction with computers, comments on the question of value neutrality in the following way:

> I have often been asked, "Are computers good or bad?" The question was usually asked in regard to children, but as home computers moved aggressively into the workplace, I was increasingly asked to answer this question in regard to adults. The question deserves some comment. No one asks whether relationships with people are good or bad in general. Rather, we seek out information to build our own model of a *particular* relationship. Only then do we make judgments about the possible effects of the relationship.... Computers are not good or bad: they are powerful.[2]

The crucial point is that it does not make sense to talk of good or bad machines outside of any reference to the particular ways they are being used.

Why do critics get so hot under the collar when it comes to this issue of value neutrality? Why do they devote endless pages to arguing this point, pages thick with quotations from Hegel, Weber, Marx, and Cassirer? I understand their fear well enough: that science is an arena without ethical values; that science deals with truth and falsity, not good and bad. This is a dangerous misperception. Science is a human activity and as such deals with right and wrong, good and bad. But the critics further confuse the issue by saying that ethical values are inherent in tools. I can use a pencil to write a beautiful sonnet, or I can use it to stab someone. Similarly, I can use a computer to write a novel, or I can use it to embezzle funds from someone's bank account. By focusing on the machines themselves, the blame-the-tools argument directs attention away from what should be the real concern of ethics: human actions and their consequences.

I believe that children of all ages should have access to the tools that adults use in our culture, and the computer is one such tool. However, when people ask at what age child computer use is appropriate, they are often talking not about access but *exposure*. This is something very different. Exposure usually means *having* children use some sort of educational software that is supposed to "teach" them something. This being the case, adults then start worrying whether this or that program is "too hard" or "too abstract" or "too divorced from reality" or "not tactile enough," according to some preconceived, idealized notion of child development.

The assumption here is that only adults know what is good for children. The children themselves are not to be trusted: They do not know what is good for them; they do not know what they want or need. I disagree with this. If given free access—not exposure—to computers, with as much help and assistance as is asked for, the child will show us what is appropriate and what is not. No child will work on something that really is too hard, too abstract, or too boring, provided that he or she is *free to leave* the computer.

However, this is almost never the situation in schools, where exposure is the rule. Children are *told* to work on the computer or are brought into the computer lab for forty-five minutes; they are not free to leave. In a home schooling situation, we can give children a choice, and by their choices, they will show us what is appropriate and what is not.

The type of educational software or "courseware" where the computer fires questions at the learner is certainly to be avoided. Similarly, parents or teachers should not use this instructional method. The point here concerns courses of action rather than tools: What shouldn't be done, shouldn't be done at all. A computerized workbook is just as bad as a paper one. The real problem with workbooks, whether on the computer or off, is that they convey a bad model of learning. When children respond to questions and exercises in workbooks, one of the things they are learning—regardless of the content of the workbook—is the very idea that learning itself consists of answering other people's questions rather than your own. This image of learning is ultimately harmful and is one of the many elements that leads people to view learning as a passive process, as something that is done to them.

One must be wary of saying that people are "active" when using computers because they are pushing buttons or in some way responding to events on the screen, whereas they are "passive" when, for example, they are watching television because they are just looking at it. Such a use of the word *active* or *activity* is a rather shallow one: it takes the defining characteristic of activity to be mere movement rather than volitional, purposeful, intentional action. Social psychologist Erich Fromm noted this very distinction between the shallow and deeper senses of "activity" in his book *Man for Himself*:

> Activity is usually defined as behavior which brings about a change in an existing situation by an expenditure of energy. In contrast, a person is described as passive if he is unable to change or overtly influence an existing situation and is influenced or moved by forces outside himself. This current concept of activity takes into account only the actual expenditure of energy and the change brought about by it. It does not distinguish between the underlying psychic conditions governing the activities.
>
> The person in a deep hypnotic trance may have his eyes open, may walk,

HILDEGARD ADLER

talk, and do things; he "acts." The general definition of activity would apply to him, since energy is spent and change is brought about. But if we consider the particular character and quality of this activity, we find that it is not really the hypnotized person who is the actor, but the hypnotist who, by means of suggestions, acts through him. While the hypnotic trance is an artificial state, it is an extreme but characteristic example of a situation in which a person can be active and yet not be the true actor, his activity resulting from compelling forces over which he has no control.[3]

Computer-assisted instruction (CAI) essentially places the computer in the role of the hypnotist. "Answer *this* question, solve *this* problem," it demands. The user of such a program can only react to whatever appears on the computer's screen. The learner is not *in* control, but *under* control. The anonymous programmer or software designer who devised all this is absent from the scene, and the user is asked to be blindly, passively obedient to his or her creation. In such a situation there can be no real relationship, no compact of trust and respect between teacher and learner.

How, then, does a child learn by using a computer? The answer is, the same way he or she learns by using a pencil. Pencils don't make you a better writer, but they can be used to write with. Computers, too, can be used to write with, or to draw with, or to calculate with, or to store and retrieve information with. Clearly one can learn by doing these things. One learns to write by writing, to draw by drawing, to calculate by calculation—in short, by doing things and by thinking and reflecting about what one does. The computer is one medium among many that can be used to do these things.

The philospher and social critic Ivan Illich has coined the phrase "convivial tool" to refer to tools or social arrangements that can enhance a person's freedom and autonomy. He writes:

> Tools are intrinsic to social relationships. An individual relates himself in action to his society through the use of tools that he actively masters, or by which he is passively acted upon. To the extent that he masters his tools, he can invest the world with meaning; to the degree that he is mastered by his tools, the shape of the tool determines his own self-image. Convivial tools are those which give each person who uses them the greatest opportunity to enrich the environment with the fruits of his or her vision.
>
> Tools foster conviviality to the extent to which they can be used, by anybody, as often or as seldom as desired, for the accomplishment of a purpose chosen by the user. The use of such tools by one person does not restrain another from using them equally. They do not require previous certification of the user. Their existence does not impose any obligation to use them. They allow the user to express his meaning in action.[4]

There is nothing inherent in a tool that makes it convivial or not. While it can be argued that certain tools (such as telephone networks) lend themselves more easily, due to their design, to convivial uses than do others (such as commercial television), the key to a tool's potential for conviviality lies also and especially in the social arrangements people create around its use. With a different social arrangement, telephone networks, for example, could become less convivial (through limiting access, through surveillance, or through restricting the content of conversations); alternatively, television and video technology could become more convivial (by making available cheap, compact video recording and playback equipment, plus a supply of tapes on which people could record whatever they wish and then send these tapes, physically or electronically, to others).

In some ways the design of computers is becoming less convivial. One aspect of a tool's capacity for conviviality is its simplicity or transparency, or, conversely, its complexity or opacity. When home computers started to appear in the mid-seventies, they were largely bought by people who considered themselves to be "computer hobbyists." Frequently, these early computers were bought in kit form to be assembled at home. The first Apple computer had a large lid on top which could be easily removed, revealing many "expansion slots" or places to plug in additional hardware. These early computers were designed to be tinkered with. Not so any more. On the back of today's Macintosh computer one finds a label conveying a very different sort of message:

> **CAUTION**
> **Warning**
> **To prevent electric shock, do not remove cover. No user service-able parts inside. Refer servicing to qualified service personnel.**

This constitutes a reduction in conviviality, the hallmark of which is self-reliance. The computer is becoming more and more opaque—a veritable black box. It is possible to use a computer without knowing how it works, how to program it, or how to repair it, but this limits one's freedom. One must settle for whatever the experts send our way.

With all of this in mind, how can the computer become a "convivial tool" for children in the home? One of its uses is as a writing instrument. Many professional writers today use a word processor. Why shouldn't children have access to the same quality writing tools as professional writers? The computer can turn a piece of text into a fluid, plastic substance that can be edited and manipulated at the touch of a few buttons. Revision is no longer the arduous task it once was, and ease of editing can liberate people to be more expressive and free with their writing.

Electronic mail or "E-mail" takes advantage of computer networks (often using existing telephone lines) to enhance the speed and power of regular mail. A message sent via E-mail is delivered nearly instantaneously, and sending copies to other persons—or, through the use of mailing lists, to a large group of people—is made easy through this technology. Many home schoolers enjoy writing to pen pals, and I believe many more would enjoy writing to pen pals via E-mail, especially if they received the prompt replies to their messages that the technology enables.

Learning to program a computer can, in some sense, make it a more convivial tool and can counteract the current trend toward nonconvivial hardware. Knowledge of a programming language allows one to shape the computer to one's needs and tastes. This allows for more freedom and flexibility as far as the uses of the computer and what it can be made to do.

Another major use of the computer is for entertainment and game playing. Many people find computer games fun to play. Also, many games require a good deal of skill and concentration; they are far from "mindless." However, many games involve shooting, dropping bombs, or other forms of violence, and some people (children and adults alike) seem to become addicted to them.

The issues raised by violence in computer games are identical to those that come up in discussions of children playing with toy guns. If children are happy and love life, if they are treated with kindness and respect, if they are around other people who are happy and who love life, then they will tend not to be violent and aggressive no matter what games they play. Alternatively, if children are lonely and depressed, if they are afraid of life and are treated with cruelty and disrespect, if they grow up among others who resort to violence as a matter of course, then chances are that they, too, will become violent persons. If violent computer games bother you (as they do me), then express this to your children and explain what you find disturbing.

The fact of the matter is, not all people who play computer games become addicted to them. Who does become addicted and why? Simply put, computer addiction seems to hinge on *power* and *control*. The computer offers the promise of absolute power and control over the artificial worlds constructed inside it, and such a promise may be very seductive for people who feel powerless and who have little control over their own lives. Children in our society often find themselves in such a position. So many things seem out of their control; so many things *happen* to them. Many children are treated as puppets or pets: they are ordered around by other people who have power over them. "Eat this! Sit down! Get dressed! Stop running! Time for bed!" or simply, "Behave!" (This is especially true in schools, where the control extends to *mind control*—control of one's learning.) Children, then, are perhaps the group with the highest risk of becoming obsessed with and addicted to that which is constantly denied them: power and control. John Holt commented on this matter in *Growing Without Schooling* magazine:

> There is a danger, and we have signs already of how great it may be, that some children (adults too) may so love their power over their mini-world of the computer that they will hide in that world from the larger world outside in

which they control so little. May not autistic children be in essence people who, bewildered and terrified by the unpredictability and uncontrollability of the real world, have drawn back into a shrunken world of their own making in which they can predict and control everything?

Our age worships power and control far too much, and I doubt very much that a remedy for this cultural disease will be to put some form of total power and control at the disposal of everyone—or everyone who can afford a computer.[5]

We tend to worship those things that seem to be forever beyond our reach, and if our age worships power and control, it is not because power and control are bad per se but because, as children forming our impressions of the world, we were denied the minimum degree of autonomy that we needed to lead a healthy, productive life. Having had too little when it mattered, we feel we can never have too much. In this way, power and control become our gods.

Sherry Turkle compares the psychology of computer addiction with that of compulsive dieting. She speaks of how one can use the power of computers or of control over one's body to "measure" oneself. The promise of perfection, for someone who otherwise has a low sense of self-esteem and self-worth, can be irresistible.

Most people don't become addicted to video games just as most people who diet don't become anorexic. But when they use these powerful materials to measure themselves, they are at risk. And, of course, some people come to the material more vulnerable than others. *The greater the anxiety about being out of control, the greater the seduction of a material that offers the promise of perfect response.* The body offers this type of promise. So many fewer calories will cause so many pounds to drop. Part of the "holding power" of any diet is the sense of involvement with the process itself. People go on diets to improve their appearance. They begin regimens of exercise for the same reason. But the experience of molding the body, the experience of its response, its malleability, can take over. Similarly, the experience of a game that makes an instantaneous and exact response to your touch, or of a computer that is always consistent in its response, can take over. It becomes gripping, independent of anything you are trying to "do" with it in an instrumental sense.[6]

Conversely, the person who feels content with him or herself, the person who feels "I'm basically OK" is not as vulnerable to the seductive allure of perfection, since such a person feels he or she is not in need of such "measurement."

The technocentric response to all of this would be to conclude that "computer games are bad for children." A more considered response would be to look more closely at what children are doing with computer games. Are they using the games merely as a form of entertainment, or are they using them to measure themselves, to escape from a world where they are coerced and manipulated into one where they can be in control, where they can be "perfect"? The answer to this question will depend largely on how we treat our children. If we push them around, if we convince them by our actions that they don't matter, aren't worth anything, and have no choice but to obey, then we should worry a great deal about computer addiction. However, if we treat children with dignity, if we respect them as *persons* and take them seriously, if we give them autonomy over their lives and let them make their own decisions with as much help and assistance as they ask for, then we need not worry about computer addiction. Such children will not crave power and control, will not need to retreat into an artificial world in order to find it, and will not need to test their self-worth through mastery over a machine.

Finally, a few words about what is called "computer literacy." While it is almost never clear just what is meant by this phrase, one can generally assume that computer literacy entails some sort of general knowledge about computers—how they work and how to use them. The importance of such knowledge is vastly overrated. My advice to home schooling parents is: Don't be intimidated by advertising claims that say your child will be left behind, or will be ill-prepared for the "computer age" unless he or she is "exposed" to the computer early on. This is pure nonsense. People who say such things are almost always trying to sell you something.

There are a number of reasons why computer literacy will not make a difference to your child's future. First of all, the computers of ten or twenty years from now will very probably be unlike the computers of today. Computer literacy, such as it exists now, will rapidly become out of date. The only reason to become "computer literate" right away is because you need or want to use a computer now.

Second, as a number of computer visionaries have already remarked, computers in the form of microprocessors will become absorbed into the appliances of the future. The general-purpose computer will largely disappear, and instead, machines with more specific purposes will become computerized. Just as computers have worked their way into wristwatches, toys, typewriters, microwave ovens, cars, VCRs, and automatic bank teller machines, we can expect them to seep into the woodwork of the twenty-first century. Indeed, most of us are unaware we are using computers at all when we use these devices, just as we don't stop to think how often we use appliances or devices that contain electric motors. (No one talks about "electric-motor literacy.")

These computers of the future will be much easier to use than the ones we have today. Word processors will not require much more in the way of skill than today's typewriters, nor will spreadsheet programs require much beyond basic accounting skills. It will be much easier to learn how to use computerized tools, and "computer literacy" will become a moot point.

Notes

1. Seymour Papert, "Computer Criticism vs. Technocentric Thinking," *Educational Researcher* (Jan.-Feb. 1987), 24.

2. Sherry Turkle, *The Second Self: Computers and the Human Spirit* (New York: Simon and Schuster, Inc., 1984), 322-323. Italics mine.

3. Erich Fromm, *Man for Himself* (New York: Ballantine Books, Inc., 1947), 92-93.

4. Ivan Illich, *Tools for Conviviality* (New York: Harper & Row Publishers, 1973), 22-23.

5. John Holt, *Growing Without Schooling* 31 (Feb. 1983): 15.

6. Turkle, *"The Second Self,"* 89. Italics mine.

15

WHOLE READING

Margaret Yatsevitch Phinney

I rode downtown the other day with a friend and her three children, aged two, four, and six. As we passed a gas station, the following exchange took place among the children:

Robert, the youngest, pointing to the lit-up Sunoco sign, yelled, "Gas! Gas!"

Johanna, the middle child, said questioningly, "That says, 'Gulf station,' doesn't it?"

"No, that's not 'Gulf,' " commented first-grader Elizabeth. "It's. . .it's. . .what's that called, now? It's. . .'Sunoco.' That's where Mrs. Berman gets her gas when she takes us to Brownies. See, it's too long to be 'Gulf,' and it starts with S. And it has 'sun' in it."

As a reading consultant and a first-grade teacher, I thrill at this sort of interchange, for here are three more readers taking on literacy—three more young people who have discovered that the rich world of print in which they live makes connections with their daily lives.

"Three readers?" you ask. "What do you mean, 'three'? Only one of those children read that sign!"

To me, all three children read the sign. Robert was reading just as truly as a one-year-old is speaking when she says "Muh! Muh!" as she reaches for her mother. He was associating meaning with print and the symbolic shape and colors of the sign that surround the print. He was attempting to express that meaning.

Johanna was reading with the same degree of accuracy that she uses in speech when she says, "I goed with Daddy to the store." Her message was clear, but not yet in perfect standard form. She knew that the sign was more specific than just "gas," that it was a particular *brand* of gas, but she still lacks enough experience with names of stations and with the details of print to be able to precisely identify it.

Elizabeth, the most mature reader, was able to use her memory and background knowledge—her trips with Mrs. Berman—to help her identify the sign. In addition, she has developed an awareness that letter-sound relationships and word length can be used as clues, and she knows enough sight words to recognize "sun." These two pieces of understanding helped her to confirm the accuracy of her reading.

Do we, as parents, consider that our children are not talking when their attempts to communicate with us are as imperfect as Robert's and Johanna's reading? No, indeed! We get very excited when they try to imitate us. We give them a great deal of attention for such efforts. We encourage them and model more language for them to try out! We even imitate their amusing "misses." But we certainly do not say "When will Johnny ever learn to speak?"! It would never occur to us that something so basically human as speech would not be learned by our children, unless they had a severe physiological impairment affecting speech development.

Why, then, do we treat reading as such an all-or-nothing accomplishment? Reading and writing are language processes just as much as listening and speaking are. Why do we feel that children's attempts to use and interpret print must be perfect from the first try? It is simply not reasonable to have such expectations. Yet most school reading programs *do* require mastery of one aspect of reading before children are allowed to move on. The back-to-basics and mastery learning movements are even more rigid in this regard than previous programs have been. Almost none of them are geared to the way children naturally learn language.

Many teachers are now learning that reading can be as natural a process as learning to walk and to speak. They have discovered that if children are placed in an environment as rich with print as a home is rich with speech, as supportive of attempts to read and write as the home is supportive of attempts to walk, explore, and communicate, they *will* learn to read. They will read with the same joy and confidence that they express when they babble, run, laugh, and play. And they do *not* need sequenced readers with controlled vocabulary and workbooks and hundreds of dittoed worksheets to do it. All they need are the following:

1. Books, *real* books, straight out of bookstores and libraries;
2. Someone to read *to* them, to read *with* them, without pressure or

intimidation; someone to model reading and writing for them; and someone to answer their questions;

3. A risk-free environment in which to practice;

4. Time.

Research shows that children who learn to read before they go to school have these enriched, supportive conditions in their homes. The trick is to bring this environment into the classroom.

I am what is known as a "whole language teacher." This means that I teach reading from whole to part. I do not start with letters and letter sounds; I start with whole stories, poems, chants, and songs, which I gather from the rich sources of literature available in bookstores and libraries. (We live in a golden age as far as children's books are concerned; there is no shortage of good material for teaching reading.)

I choose material that is lively, of interest to children at their grade level, and predictable. By predictable, I mean that it has elements that make it easy to remember: rhyme, rhythm, a tune, a chorus or repeated lines, or a story structure that repeats, such as the sequences in "The Three Little Pigs" or "The Gingerbread Man."

I present this material to my students in enlarged-print form so that everyone can see the print at once. This tends to duplicate the bedtime-story situation that is so natural in the home but difficult in a classroom, because a teacher's lap simply is not big enough for twenty-five children.

I highlight rhyming words, repeated endings or beginning letters, some punctuation, and other details by printing them in a contrasting color. This invites children to take note of patterns and important cues that can guide them as they gradually focus more and more on the details of print. Sometimes I make drawings as clues to word identification.

Because I love the literature myself, I read it with enthusiasm, and I invite participation by the children to the extent that they are able to join in. The more times we read a piece, the more children chime in.

Like learning to speak, reading is a gradual process of moving from general to more accurate expression of meaning. The children learn dozens of pieces of literature each month. Through daily reading and discussion of the details that they recognize, they begin to acquire sight words and strategies for using print. They employ these strategies during daily practice times, when they read their favorite pieces to themselves or with friends. Words, meaningful phrases, and grammar and phonics patterns that are recognized in one situation are transferred more and more often to other material.

Another advantage to natural reading is that children learn self-regulation and independence. They are free to reject material that is too hard and to reread material that they have been able to work out on their own. They learn to become judges of what they can and cannot handle, of when they are ready for more challenge and when they need to remain with familiar material in order to consolidate what they know.

Writing practice also plays a vital role in learning to read. The two activities are interdependent: the development of one feeds the growth of the other. I have a daily "writing workshop," during which children choose their own topics and. . .they write. They share their efforts with each other and help one another with ideas, with ways to express these ideas, and with "invented spelling." Since they have had no formal training in spelling at this age, invented spelling is their personal writing tool. When they want to "publish" something, they get the standard spelling from the teacher. In thinking about how words sound and look, they focus on print details. This focus transfers to their reading, and back again to their writing.

The long and the short of it is that by January, most of my grade-one children are addicted to reading. They learn to read by practicing reading, just as they learned to speak by practicing speech.

Helping Your Child at Home

Natural reading is no more magical than natural speaking. Just as children learn to talk at different rates and times, so are children widely individualistic in learning to read. Your child will probably *not* read, in the sense that we normally think of reading, before going to school—most children don't—but he or she will break into reading quickly and seemingly effortlessly if you provide a literacy-oriented environment throughout the preschool years.

Begin early. Just as it is vital that children hear speech from the time they are born, so it is true that you cannot start reading to your child too early. "Book language" is different from oral language. It has a vocabulary, rhythm, and flow that speech does not possess. When children are exposed to this "other language" at an early age, it

becomes part of them. If reading is associated with being held and rocked and loved, it later becomes a source of comfort and security in and of itself. Most importantly, reading to infants and very young children helps them learn to listen and attend for long periods of time. The ability to concentrate and pay attention is a major factor in later school success.

Choose a variety of stories, poems, rhymes, and songs. From about age four, keep a chapter book going and read some of it every day. For other times—naps, doctor's offices, before supper, midmorning— choose shorter, predictable materials: nursery rhymes, jingles, folk and fairy tales, and the wealth of picture books found in any public library. Reread favorites over and over again. This can become tedious for you unless you keep in mind that children do not ask for repeats unless they are in some way benefiting from hearing a story again. Children do not seek boredom! You can spruce up the reading by using different tones of voice or by encouraging the child's participation by stopping before the end of a line and inviting the child to fill in the last word or two.

Encourage memorization of rhymes, songs, and predictable stories. Memory of material provides the base from which a focus on print is later built. If your child tells you that he or she can read a story, but is clearly reciting it from memory, do not contradict. Your child is demonstrating his or her understanding of many exhibited behaviors in reading, such as turning the page, observing picture clues, and using "book language." At this point, children are simply at an early reading stage, like the early talker who gets the message across in less-than-perfect standard English.

Answer your child's questions about words, letters, pictures, signs, and the world in general. Be straightforward, honest, and matter of fact. Do not quiz your child about aspects of print.

Regularly, but not excessively, comment on interesting features of print when you read aloud. For example, if there is a sign in a picture, point to it and say, "Look, that sign says 'St. Ives.' And look, there's where it says 'St. Ives' in the poem"; or, "Look at that word 'yellow.' It has two *l*'s right in the middle." If your child is ready to tune in to print, the next time you read a passage he or she may point out these words or features independently. If not, don't worry; just keep going. Remember, as with learning to speak, you cannot force development.

Show that you value reading by letting your children see you read frequently and hear you talking about things you have read. Have family reading times. Replace TV viewing with reading as much as possible. Establish a library-visiting routine and make sure you check out books for yourself.

Above all, do *not* try to teach phonics principles or rules. These are very abstract and often confusing. With so many exceptions to these rules, especially among the most common words in the language, many children can quickly become frustrated by trying to apply them before understanding the strategies involved. In my classroom, I do not expose children to phonics generalizations until they are already reading.

Above all, use natural common sense. Remember, your children learned to speak successfully without formal instruction. All you did was model, encourage, and remain sensitive. Keep it up!

16

READING: A LEARNING EXPERIENCE THAT'S FUN

Anne Running Tabbut

W hen the topic of teaching reading comes up these days, the importance of phonics is usually stressed. Most teachers say kids must learn to read by sounding words out, or they'll suffer from a lifelong difficulty with reading. I agree that reading mastery will never be achieved without a knowledge of phonics, but I have some objections to using the sound-it-out method as a way of introducing kids to reading.

Many children are eager to learn to read before they're developmentally ready to grasp the code that phonics represents. Discrimination between the short vowel sounds, particularly those represented by *e* and *i*, is especially difficult. Some kids can't do this before they're seven or eight years old. Other children, because of a learning idiosyncrasy, have a hard time learning to sound out words and are disappointed and frustrated when reading is introduced in this way.

A few kids, although they have no trouble learning to read by the phonetic approach, have problems making the transition to the immediate recognition of words that is necessary to fluid reading and tend to laboriously sound out every word they encounter. Phonetically regular words look very much alike, and a page full of them provides few visual handles, such as different shapes and lengths, to aid recognition.

My greatest objection to the phonetic method of introducing reading is that it's not much fun. In fact, for the creative, imaginative child who thinks of books as treasure-filled tales of dreams and dragons, such stuff as "Nat the cat sat on a fat rat" is downright boring—so much so that I've seen more than one gifted child stuck in the low-achievement reading group because he was so turned off and disappointed by his initial reading experience.

So what is an alternative? While a knowledge of phonics is essential to reading, there's a way of sneaking up on it that's fun to learn and fun to teach.

First, read to your children often, beginning in the toddler years. They'll learn to love books, and they'll want to learn to read. When you and your child think the time is right to learn to read, find some simple books that have a repetitious or predictable story line, or a story in which the pictures give strong clues as to what the words on the page will be. (A good example is *Did You Ever See?* by Walter Einsel.) Read these aloud until your child has learned a story well enough to read it by himself. He'll love to do it, over and over. Don't think there's something wrong with letting a child feel proud of "reading" this way. He's getting a wonderful feeling of accomplishment, he's learning to love reading, and he's developing an appetite for more. He won't want to stay dependent on memorized books but will be eager to learn the skills needed for reading independence. This period is also a good time for the child to learn to recognize and print the letters of the alphabet.

The third step is an exciting one. It's called the "key word" method and is described in *Teacher*, a wonderful book by Sylvia Ashton-Warner. Make some large, sturdy blank cards. Ask your child what word he'd like to know how to read and write. A word he chooses will be one that's particularly important to him—a "key" word. Print it on a card. Ask your child to trace it with his finger and copy it until he can write it without looking. Then he can write it on a piece of drawing paper and illustrate it. A word a day is the suggested rate, but your child may not want to be limited to that. Keep his words in an envelope or the like; he'll love to watch his collection stack up. One of my students used to hug and pat her word collection and call it her "treasure." Bear in mind that any word that isn't readily remembered probably isn't important to the child and can be tossed out of the key word pack. (It is also possible, however, that that word represents an emotional problem area to the child.)

After the child has developed the concept that a group of letters forms a single word, you can go back to his memorized library books and ask him to identify words there. For example, after he's read a page, say, "Can you find the word that says 'giraffe'?" Repeat this process with the other words on the page.

Many people disapprove of this "sight word" method, but I believe

that beginning this way doesn't hurt. A child who later has difficulty learning phonics would have that difficulty anyway, and "sight" words can be much more interesting than three-letter, phonetically regular words.

Next, pull out a key word. Ask your child to think of a sentence containing the word. Print the sentence word for word on a piece of drawing paper and have him read it back to you. Then ask him to draw a picture illustrating the sentence. Practice reading these sentences daily. A variation here is a game in which he picks any two key words and you have to invent a sentence containing both words. This can be a real challenge! After you tell him your sentence, which will usually be pretty silly, write it down. He reads it and illustrates it. Add it to the collection of sentences he reads daily.

The next step provides the transition to learning phonics. After the child has learned several words (twenty or so), find two or more of his key words that contain the same letter-sound combination. Maybe he'll have "tiger," "Timothy," and "tahini." Show them to him and ask, "Is there anything alike about these words?" He'll probably notice that they all begin with the letter *t*. "Is there anything else alike?" Help him discover that they all begin with the same sound. Then ask,

"What sound does the letter *t* make in those words?" What is important about this process is that the child is discovering for himself, on the basis of words he already knows, the relationship between the letter and its sound.

Now ask your child to think of other words beginning with the *t* sound. Write them down so that he can see the letter-sound connection. Next, look through your key word collection together to find the *t* letter and sound at the end or in the middle of words.

As your child seems ready and interested, find groups of key words that contain other letter-sound combinations and repeat the above process. You can continue this way until all the sounds have been learned, or when your child has learned several letter sounds this way, you can begin direct teaching of the remaining letter sounds—good old phonics. But now your child has the confidence of already knowing how to read many words, and when making up sentences for reading practice, you have a fund of interesting words to use in them, as well as the words containing sounds you want to teach.

Once your child knows all the consonant sounds, you can take any one-syllable key word and place a new, rhyming word next to it for practice in learning to read unfamiliar words. For example, if "book" is a favorite, write "hook" next to it. "What do you think this word says?" Repeat with other rhyming words.

Got the idea? You're on your way. Have fun!

TEACHING YOUR KIDS TO READ

John McMahon

The last teaching situation I was in before leaving the formalized school system was a first-and-second-grade combination class. I spent two years working with children who had a wide variety of experiences with and knowledge of the English language. Some had never seen an alphabet, while others were beginning to read. What they did have in common was an enthusiasm and excitement for learning. This is the prime ingredient for teaching reading. Most kids initially have this excitement, but they can lose it through the frustration and regimentation of daily school life. If you are going to send your children to school, send them as readers. It may be easier for them if you do. If you are going to teach them at home, here is an easy way to put them on the road to reading.

Where do you start? Should you go out and round up every word written about reading and every early-reading series you can find? What you would find if you did this would be many books on the alphabet and many early primer readers that jump right into sight reading. What is missing here is a system that enables children to figure out new words without having to memorize each one.

I have found that one of the easiest reading systems to teach, and one that allows a gradual progression from the ABCs to first-grade reading, is a phonetic system with words and stories created by the parent and personalized to address the child's own world.

The major points to remember in teaching reading to children using the phonetic system are that (1) the English language does make sense and has a few basic rules that can be learned; and (2) that by knowing these rules, words that are unfamiliar can be decoded and pronounced with success. Many of us learned to read using the "sight method"—memorizing words by sight until they could be recognized repeatedly and used in a sentence. The familiar Dick and Jane stories were like this. Two of the earliest sentences we learned were "See Dick and Jane. Look at Spot run." These sentences are phonetic nightmares. There is a double *e* in *see* sounding as *e*; a silent *e* in *Jane*; a long *a* in *Jane*; a short *i* in *Dick*; a double *o* sound in *look*; and a short *o* in *Spot*. After reading this sentence, any bright student would come to the conclusion that reading makes very little sense and will be difficult to learn.

The method described here involves learning the sound of the consonants, one at a time. Then the sounds of the short vowels are learned, as they have consistent sounds. Last, the sounds of end consonants are added, establishing the basic structure for many words. Sentences and stories can then be created for your child to read. Later, more rules are learned and more complicated words are used in a slowly unfolding method that builds on itself. There are very few primers or first-grade readers that enable the student to read sentences and stories so soon after learning the alphabet without having to either memorize a book full of grammar rules or every word, one at a time, in every story.

With this in mind, here is a step-by-step method you can work on with your child, taking as long at each step as you wish and using your creativity as the only limit to the types of materials used. You can reinforce or expand the steps as much as you like and stay at any one level of understanding until both parent and child are comfortable with the progress. As your child gains confidence with each new phase, he will indicate his readiness to move on at his own pace.

First teach the uppercase letters of the alphabet. Make a set of uppercase letters for the wall so your child can refer to them. Use letters the same shape and style each time you write them. Make flash cards, and go through them until your child can recognize the letters as you point to them and can pick out a letter you call out on his or her wall set. Writing the letters is helpful in reinforcing learning.

Teach the sounds of each letter. While some letters do not make much of a sound without an accompanying vowel, for now introduce them as if they do. Be very careful with the vowel sounds. To start, teach the short vowel sounds: the sound of *a* as in *bat*; the sound of *e* as in *egg*; the *i* sound as in *pig*; the *o* as in *ox*; and the *u* as in *but*. Always use two approaches to the learning: say the letter and then ask your child for the sound; then say the sound and ask your child for the letter.

Work on recognizing initial and final consonants. ("What letter does *dog* begin with?" "What letter does *dog* end with?") Then reverse the procedure. ("Tell me a word that begins with the *b* sound.") Use familiar objects around the house. This initial and final consonants recognition is very important in discriminating the parts of a word.

Begin putting the consonants and vowels together to make a two-letter sound. When your child can understand what he is doing, add each of the five short vowel sounds to each of the consonants. This will reinforce the discrimination of the five short vowel sounds. For example: *b* plus *a*; *b* plus *e*; *b* plus *i*; *b* plus *o*; *b* plus *u*; *c* plus *a*; *c* plus *e*; *c* plus *i*; *c* plus *o*; *c* plus *u*; and so on.

When this important step is mastered, add a final consonant to the two-letter sounds you have been learning to create a three-letter word. Working through this stage can be painstakingly long, as your child will sound out every word, sound by sound, before he or she puts it all together into one word. ("*B* plus *e* plus *d* equals *bed*. *C* plus *a* plus *t* equals *cat*.") This step takes repetition and patience.

When your child can read these individual three-letter words comfortably, you are ready to put together sentences and stories that you both will have fun reading. Use individual words your child already knows, written on index cards, and let him or her put them together to make sentences. Two words that might have to be memorized at this point are the word *the* and the *z* sound for *s* in *is*, *has*, and *was*. The creation of sentences will be much easier with these helpers. ("*The cat is bad. Pat has a pet. Dan can run at the rat. Ken is a big man.*")

This step is critical in this method of learning to read. Spend weeks if you have to repeating these simple sentences. Keep the sentences short. Have your child repeat each sentence until he or she can say it without sounding out each letter of each word.

If things are running smoothly, add another consonant and create some four-letter words to add to your sentences. Examples are *stop*, *clam*, *drop*, *grab*, *jump*, and *drum*. Again, use only those words which have the short vowel sound.

After your child has read many stories using the full range of consonant and vowel combinations, you are ready to introduce the blended sounds—those consonants and vowels that, when used together, make a new sound. Some examples are *th*, *ch*, *sh*, *wh*, *ly*, *ing*, *er*, *ar*, and *ir*. These blends have to be discussed and words using them

(*when, that, chin, wish, sing, them, shirt, car, her*) introduced. Add these words to your stories.

Add diphthongs next. These are vowel combinations which make an entirely new sound when combined. Examples are *ow, ew, oo, oy, oi,* and *ay*. The double *o* has two sounds: the sound in *book* and the sound in *choose*. Some words that contain diphthongs are *boy, new, how, hay, oil, now, lew, choose,* and *blew*. Make more sentences and more stories, adding these new words and other words that use diphthongs.

The last step involves the long vowel sounds. These are the hardest because some new rules apply, rules that must be taught and wrestled with until they become second nature. Following are the three basic rules of long vowels:

1. In short words that end in *e* or *ee*, the sound of the *e* is a long *e*. It says its own name. Words like *me, be, we, see, lee, bee,* and *pee* are examples of this.

2. Most double-vowel combinations say the name of the first vowel (*beet, bean, boat, read, cream, drain, dear, feed*). Dig deep to think of

relevant sentences that make the transition from the short vowels to the long vowels as easy as possible. Talk and write about people and places that your child knows.

3. If a word ends in *e*, the next to the last vowel is long and the *e* is silent (*Jane, cane, fire, size, five, alive, drive*).

There are, of course, exceptions to these rules. However, avoid using the exceptions until your child has mastered most of these skills and is sight reading most of the words.

Take as much time on the long vowels as you have taken on the short. Work on these sounds and gently correct when the short vowel sound is used. Make up sentences that have combinations of the short and long vowel sounds: "I can drive a car." "I like to dive in the pond." "The fire is hot." "The big boy can eat five hot dogs."

How often should you work with your children? How long per session? These questions are usually answered by the children themselves. Depending on their interest and attention span, your kids will tell you when they have had enough. Don't push them. They have all their lives to learn. And don't worry if your children aren't ready to learn reading at the age you think they should be. The interest in reading and the ability to read come to different kids at different times. Children are different, but they each will let you know by their interest in words and letters when they are ready to learn more about them.

18

Invented Spelling

Margaret Yatsevitch Phinney

"IRHCXZHCGHX," writes five-year-old Nathaniel in March of his kindergarten year. The teacher, Jan, comes over to him as he is illustrating his story.

"Howdy, Nate, how's your story coming along?"

"Good," he replies. He continues to work with deep commitment on the details of a large, red vehicle.

"Would you share your story with me?" asks Jan, pointing to his series of letters.

"OK." He puts down his pencil and, running his finger from left to right under his string of letters, remarks, "This says, 'I went to the firehouse and I had fun.'"

"You liked that trip, did you? What was the best part?" responds his teacher, helping Nate to orally expand his story.

"I liked when they turned on the sirens! *Wheeeeeeee!*" came the enthusiastic response.

"That was fun! Noisy, too!" agrees Jan. "Perhaps you'd like to show that sound coming out of your fire engine when you're finished drawing. I'm going to write your story down here, so that other people who don't know how to read invented spelling can enjoy it, too."

"OK, 'cause I'm going to send this one to my nana." And Nate resumes his drawing while Jan moves on to another young writer.

In September of first grade, one of my students, Meghann, writes, "IMEFRDEVLDK." I circulate around the room, as does Jan in kindergarten, and look over Meghann's shoulder.

"You're afraid of the dark, are you, Meghann?"

"Yeah. Sometimes when all the lights are out, I hear noises and I don't know what they are."

"That's a good topic to write about. Sometimes it helps to write about things you're afraid of."

"I know, that's why I wrote, 'I'm afraid of the dark.' See?" and she carefully rereads her piece, pointing to each group of letters that represents the individual words.

"I can see that, Meghann. Your invented spelling is so close to standard that I can read it, too. I see *I-M*, which are the standard letters for *I'm*; and there are the most important letters for *afraid*—you've got the *f* and the *r* and the *d*; and *of* does have that *v* sound in it; and *dark* starts with *d* and ends with *k*."

Meghann grins and returns to her drawing. I move on, making a mental note that in another week or two, when she gains confidence and starts writing more, I will ask her to look at one or two words each time I check in, and help her to listen for more medial consonants and an occasional long vowel.

These children have a tool for writing that we call "invented spelling."

Breaking with Tradition

When my son was in second grade, I was teaching first grade in the same school. Because he was quick with his work, he spent a fair amount of time in the hallway playing board games with other children who had finished ahead of time. I asked the teacher if she would let these children do some writing in their free time. "Oh no," she said. "I can't do that. I haven't the time to do all that correcting. You know, they just can't spell yet."

This attitude is traditional: no writing until children can spell. As a result, in the past children seldom wrote, except for workbook exercises, until the upper grades. The first composition I wrote was in ninth grade. But attitudes are changing now. We realize that writing, like speech, is a developmental process and that denying a child the opportunity to write is like forbidding a young child from talking until he or she is able to pronounce every word perfectly, something no parent would ever consider doing. In fact, just the opposite occurs: we take great pleasure in hearing our children's efforts to approximate standard speech. So why are we so rigid about early writing?

The answer is tradition. We have routinely been told that our spelling and handwriting reflect aspects of our personality: neat, tidy, careful, correct writing presumably indicates a conscientious, sociable, well-educated person. There is no doubt that illegible handwriting *is* irritating for the reader who must decipher it and poor spelling *does* jar a reader to the point of losing the impact of the message. But is it right to impose such expectations on young children who are just learning the highly complex process of writing?

Two recent developments surpass the customary considerations of "tradition." The first is our newfound respect for the quality of ideas. With the increase in overall education and the enormous quantities of published material now universally available, we are becoming a nation of critical readers. We are starting to demand a higher quality of thinking behind the written material we choose to read. No longer able to believe everything we hear and read, we are learning to discriminate between a well-researched article and a diatribe.

The second is our new awareness of the developmental aspects of learning. We realize that children go through stages toward mastery. "Knowledge" is not imprinted on their brains in its finished form. Children need to work through processes such as walking, talking, reading, and writing. Beginning with general approximations of each process, they gradually refine and perfect them until they are able to manipulate the standard that is modeled in their environment. Think of children learning to walk: they use hands, furniture, walls. Then they take a few tentative steps on their own before dropping to hands and knees again to scramble the rest of the way in security. Once they are walking, they do so with an ungainly, stiff-kneed, spread-eagled gait. Gradually, the joints become more flexible, the legs come together, and balance is maintained. All learning proceeds the same way, including reading and writing. The rule is: "Whole to part; overall idea to refinement of the details."

If what we write is now as important as the mechanics of getting our message down on paper, and if writing is a developmental process, then it is essential to encourage writing behavior as early as possible. After all, it takes time to become comfortable with expressing oneself in writing. Writing, as a process, involves consideration of what is important and what is not, what is of interest to others and what is boring, what needs expanding for clarity and what is so overexplained that nothing is left to the reader's imagination. Writing has become too important for us to waste precious time waiting for our writers to first become perfect spellers. Since formal spelling lessons do not begin until second or third grade in most schools, we must accept approximations of standard spelling until the standard is learned.

Children Love to Write

By the end of first grade, most six-year-olds love writing if it has been treated as a no-risk activity. Meghann, who wrote one sentence— "IMEFRDEVLDK"—in September, wrote the following in January: "I am GoiNg to aftaR SKol GimNastikS Iam IGSatiD VaRe VaRe IGSatid I hoP that SKol is ovaR soN I hoP We Do the Rop cliM I hiK it wil be faN vaRe fan."

In four months of daily writing, during which she chose her own topics, shared her writing often with her neighbors and occasionally with the whole class, and received a bit of coaching every other week or so from me, Meghann made enormous progress. She learned word spacing, the regular—though not perfected—use of lowercase letters, many standard spellings, sound-letter representations for all syllabic units, and appropriate placing of vowels. Furthermore, almost anyone could read her message. (Did you figure out "IGSatiD" [excited] and "hiK" [think]?) Although plenty of room for refinement still remained—in punctuation, vowel choice, and so forth—who could complain with progress like this?

Four months later, at the end of May, Meghann wrote: "I'Am on the YMCA Swim teme. tonight I'Am going to the Smith Calig Pool for a rela Meat. I'Am very icsatiD aBawt it. My Parinc Are Coming to hwath Me and My Brathar Swim My Bast frand is on it too."

The refinements were coming along steadily. Punctuation marks, including apostrophes, began to appear; she was becoming aware that *c* can have an *s* sound; and she was learning about silent *e* endings (teme) and two-vowel combinations (Meat). And all of this without a formal spelling lesson! Had she been restricted to using only words that she could spell, think of how dry her writing would have been. Invented spelling enabled her to use any word in her spoken vocabulary. It allowed her to record her emotions and the important events in her life. Already she could see herself as a writer, and she *was* a writer!

Writing before School

Parents can encourage their children to write before attending school as easily as they can encourage them to learn to speak. The key word is "encourage." Even as a teacher, I do not "teach" writing to my six- and seven-year-olds. I simply provide them with the environment, the modeling, and the questions that guide their own learning. Con-

sequently, I have twenty writers at twenty different stages of development—*their* development.

To parents who wish to help their children on their way to becoming writers, I offer the following recommendations: encouragement, acceptance, sensitivity, and common sense. These four elements that made it possible for your children to learn to listen, understand, walk, and speak are the same ones that will enable them to write.

Encouragement
Encouragement means providing opportunities and purposes for writing. Children do not do anything without purpose. When they see writing as a necessary, purposeful, and enjoyable activity, they pursue it eagerly. They must see you use writing and must understand why you use it: as a memory aid (lists, recipes, reminders, birthdays, addresses), for record keeping (checkbooks), for communication (letters, memos, announcements, invitations), for giving information (reports), and for entertainment (stories, poems). Tell your children what you are writing and why. Encourage them to write with you. Suggest that they draw first and then label, if this seems easier. Let them help write the shopping list. When they ask you to buy some-

thing for them, ask them to write it down and put it on the refrigerator. Encourage them to write memos and make signs. Give them all the support they need.

Acceptance

If you accept the idea of invented spelling and the purpose behind it, then you will be able to accept, without question, all writing and spelling efforts your child makes. There must be no hesitation, no doubt, because children are uncanny in their ability to pick up nonverbal cues. My student teachers often find this difficult because, they say, they are "no good at lying." I remind them to always refer to a child's spelling by its full title, "invented spelling," to help them distinguish it from the standard form. This way, they can legitimately say to a child, "That's an excellent invented spelling of that word." Invented spelling and standard spelling are two very different skills. One is a problem-solving skill; the other is a rote memory skill.

For very young children, writing will consist of "scribbles" that the child labels as writing. Always respond to such efforts as though they were real, for to the child they are real writing, just as their early babblings were real speech. Say, "Tell me what you wrote," or ask, "Will you read your writing to me?"

As children learn some of the alphabet from listening to alphabet books, playing with magnetic letters and alphabet blocks, learning to write their names, and casual discussions about letters, they will begin to use approximations of letter forms, mixed with invented letters, as part of their scribbles. Do not worry about reversals, upside-down letters, or placement all over the page. Just continue to model the correct form whenever you write something down for your child. Children are great imitators and inventors (how else would they learn to speak?), and eventually they will pick up the pattern. Just keep focusing on the message, not the mechanics.

Sensitivity

Be as sensitive toward your children's struggles with writing as you were toward their early attempts at walking and talking. Encourage and model, but draw back and take off any pressure the moment you detect fatigue or overload. Remember, there is no urgency. When in doubt, ask yourself, "How did I handle this sort of situation when they were learning to talk?"

Common Sense

Common sense is the element you have relied on in raising your children so far. Keep using it in helping to develop the writing process. Common sense is Mother Nature's greatest gift to parents, and as long as we pay attention to her nudgings, we do a fine job of raising our young. It is when we listen too closely to the advice of "experts" (yes, including me!) that we can get confused. Only you know the limitations of your children and yourself. It is up to you to keep the balance. If they are showing signs of frustration, stop. If they want more, provide more. Also take into account the fact that children have very different styles from one another.

* * *

One last word about relatives and outsiders who disapprove. If you find that you cannot convince Great-Aunt Mary that the letters she is receiving from your children are a valuable part of their development, then quietly rewrite them in standard spelling and keep the invented versions in your private treasure chest. Usually, however, receiving the original with a translation is appreciated by most relatives. As for friends and acquaintances who may disapprove, remember that you have brought up your children your way so far, and they are healthy and happy. When it comes down to it, who knows best, anyway?

19

Easing Children into Writing

Jacque Williamson

We are better able to see children's writing for what it really is when we view writing as thinking on paper rather than as a purely mechanical process. As parents, we know children's speech develops gradually. We know not to panic when a two-year-old says, "Men's is here," and we don't tell the child, "That isn't real talk." Yet, when a young child brings us a paper with "ILM" and tells us that it says, "I love Mommy," we are apt to give some praise but may follow with a comment such as "That isn't real writing." Our challenge is to understand and respond to children's writing the same way we respond to their talking.

When I began teaching our own children at home, I didn't consider writing to be important. Having taught elementary school, I associated writing with visions of dull handwriting drills, erasers, and torn papers. These images did not represent the type of learning that I wanted for my children, so I ignored the subject altogether. Luckily, my children did not depend on my priorities. They wrote notes, wrote to pen pals, and wrote a few homemade books. I began to see a pattern emerging in their writing styles as they grew older. Increasingly curious about how children learn to write, I began looking for more information on the subject. Happily, I found some books and articles that showed me how to encourage and appreciate young children's writing.

Stages of Writing Development
The very young child draws pictures and describes them. The parent often then writes the child's words on the paper. As the child becomes aware that letters say something, he or she will scribble or write random letters and then tell you, "That says . . ."

It is very important not to expect perfection at this early stage but rather to let the child's writing evolve naturally. Just knowing that spelling will improve the more the child writes and reads will help ease the urge to always correct. What is critical is that the child enjoys writing and feels confident enough to write independently.

The following is a progression of writing "I love Mommy." Invented spellings gradually evolve into conventional spellings.

I L M—The child is aware of initial sounds.

I LV ME—First and last consonant sounds are used.

I LV MUMME—Middle consonants and some vowels are used.

I LOVE MOMMY—The child uses the conventional spellings rather than the strictly phonetic.

A six-year study conducted by Stauffer and Hammond compared the effectiveness of programs that emphasized reading widely and writing with invented spellings with programs that did not emphasize reading or writing. They found that wide reading and writing using invented spellings produced superior spellers who remained superior throughout their elementary schooling.

Ways to Encourage Writing

Read a wide range of literature to your children, including classic literature, letters, newspapers, magazines, and the children's own stories. Examine the works critically with the children, talking about story lines, characterization, plot outcomes, illustrations, and choice of title.

Provide lots of writing materials. In addition to the traditional pencils, pens, and paper, have available good-quality colored markers, crayons, colored papers, photos, newspapers and magazines to clip from, stapler, tape, scissors, printing set, and typewriter. A computer is a boon to children, as it substitutes ready-made type for the often difficult process of handwriting and makes corrections painless.

Writing tends to be an oral task. Along with the common practice of verbalizing the words as they write, some children find that the oral experience of eating nutritious snacks facilitates writing.

Write messages to your children and encourage them to give you messages. "Good morning. I love you. Strawberries are in the refrigerator" is a welcome message for the late riser.

Letters to pen pals have been a popular activity for our children. Every time they write, they can look forward to a response. Their cor-

JILL FINEBERG

respondence has included letters, postcards, birthday cards, stickers, crazy stories, handwritten comic strips, puzzles and mazes, hand-drawn maps, homemade books, recipes, photos, and newspaper clippings.

Making up oral stories and songs encourages use of language. Occasionally writing down favorites helps the child to see that writing is "talk written down."

Talk with your child about his or her own writing. First, ask leading questions or comment about the topic. This allows the child to tell you what the writing is about. The question "What part do you like best?" encourages critical thinking. Ask about the organization: "What happened next?" "Is this part talking about the part up there?" This process helps the child order the information and group related ideas and sentences.

Only after the meat of the writing has been discussed should you examine capitalization, punctuation, spelling, and handwriting—and only if you feel the child is ready for help in these areas. Limit your discussion to one or two skills for any given paper (for example, capitalizing the beginning letters of sentences and placing periods accurately). The pencil should be poised in the child's hand at all times, ready to make corrections. This enables the child to maintain control of the writing.

Help your children make little bound books of their writing. Book-binding can be as simple as stapling papers into a construction paper or wallpaper cover, or as complicated as sewing pages together and putting them into a hardback cover decorated with fancy paper or batik. Working toward a bound book often encourages children to do the best job possible. All during first grade we struggled with our son's messy handwriting and letter reversals. When he began writing little books for his friends, the reversals suddenly faded and his handwriting became quite legible.

Now, grab some writing materials and enjoy the delight of playing with words with your child. I hope you find writing as stimulating and rewarding as we have.

20

ANDY WRITES A POEM

Amy Malick

Our family waited anxiously for the edition of the children's magazine in which Matt's poem was to be published. The day it
arrived, we were beside ourselves with pride. Although Matt tests
high on intelligence tests, he has never excelled in school, so we knew
the publishing of his poem would boost his ego.

In my excitement, I failed to notice that my younger son, Andy, was
brooding. That evening, he came to me with a pencil and a piece of
paper.

"Mom, I'm going to write a poem for the magazine, too," he said.

My heart sank. Andy has a learning disability. This year he
advanced to third grade, after spending two years in second grade, but
he was still plodding along at the bottom of the class. Andy is a very
good artist, and I had always encouraged his talent, hoping that artistic success would compensate for his learning difficulties. I was sure he
did not have the skills needed to write a poem suitable for publication.

"That's a great idea, Andy!" I said, masking my concern. After all, I
thought, I am an English teacher; I should be able to guide him in his
attempts.

Andy had already laboriously printed five lines of his poem on the
piece of paper:

> On Halloween night
> The moon is bright.
> As you can see
> The spoon is light
> for the witch's brew.

Not bad, I thought as I read. Actually, pretty good. "Fantastic,
Andy!" I exclaimed. "How about changing *light* to *right*?" With my

On Halloween night
The moon is bright.
As you can see
The spoon is light
for the witch's brew.

The bubbly brew is a stew
with spider knuckles,
with Frankenstein's chuckles,
to give the witch blue
freckles, and — A drop of

tree sap to give it a blur.
She makes it
busy until she is dizzy
And her hair is frizzy.

Plop, her
freckles
are gone!

by Andy
Wood

expert direction, his poem will be all right, I mused. "I'll write while you dictate to me," I said, taking the pencil out of his hand. That will make it easier for him, I thought.

His face fell a little, and I assumed he was gearing up for the task ahead. "Close your eyes, Andy," I directed, "and imagine what will happen next. What do you see?" I speculated that if I could help him draw on his artistic visualizing skills, he would be able to come up with ideas.

"I see a bubbly brew with spider knuckles. And Frankenstein's chuckles!" he shouted enthusiastically. Oh brother, I thought. Kids always get stuck in that rhyming routine. "Write, Mom!" Andy implored. Then he dictated:

> The bubbly brew is a stew
> with spider knuckles,
> with Frankenstein's chuckles,
> to give the witch blue freckles.

"Blue freckles?" I questioned. "How about black freckles? That's scarier."

"Well, OK," he said.

"What else would make the stew real yukky?" I asked.

"A drop of tree sap," he said.

"Great, Andy. Good thinking. How could you word that to make it fit in?"

and—a drop of tree sap
to give it a blur.

Well, there goes the rhythm, I conceded. I might as well humor him. "What next?" I asked.

She makes it busy
until she is dizzy
and her hair is frizzy.

Wow! Andy's words gave me an idea. I'll really spruce up this poem, I thought. I wrote the words in a spiral, impressed with the appearance of the poem on the paper. "Look, Andy," I said, passing him the paper. "You're so clever. Doesn't this look neat?"

"Yeah," he said softly. "It looks real neat."

"Now what?" I asked.

Plop, her freckles are gone!

That doesn't even make sense, I worried. "Are you sure that's what you want to say?" I asked. "Try real hard to imagine the witch," I encouraged. "What does she do next?"

"That's it, Mom," he said, exasperated. "She stirred the stew so hard her freckles fell off."

Sure enough. I was amazed. What a great poem! I finished writing, and handed the paper to Andy. He'd done it; he had written a poem himself. "Andy, you're incredible," I said. "I didn't know you were such a good poet."

Andy took the paper in his hand and sat perfectly still while huge tears filled his eyes.

"What's the matter?" I asked, incredulous. He had just done the impossible. How could he not be pleased?

"This isn't my poem, this is yours!" he cried.

I was stunned with the realization of what I had done. Rather than showing him my confidence, I had shown just the opposite when I took the pencil from him and began writing. He had done perfectly well on the first five lines, and although he thought of the remaining words, I had written them in my skilled adult handwriting. Therefore, to Andy they were my words.

Wrapping my arms around him, I said, "Oh, honey, I'm so sorry. I know you could have done this yourself. You *did* think of all the words."

"What about *right* and *black*? I wanted *light* and *blue*," he answered. "And you're the one who thought of writing the dizzy part in a circle."

I felt horrible, and I wondered whether I could right the damage. "You copy the poem in your own handwriting, exactly how you want it," I told him. "Then it will be all yours."

Several days went by, and eventually I asked Andy about the poem. Realizing for the first time that he had a wonderfully creative command of language, I felt I had ruined the opportunity to give him confidence. By taking over for him, I had given him the message that he was small and incapable, while I was big and competent. Would he ever risk venturing out of his fragile shell again?

Finally, at the end of the week, Andy shyly handed me a tattered piece of notebook paper. On it he had copied his poem, complete with a light spoon, blue freckles, and busy stew printed in straight lines. In addition, he had meticulously illustrated the poem. It was a masterpiece! I beamed and so did he.

And I learned something important. I hope I will never again limit my children by expecting them to perform according to a label. Matt is no more exclusively "the smart one" than Andy is "the artistic one." Each one has the buds of talents waiting only to be encouraged into blossoms by someone who believes the possibilities are there. From now on, let that someone be me.

I photocopied Andy's poem and taped it on the front of the refrigerator. I mailed copies to relatives, and Andy took copies to his favorite teachers. Plus I submitted it to the children's magazine. Will it be published? Who knows?

But, then again, who cares?

21

Science in the Home

Elizabeth Wild

As a mother, ex-high school English teacher, and parent with an interest in taking an active part in my children's education, I decided four years ago to start a weekly after-school science club for my two sons, ages seven and nine. No sooner had I called the first meeting than I realized what a major job it would be. I didn't know anything about science! "Let's do pollution! Let's study ants! Can we take apart a radio?" The kids were bubbling over with enthusiasm. I was afraid I'd overestimated my ability. Merely pointing out the Big Dipper, evaporating water, or counting tree rings wasn't going to suffice. I headed for the public library.

I had read an article in *The Next Whole Earth Catalog* that said the best way to understand an unfamiliar subject was to find a book written for the fourth or fifth grade level and work up from there. After spending countless hours doing just this, I can testify that the method works. Most of these books are easy to understand, very well illustrated, and often contain suggestions for simple experiments using rubber bands, hard-boiled eggs, baking soda, or other things commonly found around the house. Frequently, they contain lists of more advanced books on the subject.

I discovered that the enthusiasm of the kids more than justified my learning the material, rounding up equipment, and generating new ideas for every week. The children couldn't wait for each session. They didn't seem to mind that there were no badges or achievement awards, and they certainly didn't object to learning without homework or grades. I felt a glow of contentment as I listened to my children rattling on about continental drift, red blood cells, and short circuits. And I was learning so much myself.

In general, our hour-long sessions, which included six or eight children, comprised two parts. In the first, I explained the day's concept carefully, making liberal use of blackboard demonstrations, specimens, and experiments, and often asking the kids to draw pictures on individual pads to insure that they understood what we were doing. In the second part, we worked on a related hands-on project: doing an experiment, making a model, or playing a game. The more active role the kids could play, the better.

The following list suggests the range of topics we were able to cover in a three-year period:

1. Testing the reactions of earthworms to light, moisture, acidity, vibration, and cold. Making a clay model of an earthworm's insides. Making a "wormery" in a jar.

2. Doing simple tests to identify "mystery powders": flour, salt, baking soda, plaster of paris.

3. Examining a lamb heart from the butcher as part of our study of blood circulation.

4. Making periscopes from small mirrors and waxed-paper boxes.

5. Making models of our teeth using clay and plaster of paris.

6. Taking apart an old telephone.

7. Siphoning water.

8. Growing crystals on sponges using ammonia and blueing (a stinky mess!).

9. Watching and drawing honeybees on the raspberry bushes behind the house; tasting different kinds of honey.

10. Making a plaster of paris "fossil."

11. Identifying bird pictures, using field guides and back issues of *Audubon* magazine.

12. Playing a food-chain game, adding on additional loops for each new species in the chain.

13. Experimenting with heat, air, and water. (Children's science books are full of ideas for these).

14. Making a simple pinhole device to show an inverted image.

15. Composing a poem as a group to help memorize the names of the major bones in the body ("In your cranium is your brainium").

16. Comparing concave and convex lenses. Predicting the image by feeling the lens in a paper bag.

17. Making "constellations" appear on a darkened ceiling by shining a flashlight through an appropriately punctured tin can.

18. Making a simple electrical circuit with light bulb, battery, and circuit breaker. Testing various materials for conductivity. Magnetizing a nail.

19. Making Playdough landscapes showing the effects of glaciers.

20. Making bird feeders and peanut butter-suet-sunflower seed food.

21. Making a thirty-foot time line from the earth's origin to the present with adding machine tape, noting the various geological periods and emphasizing how briefly man has been on earth.

22. Testing household substances (vinegar, detergent, etc.) with our own litmus paper made from coffee filters and red cabbage juice.

23. Making booklets of common optical illusions to try out on friends. (There are some especially good ones in color.)

24. Playing with mirrors. Making prisms using mirrors under water. Angling a series of mirrors to see how long you can keep reflecting a beam of light. Making kaleidoscopes.

25. Building terrariums using large glass jars from restaurants.

26. Watching changes in air pressure as registered on a homemade barometer (balloon stretched over the open end of a glass bottle).

27. Sorting rocks to match those in a collection.

28. Testing our sensitivity to heat, cold, and pressure, by touching appropriate pins to a tiny gridwork drawn on the skin.

29. Showing the pattern of continental drift by decorating styrofoam balls with glitter (an unusual Christmas tree decoration!).

Once we were into a subject, logical field trips suggested themselves. We peered through a neighbor's telescope, dissected worms at a local high school, and visited the zoo, a blood bank, the telephone company, and a research laser facility. We visited a farmers market with an observation beehive and familiarized ourselves with the geology section of our local museum. We went on a fossil hunt and a winter bird walk with area naturalists.

The more we learned about a subject, the more there seemed yet to discover. For me, as much as for the children, science was lifted off the pages of a dry text and became a fascinating study of the world around us. I was amazed to have stumbled upon this interesting new terrain. No longer could I see a tree without thinking of the tangled maze of root hairs buried in the soil, watch bees without being aware of their various roles in the hive, or gaze at the moon without wondering at the catastrophic collision millions of years ago that resulted in its present smudged appearance.

There were many projects we never did. We never found a ham radio operator or wrote letters crosscountry for rock and plant specimens, talked about solar energy, or lifted the hood of a car. I still find myself reading articles on earthquakes or gene splicing and wondering absentmindedly how I could work this into next week's meeting. And I miss that satisfying, heartwarming feeling that I am in some small way nourishing the lives of my own children. If you're tempted, start a science club. It will surely be worth it.

Suggested Reading
Blake, Jim, and Barbara Ernst. *The Great Perpetual Learning Machine, Being a stupendous collection of ideas, games, experiments, activities, and recommendations for further exploration.* Boston: Little, Brown and Company, 1976. This book is exactly what it says.

Boy Scouts of America. *Webelos Scout Book*, 1981. Activity badge section will help guide the adult uncertain of the capabilities of the fourth or fifth grader. Good suggestions under the engineer, forester, geologist, naturalist, and scientist badges.

Brown Paper School Books. Little, Brown and Company, Boston. A series of books with unusual ideas for helping children and grownups learn together and have fun doing it. Useful titles include *The Reasons for the Seasons, Blood and Guts,* and *The Night Sky Book.*

Herbert, Don. *Mr. Wizard's Supermarket Science.* New York: Random House, 1980. More than one hundred experiments using common items found around the house by the veteran of the popular *Mr. Wizard* television program.

Stein, Sara. *The Science Book.* New York: Workman Publishing, 1980. Sourcebook of science activities that run the gamut from electricity to bedbugs.

UNESCO. *700 Science Experiments for Everyone.* New York: Doubleday and Company, 1958. Straightforward instructions for hundreds of experiments using homemade equipment made of low-cost materials.

22

Nurturing Art

Claudia Bumgarner Kirby

The basic human need to express oneself artistically is present in a primal, nonintellectual, gut-level state in small children. Their interest in what is normally called "artwork" is purely love of process. The two-year-old with a crayon or a handful of dough is not interested in "creating art" or "communicating." This child is interested in the *act* of coloring, in the feel of dough squishing, in seeing what effects hands can have on materials. Children generally prefer the crayon that makes the boldest mark. A two-year-old can be transported by a black magic marker. This is play in its purest form, a simple joy in the material and the act, with no thought of product or accomplishment.

The adult question "What is it?" or the better, less threatening, "Tell me about it" shifts the child's focus from process to communication. Taping a cherished drawing to the refrigerator door brings the focus around to "product." This adult-child interplay is a necessary and natural part of artistic development.

Our children's school experience with art is under a serious and twofold threat. The current back-to-basics movement sees artwork as playtime and therefore unnecessary. Schools suffering from budget cutbacks often see art and music as "frills," and these programs are among the first to be eliminated. However, many educators and art therapists who understand the primal force of art in young children are fighting back, and some schools offer daily art, music, drama, and storytelling.

The role of parents in this area is to provide materials and stimulation to the small child and to observe and supplement the school experience of the older child as much as necessary.

As in most things in life, the middle road here is preferable. Children who are overdirected (constantly told to "stay in the lines" or always given planned-out projects) will eventually lose interest in art or have their creativity seriously crippled. Alternately, totally undirected children miss out on very valuable learning experiences and may lose interest out of frustration.

Children need just enough technical advice to give them confidence with materials. Teach them how to hold and use scissors; how to keep a brush from dripping or drying out; how to pour without spilling; how to hold a crayon without breaking it; how to get broad and narrow lines with a marker; how to color with the side of the chalk; how to hold the paper still so it won't tear; how to control a paper tear rather than yanking it apart; how not to poke a pencil through the paper. These are skills that will greatly reduce frustration and open the way to freer expression.

If you do artwork with your children or let them work near you, you will notice when the scissors aren't working or the paper is tearing, and that will give you your cues for when to teach each skill. Don't force information on a child who isn't ready. The little one who is struggling with scissors will be much more grateful for some simple advice than one who is taken away from the crayons for a "scissors lesson." Also, many art supplies are sharp, toxic, or messy, and these need safety supervision at the time they are being used.

Children should always have paper and some writing instrument available to them. Fancy drawing paper is nice but definitely not necessary. Small children are just as happy with the backs of junk mail, outdated flyers and posters, wrapping paper, unused snipped-off sections of notepaper and stationery, printer's trimmings, cut-open paper bags, and, unfortunately, walls. One of my own most cherished early drawings was done on the back of a piece of a cereal box.

The best writing instrument available to children is still the crayon. However, some children are simply not very compatible with them, becoming destructive or hungry when left alone to draw. But, please, supervise rather than forbid the use of crayons.

Take advantage of any opportunity to expose your little people to new materials. Chalk, pencils, pens, markers, and paint are all good alternatives to crayons. Try clay, dough, rubber stamps, and glue and scissors. Keep a box or a drawer for yarn and fabric scraps, odd buttons, sequins, colored paper, old magazines, pretty rocks, empty spools, paper rolls, empty plastic bottles, and other interesting odds and ends.

And don't throw out the coloring books! It has been fashionable for some time to berate coloring books, but they have their place as long as they are supplemented with plenty of blank paper, and the kids aren't pestered to "stay in the lines." They are great for quiet times when a child feels like coloring but hasn't got the energy to face a blank piece of paper. They are a nonthreatening way to explore color or simply develop crayon dexterity. They also give children a chance to make a very recognizable image (we never say, "What is it?" to a coloring book picture). And coloring books can often be a two-person activity, which is an added benefit.

Most art materials are available in appealing, brightly colored, expensive packages at toy stores, but perfectly acceptable substitutes are available at thrift stores, flea markets, in the backs of desk drawers and tool boxes, and from adults who will part with almost-empty paint cans, markers, pens, spools, and all sorts of good scraps.

As for project ideas, any library or bookstore can provide books and magazines with ideas for kid's art projects. You don't have to be a professional, and you don't have to come up with a new project every day. The books are there to help. Even the most creative teacher has dry days. The books not only teach projects but also set your mind on a creative track; they may prompt you to discover interesting variations and offshoots of what they describe.

But—and this is important—very often the materials themselves will be all the motivation a child needs. As an art teacher with a planned project, I have been put in my place more than once by the fresh and unencumbered ideas of a child caught up in a joy of materials.

I have learned, however, not to overwhelm children with too many materials at one time. The child faced with a cabinet full of supplies and no restrictions will more often than not be overcome with the desire to experience it all at once and wind up with a shapeless, ragged, grayish-purple unidentified object and a mood somewhere between disappointment and rage. This experience is very common, but we should try to minimize the number of times it happens because it tends to discourage interest.

Stimulation and motivation are the most important materials you can provide. The child with a wide range of experience simply has more to draw upon when faced with a blank sheet of paper or a shapeless lump of clay. The child who has been read to; taken shopping to

JILL FINEBERG

all sorts of stores; played with; taken to exhibitions, fairs, flea markets, and celebrations; allowed to walk slowly and examine bugs and sticks; and permitted to look out high windows, watch rainbows, play in the rain, dig holes, taste things, and touch everything possible will be bursting with images and experiences to put into form with clay, string, words, musical notes, steps, or whatever artform is offered.

The desire to decorate and to create images is easily encouraged and readily satisfied. Be open to any form it may take. "Painting" on a hot sidewalk with water can be great fun. "Drawing" on a carpet with yarn scraps or decorating a little bather's legs and belly with soap patterns; putting catsup on food in fancy patterns; pouring honey in a spiral; finger painting in the syrup after the pancakes; arranging the salad to look like a face; drawing in the window steam or furniture dust; raking the yard in a pattern—all are responses to the primal human needs to decorate, to make images, and to play.

Allow your children to experience as many different teachers as possible. Give them what you can yourself; take them to art shows and exhibits; show them projects in magazines. Let them take classes through schools, churches, community organizations, and teaching artists. For young children, look for classes and teachers who will give them a wide variety of materials and adequate (but not stifling) direction. Try to avoid teachers who put out the paints and retreat to a corner as well as those who hover and direct which color to use. These classes should place an emphasis on play and exploration.

Classes or lessons designed to teach a specific skill, such as figure drawing, water color, wood sculpture, or landscape painting are best reserved for the older child who has expressed an interest, shown a talent, and wants to learn. These classes can, through many interesting exercises, teach a young artist valuable lessons in seeing and interpreting the world and in the skills necessary to deal with complicated processes. However, for the child who is not ready, these classes will be much more like work than play and may serve to turn him or her away from, rather than toward, art. As always, watch for the cues your individual child is giving, and follow them as best you can.

Last, and most important, if you find that you have very good experiences doing artwork with your own child, please consider sharing your talent with your child's friends or even volunteering to lead a project at school. Even schools that consider art teachers a "frill" have a hard time turning down volunteers, and the teachers who recognize the value of art for children will love you for it!

PART IV:
HOME SCHOOLING STORIES

23

IN LOVE WITH LEARNING: A HOME SCHOOL STORY

Patricia Savage

There are no bells, no blackboards, no tests, or other conventional signs to indicate that school is in session. Yet, despite the lack of these assurances, learning is the task at hand in our home. The rising sun is our bell; the kitchen table, the bathtub, or the backyard may be our workplace; and an ever-blossoming repertoire of skills is the measure of our progress.

In September 1981, the local school board approved our decision to continue to educate our seven-year-old son, Jamie, at home. Being the first ones in our circle of friends to have braved the legal frontier of home schooling, I feel much as my parents must have when they got the first TV on the block back in 1950. Everyone wants to know, "How does it work? Will it last?"

One of the delightful paradoxes of parenthood is that humility is the most responsible attitude one can have. The parent and the child are born at the same time. We are in process as much as the child. We cannot know the answers to all the questions that will face us as parents upon the birth of our child. Indeed, we cannot even anticipate all the questions! Likewise, we cannot know what kind of educational needs our child will have ten years down the line. Although my husband and I have an educational philosophy that is long-range, we feel most comfortable deciding year to year whether our children's needs will be best met at home or in an institutionalized setting.

When our children ask us questions that we cannot answer or desire to develop competence in an area in which neither my husband nor I am proficient, we direct them to other sources. If you want to learn something, go where people are doing it. My son is an excellent fisherman, and he has learned mostly from doing but also from the people he meets while fishing. He has learned to do macramé from our neighbor; to draw from the "Captain Bob" TV show; to do wood-work and play baseball from his father; to cook and bake from me. Our responsibility to our children as their "supervisors" is to respond to their needs and help them to find the resources needed to develop competency and excellence in the areas of their interest.

"Learning by doing" is a phrase commonly heard in home educa-tion circles. What that means in our house is that I never have elbow room at the kitchen counter or the breadboard. It means that the typewriter never comes out without everyone having a turn. It means the kitchen table is never clear; when I sit down to write or do art-work, the children get out their pads, felt tips, scissors, and paints. It also means that four-year-old Katy helps to bring in firewood, that Jamie cleans the kitty litter, and that everyone picks up after her or himself. It would be great if I could add, "And all runs smoothly." As in most homes, our children have to be continually reminded of their responsibilities. Still, the development of a sense of order, coopera-tion, and responsible participation is as important to us as is the blos-soming of creativity, intelligence, and an appreciation of beauty.

It has been my observation that the most creative cooks, artists, and craftsmen work in a total whirlwind of a mess; it has also been my feeling that clarity comes from order. I try to always start with an orderly kitchen before I cook. I clear my workspace before I bring out my writing. I bring all my art supplies to the table before starting a project. I totally immerse myself in what I do—is there any other way to enjoy it?—and the result is always a messy workplace. Before I go on to anything else, however, order is restored. This is the message I give my children as well: Make as big a wreck as you want; just pick it up when you are through. And the children respond to order. I have observed more than once that when their playroom is disorderly, no one spends any time in it. As soon as it is reorganized, interest is dra-matically renewed.

Volumes have been written on how to instruct, on what should be introduced when, on which materials should be used, and what approach is best. As mentioned previously, I feel that attitudes are more important than method in creating a climate of growth. How-ever, we have tried various ways of structuring our day so that our educational goals (as loose as they may be) are met.

Our arrangement with the public school system is to present a yearly curriculum and to have periodic evaluations with the superintendent and a teacher. I keep a journal of our daily activities, which probably will be valued as a family history in future years. In addition, Jamie has a scrapbook of newspaper and magazine clippings and stories he has written, an art portfolio, and a file folder with language and math worksheets that I have designed. We also keep samples of his crafts to show the visiting authorities. These records have to date provided a satisfactory way to indicate progress to the school. However, I always feel that these products are insufficient measures of what is going on; the everyday process of growing up is so much more interesting, mysterious, and intangible. When Katy says, "Want to see me draw a cat?" she means, "Watch me while I draw it," not "Look at the finished picture." Very young children know what we often forget: the fun is in the doing.

We have not developed a rigid schedule, although there is some structure to our day. In the early months of this "school" year, we found sitting together at the kitchen table for an hour of academics was helpful in getting us in touch with Jamie's abilities. Usually we had a half hour of language games: "hangman" or scrambled letters or writing a letter or story. The second half hour was spent reading history books geared for youngsters, having discussions referring to our globe or map, or working on a nature project. Jamie has acquired an array of skills as he has needed them through the years, such as telling time, adding, subtracting, multiplying, dividing, and working with fractions. Most of his nature projects are self-propelled, such as making a vivarium, collecting and drying fungus, or growing sprouts. This morning, for example, drunk on the first spring air, he found some vegetable seeds from last year and planted them in egg cartons.

When I became pregnant with my third child, my energy was very low in the morning, and structured time was phased out. Interestingly, Jamie exhibited qualities at this time that were invaluable to me. He would start breakfast for himself and Katy, bring food to me in bed, and generally take responsibility for many things I normally would have thought only I could do. This illustrates a real advantage to the home curriculum: it is flexible, with "real life" frequently dictating what needs to be learned. Once I started feeling better, we started spending more focused time together again. I developed a more relaxed attitude, confident that we could rely on a more spontaneous schedule. Each family and each child is different with regards to goals and motivation. For us, continuing to trust that we can each be left to do what we have to has been the way to flourish.

Frequently we are asked if we worry about the limitations placed on our children's experience by keeping them out of school. But there is a paradox here: rather than home-based education being a sheltered experience, it is one where all possibilities are kept alive. Because our children are not required to sit in a classroom for 180 days a year, we have tremendous freedom. Each day is different, and the possibilities are very wide. We can go to the library, a museum, or a park during school hours. The truth is, however, that we put a lot of energy into our home and we like being here; for us it is an interesting place to be. Every home is potentially interesting because of the people who live there and the efforts they put into making the environment livable and unique. If a parent has many interests and is expansive rather than reticent about them, then it is likely that the child's natural curiosity about the world will be nurtured.

We have been blessed with two children who are creative and self-motivated. They frequently go off in a corner to express some part of their imagination through artwork, dance, or fantasy play. For me, the development of a creative personality does not necessarily mean that one must become proficient in an area that is commonly thought to be "artistic." Being creative means being able to look at the world in a certain way, with freshness and openness.

But there is no doubt that offering a wide variety of artistic experiences increases a child's options for expression. I read a lovely saying by Henry Van Dyke the other day: "Use what talents you possess: the woods would be very silent if no birds sang there except those that sang best." We try to provide opportunities for our children to sing or dance or skate or draw, not so much to encourage future opera stars or Olympic champions, but because with these skills their lives will be more enjoyable. I could never sing professionally, but I thoroughly enjoy every hour I spend singing my heart out at the piano. Song, color, and movement have effects on the spirit that defy logical explanation.

After we dealt with the decision of home school or formalized school last summer, a more cogent issue presented itself: teaching versus nonteaching. How much should we interfere with or direct the natural unfolding process of learning? Sometimes I think that the children learn in spite of our efforts rather than because of them. I

read a passage by Anne Herbert in *The Next Whole Earth Catalog* not long ago that I find myself turning to often:

> The only thing to teach is how to fall in love, how to be ready to fall in love, what to do then to make it last, make it a lifetime thing; to teach how to find out more about the beloved, to build something with the beloved, within the beloved; to teach all this before love ever happens, so that when love comes, be it of caterpillars or dead painters or wood and nails or computers that talk back, when it happens the feeling doesn't dissipate into a hopeless infatuation —"it must be wonderful to do that, to know about that, but I can't"—but is a release of power like real love that leads to knowing more because you know where to find it, cherishing and building in this love because you know that someone can tell you how to do it and you keep looking until you find the one who can."[1]

We do, of course, teach our children lots of things. That is our responsibility. The point is that what we teach them is not so much what we instruct them in as how we live. Our responsibility is to wake up every day "in love," to feel fresh with the newness of morning, reassured by all the wonders at hand, which exist despite our manmade worries. One of the real pluses of having children is that they keep you from doing the "shoulds" and getting caught up in the "only-if-I-coulds." With only two inches of snow on the ground, the attic is stormed for toboggans and hockey sticks and warm woolens. When the children learn to make macrame necklaces, they use up all the new cord in one day. One day, they discover how to make "God's eyes," and the next you have no string in the house. When they play store, they need *all* the vegetables from the refrigerator, not just the carrots. You see, children are so eager to fall in love.

Notes
1. *The Next Whole Earth Catalog* (Point/Random House, 1980), 77. Originally published in *Rising Sun Neighborhood Newsletter.*

24

HOME SCHOOLING DAY BY DAY

Kate Kerman

When asked, as I have been many times, "What is a typical day like in your home school?" I always groan or grimace. Today, for instance—was it typical? Ed made breakfast while I folded laundry. The kids—Ada, age 9; Hannah, age 5; and Jesse, 2½—gradually woke up and ate. Ed and Ada left for a day at the library. Ada planned to work the same hours as Ed and to do some errands for me on her breaks and lunch hour. Hannah and Jesse ate a little, then I read *Knights' Castle*, by Edward Eager, to Hannah while Jesse nursed. I next read a Richard Scarry book to Jesse and returned to housework. Hannah washed dishes while I read to her, after which I washed dishes and read another book to Jesse. Hannah and Jesse played with a shapes puzzle; I did laundry and wrote a letter. They asked for something exciting to do, so we made play dough, and they spent some time with that. Ada called to check the details of one of her errands. We ate lunch. Hannah and Jesse dressed up in some old tights, slid around the kitchen, and practiced some "clown tricks." We settled down to read and nurse some more. A hunter knocked at the front door to report that there was a fire in an old bus parked at an unoccupied house up the road. I called the emergency number, and we walked up the road to watch the fire fighters at work. When they all left, we walked home. Hannah and Jesse played outside, while I cleaned the porch. We came in, nursed, and read some more. Amazingly enough, both kids then fell asleep.

This report does not include the questions I answered ("Why would someone want to set fire to that bus?" "How did they fill this ballpoint pen?" and so on), the role-playing involved in using clay and dressing up, or the discussion on how and when to use the emergency number. Nor does it describe Ada's activities: doing some statistical gathering for Ed, checking shelves to see that the books were in order, as well as having a chance to see what the rhythm of his day is like.

As to whether all this is typical, or whether there is a more typical day I could report, it's difficult to say. Sometimes we have a more structured day and do projects together that look a bit more "schoolish"—although we do not use textbooks at all any more, rarely use workbooks, and have long since given up on having a special school location, since we always end up at the kitchen and craft tables anyway. Sometimes the kids get deeply involved in their own activities. At times we go traveling, visiting, or sightseeing. Occasionally I get immersed in my own projects, and the kids must suffer slight neglect or work with me. Ed joins in on some days; at other times we have friends or relatives involved.

Much of the structure I've evolved in learning with my children at home has been for my own reassurance. I keep a school journal and compile a quarterly or semiannual report that roughly divides our activities into subject areas. This addresses my fears that "nothing is happening" and gives us something concrete to show to anyone else who is interested—friends, relatives, school officials, other home schoolers. When I assemble a report, I'm always amazed at how many interesting things we've done.

Home schooling can be boring, difficult, and frustrating for me on a daily basis. Now and then I have almost despaired over the conflicts between the kids, or between them and me, concerning the messes that busy people generate—also, over a sense of philosophical and political isolation from our community. The journal keeping, reports, and the school meetings that we have evolved are my crutches. Rather than being learning tools for the kids, they are my way to feel "on top" of things, in touch with the broader picture.

That broader picture as I see it now makes me more able to deal positively with daily exasperations. At nine, Ada is an aggressive learner, heavily involved in academics, competent with her hands, and able to assist with housework, be responsible for her younger siblings, and do needed volunteer work at the library. Although she's had ups and downs socially, she now gets along well with people at home and in public. Most important to me is the fact that when she's among other children she doesn't feel the need to take their values and desires for her own.

Our hope as parents is to raise good choosers—thinking, evaluating, caring people. Our attempts to do so revolve around a democratic form of family government. As we come up against small and large decisions, we try to involve our children in ways appropriate to their ages. We have a weekly family council for setting up menus and chores, planning family trips and celebrations, and ironing out diffi- culties. Attendance is voluntary. Ada is a full participant; Hannah and Jesse come and go. Jesse now and then participates by asking for a certain favorite meal or expressing an opinion. Hannah brings up issues, expresses opinions, and volunteers for jobs. She needs help with these jobs but is gradually learning how to do them. One of the standing agenda items for the family council is school issues: schedul- ing, general satisfaction with what's going on, field trip plans, and the like.

We decided early on that our kids would have a choice about going to public school. (After all, we are trying to raise choosers!) We set age eight as the earliest time they could choose, figuring that we would have had our major influence by then. As Ada approached the age of eight, she decided to try out third grade in public school. The spring before she started, we checked around regarding teachers and chose one in a first-, second-, and third-grade team with a "semi-open" classroom that seemed suited to Ada's independent learning style. We interviewed this teacher and Ada spent a day in her class before we decided to go ahead. The school agreed to Ada's and our request that she attend part-time. She went full-time for the first month as a chance to get into the routine and establish a social niche for herself. After September, she attended four days a week. This year, having gone through a similar choosing process, Ada attends fourth grade two days a week. She has done well academically and has made enough friends for her social needs. She expects to have a similar choice each year from now on.

I had many qualms and a lot of hard adjustments to make in seeing Ada off to public school, but I feel good about the way she has been able to adjust. Her strong sense of self-worth and her values remain intact; indeed, I think they have been strengthened by coping with teasing, school rules, social "niceties," and the reality of being with so many people much of the time. I also think that this kind of coping probably would have been difficult for her at the age of five.

Many people raise the question of "socialization" with us. We have had rough times with our children (who hasn't?) and, in fact, until the age of 7½, Ada had on occasion some pretty wildly "antisocial" approaches to social problems! I gritted my teeth and wondered if we were doing the right thing. But a family has the love and the long-range commitment to deal with problems and to create responsible, caring people, while a school must have a less personal and supportive approach because it deals with large groups of children. In looking back, I feel sure that spending those years in school would have created more problems for Ada than it could have solved, although I sometimes regret that we didn't create more informal social times for her then. In any case, Ada went to school when she was ready to go, having built up a lot of self-confidence.

Our relationship with the local school district has been generally very positive. Knowing before we had children that home schooling was our goal, I was able to approach it from a strong position legally by getting my Michigan teacher's certificate. When Ada was five months old, I returned to college as a midyear sophomore, taking advantage of an excellent independent study program available at Aquinas College in Grand Rapids, fifty-five miles from our home. This met my desire to be a full-time mother and a college student simultaneously, and Aquinas's innovative and humanistic education was exciting and helpful to me. I was able to do my student teaching in a five-pupil alternative school run by friends of ours, with Ada (then going on 2) participating as a tagalong.

Supplied with a teacher's certificate and a good knowledge of Michigan's tutoring law, we were able to present a convincing proposal to the local school when Ada reached the age of 6. The local superintendent suggested from the start that Ada attend part-time, so although we didn't want that at the time, it was easy to approach him with that request two years later. Ada's teachers were initially dubious but willing to try having a part-time student, and it has worked out very well, even in the more traditional "self-contained" classroom she attends this year.

I think there are many reasons why we have been able to deal positively with the schools. We started out from an unassailable legal position and really knew more about the laws relating to home schooling than the local folks, who had never before dealt with it. Home schooling often falls into a legal gray area, and it pays to do some boning up.

A second advantage we had was the fact that we are home schoolers for religious reasons. As Quakers, we desired a religious education for

our children, and the nearest Quaker school was two hundred miles away in Detroit. This argument is well-understood in our community. Part of the cooperation we've experienced has been because we have given advance notice of our intentions and have always been willing to provide the schools with information about what we do, sometimes even more than they have asked of us. (As we have been on firm legal ground, this has been a good policy for us. It wouldn't be for everyone!)

Part of our success, I think, lies in the fact that we are not attempting a frontal attack on schools in general. We don't see "school" as monolithically evil. It is a large institution and provides a structured approach with many rules and inevitable value clashes. However, we have been impressed with the flexibility of our local school as it has dealt with us. There are good teachers (and in our district parental requests for specific teachers are taken very seriously) and friendly administrators. In talking with other home schoolers who have had good relationships with their various school districts, I find that the most successful have either accidentally or on purpose come in con-

tact with the administrators or teachers most friendly to home schooling and have worked with those people to establish a program satisfactory to all involved. I would like to emphasize that what has worked
well for us would not work well in every situation, and I would urge
people interested in home schooling to do some research before deciding on the best approach for them.

In working with Ada to develop a positive experience for her in
public school, we have tried to keep certain ideas in mind. First, we
don't expect too much from the school; we have, after all, already
taken major responsibility as a family for her social, religious, and academic upbringing. Ada was seeking companionship and has found
that to the degree she wanted. School has given her many opportunities to think about our values and lifestyle in comparison with those
of other people, and I believe that one reason she chose to go was to
test herself out against a new set of givens, having come to grips with
the environment we had to offer.

We all had modest expectations concerning academic challenge in
the school as compared to the excitement and satisfaction of Ada's
home projects. School offers her a standard educational curriculum
that gives her a common "language" with others. Her self-learning, in
contrast, can give her the tools to analyze and accept or reject the
validity of the elements of this common language.

When Ada has had problems with school, we have tried to talk with
everyone involved (if we felt she couldn't cope with the situation herself), and by being interested and involved parents, we feel that we
have helped her get what she wants from school. We volunteered in
her classroom last year and both years have talked with her teachers
often enough to feel we could relate well to them, thus giving us a
good start on any problem-solving that needed doing.

I believe that one of the most powerful ways of learning values is by
watching the people you admire in action. As a parent and teacher, I
feel it is essential for me to be a learning, growing person. The process
of learning and the confidence it brings is what is important, not
specific subjects. Home schooling has shown me the importance of
being a good model for my children. This means trying out new and
frustrating things (and sharing my approaches and frustrations), so
they can see that adults can be beginners, too. It means sharing my
ignorance and my questions, so they can see that adults don't have all
the answers. It means asking for and accepting the instruction of my

children and asking them to instruct each other, so they can become competent in sharing their skills with others.

I work on my own projects in and out of school times. Over the past two years, I have felt a surge in my own creative forces and have happily explored things I never dared try before—drawing, poetry, songwriting, t'ai chi—and some I've wanted to try for years, such as playing the hammer dulcimer, typesetting and printing, and developing photographs. Often the children join me as I learn new skills, but whether they participate directly or not, the important point is that I create space and time to keep my mind and body alive and learning, so they can see learning as a lifelong engagement. In turn, as I live with my children, I have been humbled and freed by their joyful curiosity and intense emotions, as they reach out to establish themselves as increasingly competent human beings.

25

HOME SCHOOLING'S UNIQUE STRUCTURE

Nancy Wallace

The other day during a summer storm, when I'd finished all my inside work and couldn't get out to weed the garden, I sat down and ordered twenty-five dollars worth of textbooks for next year: an eighth-grade math book for Ishmael, as well as an introductory algebra text in case he ever should feel particularly ambitious, and two fifth-grade math books and fourth-grade spelling and language books for Vita. When I was finished, I sat back feeling very self-satisfied and said to myself, "Nancy, you are smarter than I thought." Now I'm not ordinarily given to that sort of self-flattery, but in a way I really think I deserved it. After all these years I had finally decided *not* to feel apologetic about ordering textbooks. After all, textbooks, and the ordered learning they represent, have really had a hand in making our home school as successful as it is.

This wasn't always the case, however. In fact, until a few years ago, I would have said that textbooks seemed more like a noose around our necks than anything else. When we first started home schooling in New Hampshire, we were very much under the thumb of our superintendent and the school board. I had to write a detailed curriculum at the beginning of each year (which wouldn't be approved if it looked like we were going to have too much fun); twice a year, Ishmael (Vita was not of school age) had to undergo testing by the classroom teacher who normally would have been responsible for him; and twice a year, the assistant superintendent looked over Ishmael's work and grilled me about what I was "teaching" him. As if all this wasn't enough, poor Ishmael also had to take a standardized test each spring.

From the day we took Ishmael out of school, we noticed that he learned far more from reading for pleasure and being read to, making things, talking with people, and exploring the world in his own way than he ever learned from a textbook. However, we were afraid to put textbooks aside altogether, since the only skills that the school people seemed to be interested in were the ones that ordinarily could be learned only from a textbook.

So even though we were pretty sure that we knew what the ideal home schooling situation would be like—one in which Ishmael would be free to learn in the same way that he had been free to learn when he was too young for school—we didn't have the courage to give him back that freedom entirely. But despite my frustration with the structure that the school authorities imposed on us, it was obvious that Ishmael had changed dramatically now that he wasn't in school. He was happy, active, inquisitive, and friendly. The only time I ever saw a trace of the irritable, depressed child that he used to be was when the assistant superintendent came over to inspect his work. Finally, Ishmael was free to read as much as he liked and could write stories and plays without worrying about how his handwriting looked. Best of all, on nice days he could play outside with Vita, even during school hours.

At the same time, I had to admit that Ishmael seemed to enjoy the schoolwork that we did each morning. He learned to write neatly by copying his favorite poems into his handwriting notebook, and we taught him the parts of speech by playing Scrabble and Spill and Spell. We thought that science and social studies textbooks were useless for the most part since they were so arid and boring, so we relied mostly on books from the library and magazines like *National Geographic*.

But language and math textbooks came in handy. Among other things, the language textbook explained rules for using proper punctuation, writing formal letters, and dividing words into syllables, and although I didn't make Ishmael do all of the written exercises in the book, we skipped around and read up on whatever I thought the school people would expect Ishmael to know. I searched and searched until I found a decent math textbook—one that explained why arithmetic works the way it does—and we went through the book page by page, making sure that we didn't skip anything and yet only doing as many problems as it took to make sure that Ishmael understood what was going on. The drill work that he'd done in school had made him hate math so much that I was wary of making him do too much. I soon realized that if Ishmael really understood a concept, it stuck in his brain *without* the drill.

What surprised me during these first few years was that Ishmael seemed to *want* to do school work—partly because he was afraid that if he didn't, the school authorities would force him back into school and also because he genuinely felt that he needed to grow up knowing all the things that everyone else knew.

Vita, meanwhile, was desperate to do schoolwork just because Ishmael did. Textbooks for her, however, initially did more harm than good. When she was four, I bought her a math workbook, and although she quickly got the hang of adding and subtracting on paper, I often found her putting just any old answer down, since she couldn't understand why marking in the correct answer was important. Comparing the amount of wood that she had split in a day to the amount that Ishmael split was important, yes, but who really cared about numbers on paper? By the time she was five, she was writing great stories, although her spelling was ridiculously bad. But when I bought her a spelling book, she became so hung up about spelling correctly that she stopped writing altogether. You can imagine how I felt!

Meanwhile, I kept wondering what would happen if the school left us in perfect freedom so that we could do what so many other home schoolers were doing: just letting their kids be. Would Vita and Ishmael still want to read history and science with Bob at night? Would Ishmael become less conscious of "what everyone else knew" and lose interest in keeping up with math and grammar? And would Vita eventually learn to spell and write neatly?

I finally had my chance to learn the answers to these questions when we moved to Ithaca, New York, where the superintendent was not only sympathetic but trusting enough to leave us mostly to ourselves. All he did was tell us that we had to teach the subjects that were required by state law for five hours a day, kindly pointing out that we could use whatever teaching methods we pleased, and he asked us to send him quarterly reports describing the kinds of things that the kids were doing.

Ithaca was such an exciting place for us at first that between concerts, museums, hiking in the gorges, and all the classes that Vita and Ishmael signed up for—art, music, dance, and German—we didn't have much time to think about schoolwork. Still, Vita, who was barely reading before we moved, managed to learn to read well enough so that she could read just about anything in the children's room at the library. Bob still read to the kids at night when there was time, and although he didn't carefully restrict his reading to history and science as he had before, they didn't seem to care what he read, as long as it was interesting. I began spending more time working with Vita and Ishmael on their music, which had developed into a very serious interest of theirs, and Ishmael wrote a musical play. Amazingly enough, this play, "Love's Path is Lumpy," was accepted for production at a local theater, and both kids were given small parts. Naturally, this put an end to Bob's reading sessions, since the kids now spent every night at the theater rehearsing.

Despite the lack of formal schoolwork, it was easy to see that all during these first months Vita and Ishmael were incredibly productive. All the same, as I watched the other kids in the neighborhood going off to school each day, I often worried that we were somehow neglecting Vita and Ishmael. I tried to tell myself that I was being silly—that the neighborhood kids spent most of their time in school standing in line, passing in papers and waiting for papers to be passed out, filling in the blanks on mimeographed worksheets, and generally learning how to put up with boredom. Certainly I didn't want that kind of schooling for Vita and Ishmael, but I did feel that something was wrong.

For one thing, despite the fact that I now spent a good deal of time working with the kids on music, I still found myself missing them. Now that I think about it, I suppose that we were still spending much more time with each other than most families, but it just wasn't *enough* time. Bob kept pointing out sadly that he and the kids hardly ever had a chance to read together anymore. As for me, I often found myself thinking fondly of the mornings that we had spent in New Hampshire reading, writing, talking, and playing—uninterrupted by the phone, friends, or outside classes with their fixed schedules.

Meanwhile, I noticed that Vita and Ishmael had begun feeling unexpected pressures that seemed to be aggravated by our lack of attention to "formalized" schooling. Visiting relatives, for example, often wanted to play math games with the kids, hoping to take part in our home school, but Vita and Ishmael felt badly when they made too many mistakes. I think they felt more insecure than they would have otherwise—guilty even—just because they hadn't worked on math in such a long time. When the kids started taking German, I

noticed that Vita felt an incredible relief because she could already read German. She felt humiliated, however, when she had to translate German sentences into English because her spelling wasn't as good as she thought it ought to be. She felt anxious, too, because the teacher not only assumed that she knew all about nouns and articles, but expected her to know what direct and indirect objects were. And poor Ishmael definitely felt funny when his piano teacher showed her surprise at discovering that he still couldn't tell time.

Having no structure to our home school wasn't working too well, but, fortunately, now that we had a better understanding of our needs, we really were free to experiment and find out what kind of structure suited us best. After three years and concerted efforts to cut down on our outside activities, certain patterns have developed that can't exactly be called "structure" in the usual sense but that definitely reflect a certain order. The only way that we have been able to make this seemingly haphazard structure work is to admit that it is a structure and to make time in our day for it.

When I think about what we are doing these days, I am reminded of the experiment that Adelle Davis described in her book *Let's Have Healthy Children*.[1] For months, babies were offered three well-balanced meals a day, consisting of only wholesome natural foods. No food was salted, but the babies were offered salt separately. They weren't given any sugar. Most important, they were left totally free to pick and choose what (if anything) they wanted to eat from the foods that were offered.

"All of the children," Adelle Davis wrote, "went on food binges. They would sometimes drink quarts of milk one day and eat little else; the next day they would perhaps scarcely taste milk. One child ate 11 eggs at one meal; another ate 13 bananas at one time. Again and again certain foods would be avoided for a period and then eaten heartily."[2] From day to day and even week to week, they found that the children's diets were imbalanced in the extreme. But when their total food consumption was analyzed over a period of months, it was found that they had eaten a remarkable balance, supplying all the nutrients that they needed.

Like the children in this experiment, Vita and Ishmael do much of their learning in binges. If Ishmael spends three or four months writing a play (he's written three so far), he won't normally do any more writing, except for occasional letters, for another three or four months. Vita may spend weeks "making things," from woven belts to popsicle stick houses to cardboard and cellophane stained glass windows. Then, perhaps for the next month, she'll spend all of her free time reading about whales and porpoises. And like the child in the Adelle Davis experiment who avoided salt for days and then ate it in handfuls, grimacing all the while, so Ishmael will spend weeks at a time doing math. He has actually begun to enjoy math.

Music is the one activity, other than their nightly reading with Bob, that Vita and Ishmael do on a regular basis, day in and day out. This is partly because it is what they love to do best, but also partly because serious musicians, like serious athletes, have to work consistently in order to develop and then retain their muscular strength and coordination ("technique," as they call it in the music world). The kids have worked out a regular daily schedule as well, since they play for such long hours—Vita for two hours each on the violin and piano, and Ishmael for four to five hours on the piano. If they didn't, they'd always be competing for time at the piano. Despite their seeming regularity, though, Vita and Ishmael learn their music in binges in much the same way that they learn most everything else. For weeks at a time they'll make amazing creative and technical progress, and then, of course, they'll need a rest. Almost surely their practice time will diminish as they tire more quickly of playing, and they won't do as much improvising or playing just for fun.

Although Vita and Ishmael are for the most part free to do their learning in binges, even during their periods of rest they tend to be productive. Once again, I am reminded of the food experiment where, although the babies were allowed to eat as much or as little as they liked, they were offered only healthy foods. In the same way, our home environment offers Vita and Ishmael healthy things to do: no TV, plenty of books, paper, records, art materials, and musical instruments. Vita may spend every afternoon for a week reading *Little Women* on her bed, and when she's finished with it, she'll just turn back to the beginning and start all over again. Or Ishmael may spend days writing opening paragraphs for stories that he never finishes. These kinds of activities may be called aimless, yet they provide the kids with the rest and nourishment they need for their later creative outbursts.

It would be misleading to give the impression that Bob and I are passive bystanders, merely creating an environment for the chilren's growth. Just as the babies were offered three meals a day—they never had to go to the refrigerator and search out their food for themselves—so we offer the kids schoolwork of one kind or another on a regular basis. Unlike traditional teachers, we never suggest schoolwork to Vita and Ishmael if they are engrossed in something else, and they know that they are free not to do the work if they don't feel like it. Usually, though, they do. In fact, Vita and I have a little ritual that we perform when she's bored. Before I can open my mouth she'll say, "Don't tell me! I know what you're going to say already! You're going to tell me to do some math." Then we laugh, and she runs off to get her book.

John Holt said quite often that parents shouldn't try to teach their children unless the kids specifically ask to be taught. I think he would agree with me that kids don't always know how to express themselves verbally, and so it's unfair to always wait for them to ask for help out loud. In fact, it could even be harmful, since they might very well grow up feeling neglected or uncared for. When Ishmael, at age eleven, had the mortifying experience of discovering that his piano teacher couldn't believe that he didn't know how to tell time, I suggested that he learn how, and I gave him as many opportunities to practice as I could, even when they seemed to be a bit artificial.

Likewise, because I know that Vita wants to learn to spell properly, I'll often help her correct her spelling when she's written a story or a letter, even when she hasn't asked me to. Of course, I have to be quite sensitive about this. Now that she's older, I often suggest that she do some work in her spelling book. Fortunately, working in the spelling book doesn't cramp her actual writing anymore, since she has now learned to write in two ways: fast and carelessly if she has some thoughts that she wants to get down before she loses them or more slowly and carefully if she feels that she can spare the time.

These days, it's Ishmael who helps *me* with *my* spelling, but I do spend a lot of time with him going over his writing, working mostly on clarity and style. And although it's usually I who says, "Hey, can I see what you've written?" I know that he appreciates my interest and help. Every few months I'll suggest that he experiment with different types of writing—poetry or perhaps a research paper.

Day in and day out, I keep track of what Vita and Ishmael are doing much in the way that I keep track of the food that we have in the refrigerator—not like a teacher, but almost by osmosis. And like the shopping lists that I keep in my head, I keep lists of the things that I think the kids should be getting around to soon.

Over these past few years, Vita and Ishmael not only have been happy about what they are doing, but they've felt really happy about themselves. They feel satisfied that they are learning, or are at least aware of, the basic skills that society expects them to acquire, and these feelings of satisfaction and self-confidence have helped free them to pursue their creative urges—music, writing, and art—with a mixture of seriousness and fun that I don't see in many other people.

The moral of this story, however, is *not* that textbooks and structure are what make successful home schools. Despite the fact that we are really pleased with the way our home school is working, I wouldn't necessarily recommend to other home schoolers that they do things our way. Because all families are unique, all successful home schools have to be tailor-made to fit the needs of each family, and no book or article can pretend to tell us how to do it.

Still, there is a lot that we can learn from each other. For example, there is a family of five children mentioned occasionally in John Holt's newsletter, "Growing Without Schooling," and except for the oldest one, who is now fifteen, none of the other kids can read. Because they live on an isolated farm and the parents have included them in their own work and given them a lot of responsibility around the farm, all the kids know how to raise and care for animals. They all seem to be budding naturalists. In their "world" they are certainly competent, and they feel good about themselves.

And feeling good about what we are doing is really the goal of all home schoolers. What we have to keep in mind, though, is that whatever works for our family is fine—even if it's something as traditional as textbooks!

Notes

1. Adelle Davis, *Let's Have Healthy Children* (New York: Harcourt, Brace, Jovanovich, 1972).

2. Ibid., 270.

26

BEYOND THE CLASSROOM

J. David Colfax

We've just finished lunch on a hot Saturday in July, and none of us is eager to get back to work outside on the ranch. Drew, seventeen, picks up a Dos Passos novel he's left on an end table. Reed, fifteen, is examining a computer printout of a program he'd done for a 4-H project. And Garth, nine, is leafing through the latest issue of *Natural History*.

Jason, fifteen, who is spending the week with us, slouches in his chair, frowning. "What's going on here?" he suddenly exclaims. "You guys are all *reading*. You're not supposed to do schoolwork in the *summer!*"

Jason is no dullard. He attends an elite Eastern prep school and plans to be an engineer. But his attitude is one that is shared by many children and their parents: school is school and home is home, and they should be properly separated. Education is for schools, nine months a year, and schooling should be left to the experts.

This attitude is being steadily eroded as parents become increasingly concerned about and involved in the education of their children. In part, this is the result of a generalized dissatisfaction with the quality of the schools—the "decline of American education," as it is widely, and not always accurately, portrayed by the media. Some parents worry about violence in the schools, and others object to the values transmitted by peers and teachers. Still others, aware of the increasingly competitive character of American society, are unwilling to entrust to the schools the task of equipping their children to compete effectively.

Some parents, like Jason's, send their children to carefully chosen prep schools. Others teach their children at home, as we've been doing for more than a dozen years. And some families are able to relocate to suburbs where the public schools are known for their excellence.

But for many parents, these are not options. These choices require time, money, and mobility. So what are parents, in the interest of having their children make the most of these crucial formative years, to do? What, if anything, can parents do to make a real contribution to their children's intellectual growth?

A recent series of TV commercials suggests that Dad and Mom need only to run and buy the advertised personal computer, install it in their child's room, and sit back and wait for genius to unfold. Another commercial suggests that all that's needed is a set of time-proven "great books," which, when purchased in expensive bindings and displayed prominently in the living room, will assure a child's future. Or, how about a few weeks at music camp?

These gimmicks, probably harmless enough, are nevertheless unlikely to contribute appreciably to the child's learning. However, there are a number of steps that parents *can* take to provide their children with a nurturing, educationally enhancing environment in the home. Some readily available and relatively inexpensive materials are perhaps obvious, yet they are lacking in many homes. Other home enrichments require that parents pay close attention to the total learning process rather than rely exclusively on the advice of experts.

Hardware and Software

Ideally, every home should have some sort of basic learning center—even if it is not designated as such—comprised of books, books, and more books. At the core of the center should be a usable—and *usable* is the key word here—multivolume encyclopedia set. By this I don't mean those antique volumes that Aunt Harriet willed to the family, or the set that you picked up one-volume-at-a-time at the supermarket. What you want is an attractive, informative, and up-to-date set that children are inclined to pick up and *use*—and use hard, knock around, carry into the bathroom, read in the backyard as well as at the desk. Unfortunately, fewer than 10 percent of American homes have a good encyclopedia set, although nearly 100 percent have one or more television sets. The prevailing assumption seems to be, "Who needs them, when you can look things up at school or in the library?" But this misses the point. A sturdy encyclopedia set should serve to encourage curiosity and foster the habit of looking up answers to questions that arise in everyday conversations, experiences, and reading material.

The *World Book, Merit,* and *Compton's* encyclopedias are all good choices, but consult a buying guide before making a purchase. Consider purchasing a used set that has been updated with annual supplements. Some bookstores in larger cities specialize in used sets at reasonable prices. The "children's encyclopedias"—*Childcraft* and the *Book of Knowledge,* for example—are worthwhile, but they are expensive and quickly outgrown. Money might be better spent on a wider mix of children's books from a variety of sources.

Next, add some standard reference books. Consider a couple of dictionaries, a world atlas, a current almanac, a book of world records, *Bartlett's Familiar Quotations,* a thesaurus in dictionary form, and some specialized reference volumes—on sports, art, or music, perhaps—corresponding to the children's interests. For younger readers, include the *Golden Nature Guide.*

Surround these with books of all kinds—novels, mysteries, how-tos, classics, best-sellers, and throwaways. Most of these can be picked up at used bookstores and exchanges for next to nothing. Annual library sales are an especially good place to obtain worthwhile books that have been donated to the library. Also try the various publisher's clearinghouses and remainder tables in bookstores. Unfortunately, since good children's books typically are worn out, few end up in used bookstores. Parents should therefore be parepared to purchase books for younger readers at near premium prices. A comprehensive source of information on new titles is the annual children's book issue of the *New York Times,* which comes out in early November.

Now, supplement the books with a variety of periodicals. Children should be encouraged to subscribe to magazines that appeal to their interests. *Running, Astronomy, Linn's Stamp News,* and the *New Yorker* are current favorites around our home. Remember that subscriptions are not forever; as interests change, so should reading matter.

However, building up a library is more than just going out and buying a slew of books and magazines. It is really an integral part of the learning process, and children should be involved in it beginning at an early age. Parents can encourage their children to browse in old bookstores and search out bargains. Visits to the library can provide opportunities for checking out numerous books that can be examined at home, inviting children's exploration and discrimination. Parents should be prepared to deal with rejection (our favorite children's books, with a few exceptions, have not turned out to be our children's favorites) and misuse (we've had encyclopedia volumes barely survive all-day rains after being left outside, where they were, after all, being *used*). Most importantly, children should regard books not as venerated artifacts, but rather as "user friendly," as tools, some of which are worthwhile and some of which are not. Appreciation for fine books can come later.

Also important is learning-center hardware. We do not have that newly ubiquitous item, the personal computer, only because of twelve-volt interconnect problems (we obtain our electrical power from photovoltaic cells). Nevertheless, our children are "computer literate" thanks to a 4-H program run by a local expert. We also have made a tradition of providing each child with a new typewriter on his twelfth birthday, something that encourages the early acquisition of an important skill, although it does not help penmanship.

As interest develops in different areas, we make every attempt to provide quality hardware: glassware from a chemical-supply house, specimens from a biological supplier, clay from an art-supply cooperative. We try to avoid prepackaged kits of all kinds, preferring to have the children seek out and purchase raw materials as their needs and interests expand. Locating quality hardware takes time, and items often seem expensive, but most children will appreciate the difference between "real" and "kid's" stuff. Quality materials tell them that their intersts are being taken seriously.

Parental Provisions

"OK, so you get all of these things. You've still got to motivate them," says a friend. "That's the hard part."

Of course it is. Books, magazines, typewriters, beakers, and microscopes cannot do the job alone. The parents' role is crucial. If the hardware and software are to have any impact at all, the parents must invest what may seem like excessive amounts of time and energy in order to recognize and cultivate their children's interests and talents. In an era when many parents become aware of their children's intellectual performance only at report card time, this is no small investment. Parents who take their children's educational development seriously come to appreciate the inherent limitations of schools as institutions, and they make adjustments accordingly. Schools are

necessarily bureaucratic; their programs are designed for categories of children rather than for individuals, and even special programs tend to become ossified over time. The problem is not that teachers are uncaring, but rather that organizational needs tend to take precedence over individual needs. And in the process, individual needs, abilities, interests, and talents are often lost.

Parents can do what schools cannot do. They are uniquely positioned to identify the needs, interests, and talents of their children, provided that they take the time and make the effort to do so. Parents, unencumbered by organizational imperatives, can provide what even the best schools cannot. How? Simply by showing interest and providing opportunities.

For example, a grade-school child with an interest in art can be encouraged through association with a local artist who is willing to give art lessons. Books on art can be borrowed from the library. Art supplies can be purchased. Even if the interest fades, nothing will have been lost. Other interests will emerge, some of which will in their turn fade and some of which will endure.

The child must be given his or her own lead. We all know of parents who have grimly provided their children with "opportunities," the most universal of which are probably those often-despised music lessons. It is not enough for well-meaning parents to prescribe what they think is "good" for the child. Interests must evolve out of close and caring relationships and through a genuine appreciation of the unique qualities of each child.

Of course, the object in encouraging children to develop their own interests to the fullest is not to create precocious overachievers or grade-school experts. It is to provide each child with a "frame of confidence" that allows expansion and growth in other areas as well. The child who becomes interested in American Indians may, with encouragement, become increasingly interested in other cultures, archaeology, or American history. The nine-year-old who takes apart an old lawn mower engine and tries to reassemble it may go on to other mechanical projects. The thirteen-year-old who borrows fifty dollars to start his own stamp company and fails has learned something about real-world economics. The youth whose interest in raising pedigreed dogs is encouraged and supported may develop management skills, write articles on canine lore for specialty magazines, or develop an enduring interest in zoology.

This is not to say that parents should indulge their child's every whim and fancy. An interest or two, cultivated and nurtured, will provide a firm basis for future learning and growth, much more so than a half dozen undeveloped interests will.

How does one get the child to this point? Sometimes it takes imagination. Education is, after all, "drawing out," and occasionally parents may have to take the lead in linking skills with interests. It doesn't always work, but it did for us one Christmas when we were at a loss for a gift for Drew, who was then thirteen. He was interested in math and loved nothing better than to be involved in building projects around the ranch. Somehow a truckload of two-by-fours did not seem to be an appropriate gift, and he already had a complete set of carpenter's tools. He had shown some interest in astronomy, so we considered buying him a telescope, but the owner of the optical supply house had a better suggestion. Since Drew was adept at building things and could handle the math, why not give him the *materials* to build a telescope?

So, on Christmas morning, a puzzled Drew worked his way through a carefully arranged sequence of packages containing grits, a glass blank, a pitch lap, and—several packages later—a manual that described how to put all of this together. He spent the next year reading, grinding a mirror, and locating parts for the base. The following year, he designed and built an observatory and wrote a weekly column for the local newspaper. Next year he plans to enter college and study physics.

Not all parental efforts in providing support are as successful. It is a trial-and-error process, jointly engaging child and parents. Sometimes the magic works and sometimes it doesn't. But even when it doesn't, the process of working together has its own rewards; it tells the child that the parents care and are there to provide support and encouragement.

Schooling Options

But what about schoolwork? Shouldn't it come first? The answer is a resounding "maybe." Folklore abounds with tales of children who did poorly in school and went on to financial or creative greatness. Although these stories may be true enough, they are not reassuring to parents whose children are not doing well in school.

Perhaps it is worth considering the possibility that the child who is doing poorly in school is behaving in an appropriate manner. Subjectively, school may be boring, undemanding, even stultifying. Maybe it's time for the child and parents to take on primary responsibility for the child's development. Some teachers may agree to contract with the student so that he or she may engage in a particular course of study or special-interest project; others might allow the student free time to work on projects that extend beyond the regular curriculum. (We know of one boy who spent most of his senior year carving a life-size figure out of limestone in the high school boiler room.) Actually, once the parents come to regard the school as a resource rather than an immutable setter of standards, the battle is half won. Instead of having conferences during which they worry over why Johnny is doing so poorly in algebra, parents and teacher can meet to determine just what Johnny really is interested in and what he could be more effectively and constructively doing.

Although many teachers and administrators will welcome parental involvement, few have the time or resources to devote to the child or parent who makes extraordinary, even if legitimate, demands upon the system. Overbearing, know-it-all parents, with their potential superchild in tow, are likely to find that even the most responsive of school systems will not cater to their demands. Unfortunately, however, even the most diplomatic parents sometimes encounter resistance, only to discover that some teachers and administrators regard parental involvement as an unwarranted intrusion into the professional educator's area of expertise.

When encountering resistance at a local public school, it is important for parents to recognize that other options are still available to enable their children to obtain an adequate education. Sometimes the easiest solution is an out-of-district transfer. Most school administrators, anxious to avoid conflict with dissatisfied parents, will authorize a transfer when a parent firmly demands it. For example, in one rural school district, parents who are unhappy about the quality of teaching and the limited number of courses offered at the local high school are routinely allowed to send their children out of the district to a more comprehensive high school in a nearby community.

Another option is a local private school. Some inner-city parents, whose children were consigned to inferior schools, have been sending them to the often-superior parochial schools in their neighborhoods.

Private boarding schools are not for everybody, but they are another alternative and one increasingly open to children from less-than-affluent homes. Typically well-endowed and sensitive to charges of being bastions of privilege, these schools are usually generous in providing financial aid to needy but outstanding students.

And there is the increasingly popular home schooling option. It is estimated that one hundred thousand or more children are being educated at home. In some areas, it is condoned by the local board of education, while in others, it is vigorously (but usually unsuccessfully) opposed. A middle ground has been established in Washington, where fully credentialed teachers are contracted by an intermediary organization to work with home schooling parents.

Home schooling is a demanding alternative because the burden falls squarely and inescapably on parents and child, but the rewards are usually worth the effort. Once rare, home schooling is becoming mainstream in many areas. And most observers predict that within a decade it will be regarded as an entirely legitimate alternative in most school districts across the nation.

Who Is Responsible?
Parents need not resign themselves to turning their children over to the so-called experts and hoping for the best. Ultimately, it is the parents who are responsible for the quality and content of their chil-

dren's education; and in order for them to adequately meet this sometimes awesome responsibility, they must be firmly in control of the process. If children are to grow up to become creative, talented, and socially responsible adults, they need more than what the schools are capable of providing. While there are no quick fixes, parents who are flexible and supportive in their relationships with their children, who set an example in the conduct of their own lives, and who are not afraid to share their concerns, aspirations, and values with their children cannot go too far wrong. All it takes, like so many things, is time and effort.

27

FIRST DAY OF SCHOOL AT
THIRTEEN

Heidi Priesnitz

M y entire life had been like a long summer holiday. I was one of a
number of kids across the country who have never been to
school but, instead, receive their education in the "real world." I
learned by doing, so to speak. Although I never sat down to a "real
lesson," I still learned math and history. If I felt the need to know
something, then I would either look it up in a book or ask someone
who knew.

And so it went until I was thirteen. At that time, my parents
(mostly my dad) encouraged me to try high school. I really didn't have
a clue as to what it would be like and at first rejected the whole idea.
But after becoming familiar with the idea and agreeing with my parents that I could quit at Christmas if I didn't like it, I decided to give it
a try. I guess my parents felt that at that point in my life I was old
enough to decide for myself whether I wanted to go to school or not,
but that a fair decision wasn't possible without knowing what school
was really like. Perhaps I felt that there must be something wrong with
school and that was why my parents had kept me away, but otherwise
I had no prejudgments.

We decided that I should try a local high school with an arts bias
and a liberal reputation. At the beginning of August, my mom and I
went to the school to talk with the head guidance counselor. After
talking with me for a short time, he placed me in all advanced grade-
nine courses except for two, one of which was an advanced grade-ten-
level accounting course. The counselor said that he expected me to be
ahead in English and related subjects but that I might be behind in
math. Both proved to be true, but of no problem or even significance.

My experience on the first day of school had many parallels to that
of a five- or six-year-old starting kindergarten. I was nervous and yet

excited and impatient. My first couple of hours proved to be some of the most frustrating of my life, due to what I later discovered was the disorganization natural to the first weeks of school. No one went to first class that morning because no one had a timetable. First impressions are extremely important to me, and I was not impressed.

After the initial culture shock, I actually started to enjoy school. And as I told one of my teacher friends later in the year, "I hate to admit it, but I think I'm hooked!" By the end of September, I had started a school club and been elected its president, become good friends with a large number of staff and students, and was getting good marks.

Christmas came, and I told myself and my family that I wanted to keep going until the middle of February, when the semester was over. Exams passed and so did the end of the semester. I decided, though it was a little difficult, to finish off the year. And so I did. In June I ran for student council and organized a good campaign. I ended up coming in second to a "cute guy," and that made me happy.

In class, things improved as the months went by. At the beginning of the year, I had had some difficulties because I didn't have experience in writing tests and putting up my hand before speaking or going to the bathroom. I caught on pretty fast, though. One day during the first week I decided to go home. So I asked the teacher if I could make a phone call. I called home to arrange for a ride, went to my locker, got my stuff, and left. Not until the next day, when my teacher asked me why I had "skipped" class, did I realize that I was expected to sign out of school and that I couldn't just go home. I didn't do that again!

One thing that I found very interesting was the reaction of staff and students when they discovered that I'd never been to school before. The first question students usually asked was, "What did you do all day?" I always told them it was like having a summer holiday all year round. Their reaction then was, "Boring!" They always asked if it was legal, and I always quoted the section of the Education Act that deals with that. Sometimes they said stuff like, "I wish I had your parents." I never knew what to say at that point.

Teachers' reactions were interesting also. I heard comments like "Let me know if you need extra help" or "If I had the guts, I wouldn't send my kids to school either." My teachers seemed to like to talk with and help me because I was interested and wanted to be there.

The place where I think that my home schooling has really paid off is in my attitude and my outlook on life. I feel that because of home schooling, I have a lot more confidence in myself and in others as well. I also feel that I have a better relationship with my family than I would have had otherwise, just because I've been with them a lot more.

Overall, I'm really happy that I went to school last year, but I'm glad it was my first time. And I'm going to grade ten this year, no doubt about it!

28

THE HOME SCHOOLED TEENAGER GROWS UP

Penny Barker

A concern among many home schoolers with older children is the teenage years and the transition into adulthood after a life somewhat separated from the mainstream. Does the philosophy of living each day to its fullest, rather than of constantly preparing for the next test or for college entrance exams, make as much sense for our teenagers as it did for our blossoming young children? Looking at the home schooled teens whom I know, I cannot help but think that it does.

Our home schooled teens have benefited immensely from the wide variety of experiences we provide for them. Both their growth and sense of direction have been enhanced. I remember that when my daughter Britt was fourteen, she was writing a weekly puzzle column for our local newspaper and selling articles to the *Mother Earth News*. People asked her if she planned to be a writer when she grew up, and she would say, in the most unassuming manner, "I am a writer." At fourteen, this answer was accurate; it reflected where Britt was at the time. Now that she is nearing eighteen, when asked the same question Britt ponders over it and truly wonders about her adult life. Similarly, being applauded and lauded for her piano playing at eleven was very different from now considering making piano performance her life's work.

When Britt was sixteen, she decided she wanted to pursue biology and nature art in a serious way. Fortunately, she was able to travel across Canada for eight weeks with a Canadian nature writer and watercolorist and her field-biologist husband as they gathered material for a book. Britt came home disillusioned with the field of biology, feeling that it meant dissecting a world she had always been taught to see as whole and spending hours engaged in *reading* when she had always placed emphasis on *doing.*

At first I felt a sense of failure: perhaps I had not prepared her adequately for meeting the demands of the "world out there." I now see that the encounter was good for Britt because she was able to experience the field of biology firsthand and realize it is not what she thought it would be. Otherwise, she might have spent years preparing academically for a career as a biologist, only to find out after leaving school that it was not for her. Furthermore, Britt's Canadian experience provided her with much inspiration and material for a naturalist column that she was able to sell to the local newspaper.[1] This column has since become a weekly favorite among people in our county.

Britt also works in the layout department of the local newspaper office and as a waitress in a nearby inn. She has learned much and met many people of all ages and from varying backgrounds. The innkeeper often asks her to stop her waitressing work and perform at the piano for some of the guests. (This woman, who has taken Britt under her wing, seems to feel that the combination of performing pianist and breakfast waitress is a wholesome one.) It is good to know that Britt does not prioritize her writing, her piano playing, or her waitressing. To her, they all seem to be jobs that need doing.

I watch as Britt ponders what she wants to do with her life. In fact, the little girl who was once an adamant spokesperson for the "I'm living today" philosophy has begun to fret about her future and wonder, "What will I do in the fall?" I no longer think this fretting is a bad sign; it probably signals the beginning of the separation process. Britt will soon leave the nest and become independent.

Other home schooling families with teens see various choices developing. Indeed, the range of these choices makes one wonder what prompts different teens to look in different ways toward the future. One family I know has five girls and lives on a large farm not far from our home. The two teens, Ranata and Rachel, are in charge of the household—meals, gardens, laundry, and so on. I once spent an afternoon at their home eating delicious homemade butter and cheeses that they had prepared themselves. Ranata and Rachel want nothing more than to marry and settle with their mates on the large piece of land owned by their family.

Another friend with four teenagers who have always been home schooled finds that each one seems to be following a different path.

At eighteen, the oldest boy began to question his entire home schooling background, wondering if he could meet the requirements of the world "out there." His mother was somewhat disturbed by his doubts, but she allowed him the freedom to seek the answers he seemed to need as he moved into young adulthood. He enrolled in a local college after taking an entrance examination (without being asked to produce a high school diploma!), and, having been in college only a short time, he was granted a scholarship for high academic achievement.

It was during this year that the young man commented to his mother, "It's true, isn't it, that you can sit in a class in college and listen to someone talking about a subject, but unless you are really interested you will retain little and learn less." He was amazed at the disinterest of the students who were there of their own free will, just as Britt is repeatedly amazed at the disinterest and blasé attitude often shown by other students in her piano performance class. Both teenagers are also taken aback by the lack of respect shown to instructors by their students and the unwarranted hostility and disrespect often paid to employers by their employees.

This same mother is now busily searching out a suitable apprenticeship for her seventeen-year-old daughter, who is skilled in the arts of homemaking and yet, unlike Rachel and Ranata, is not content with staying at home and now wants to reach out into the world. Sixteen-year-old twins in the same family are happily studying small-engine repair work with a neighbor and will be able to make this skill their breadwinning occupation if they so choose.

Home schooled kids wonder what they are going to do with their lives as much as other kids do; however, they may have the advantage of coming to grips with the issue earlier and before thousands of dollars have been spent toward their "futures." Apprenticeships are a good way to let your older home schooler experience various lifestyles, acquire new skills, and meet new people.

Dick Gallien, a home educator interested in older home schoolers, and his wife, Nadine, recently offered to let young people join their family and live in a cabin on their farm in Wisconsin "to see if there is some aspect of it that interests them." He writes of one girl who stayed with them for five months, "I have complete faith in her milking our twenty-five cows; she has learned the printing business by working for a printer in town; right now she is helping tear down thirteen

MARILYN NOLT

greenhouses, partly for pay and also to get enough greenhouse glass for her own future building; she is reading and doing things constantly. This afternoon she will be with a beekeeper. Yesterday she sheared part of a sheep."

A good way to secure apprenticeships and related experiences for older children is to begin while they are young. Make a point of keeping track of various people you know or meet along the way who are lovingly dedicated to their work or a hobby. Many people with interest and expertise in a given area will gladly share their knowledge and skills with others. For example, I have already made the initial steps to have my eleven-year-old one day study the cello, which he enjoys so much, with a wonderfully talented cellist who loves music and children, too. Interests may change, it is true, but having this musician's name and address recorded in my notebook will give me access to the opportunity should I wish to pursue it.

My daughter Maggie has a strong interest in sheep and sheepdogs and presently spends a day or two a month helping a wonderful man work his border collies. My eyes are always open to opportunities for her to further this interest, on sheep farms as distant as New Zealand and as close as our own Ohio. True, it would take money to travel to New Zealand, but as a capable teenager, Maggie will be able to earn that money, especially if she has a strong interest in pursuing a New Zealand sheep farm experience.

Such opportunities exist for rural and urban home schoolers alike. In fact, the commerce and activity of a city provide many opportunities for teens. I have a sixteen-year-old home schooled friend who lives in Cleveland. In the past year he has been able to apprentice with a roofer, arrange a possible apprenticeship with an architect in Oregon, and travel and backpack through the canyonlands of southern Utah and the mountain country of southwestern Texas with our family for eight weeks. Until this time he had not been west of the Mississippi River. These experiences have given him a broader world view; they will help him make future choices. He is currently earning eight dollars an hour working for a draper so that he will have the funds available to pursue his plans, whatever they prove to be.

Home schoolers Dan and Harriet Shultis of New Mexico are busily working out a network whereby older home schoolers can come into contact with opportunities, apprenticeships, and one another.[2] Keep yourself informed of possibilities along these lines that come into your own life, and begin a notebook of names and addresses of people who might prove to be sources of growing experiences for your teenager.

Notes

1. This material is published in Britt's book, *Letters Home*, available from Home Education Press, P.O. Box 1083, Tonasket, WA 98855.

2. For more information on networking and apprenticeships for home schooled teens, write to: Dan Shultis, P.O. Box 167, Rodeo, NM 88056.

HOME SCHOOLERS AND COLLEGE

Patrick Farenga

The most celebrated case of a child going directly from a home school to college occurred in 1983, when Grant Colfax, a boy who was taught at home by his parents for eleven years, was accepted to Harvard University. The reputation of his schools, the detailed transcripts of his test scores and course grades, and the official recommendations of his high school teachers had nothing to do with his acceptance, since they did not exist. It was a combination of his life experiences, his interview with a Harvard admissions officer, and his mid to high (600) Scholastic Aptitude Test (SAT) scores that tipped the scales in his favor.[1]

Still, critics say that the Colfax family is extraordinary—an exception to the rule, one in a million. How do other home schooled children fare when they apply to college? A growing body of research and personal case histories provides encouraging and surprising answers to this question.

Meeting Admissions Requirements

To begin with, standardized tests usually require standardized study—a discipline readily available through public and private institutions of standardized learning. Indeed, many American high schools and all of their more exclusive relations, college preparatory schools, gear their curricula toward subjects needed by their graduates-to-be for peak performances on the SAT and other standardized achievement tests. In addition, these schools provide college admissions counselors, practice tests, and special seminars to ensure a good rate of college acceptances for their senior class. In light of this, one wonders how home schoolers can compete with these resource-rich institutions for college admission slots? How do they "make a good case" for themselves?

A dissertation on the admissions requirements of 210 universities and their impact on home schooled applicants reveals some hard facts. "The universities that had admitted [home schooled] applicants accepted subjective criteria in lieu of high school transcripts. The admissions officers from the universities believed that these students were as likely as any others to succeed and did not feel that additional policies were required."[2]

The findings of this study support the Colfaxes' claim that "a home schooled student who does reasonably well on a few standardized tests and can make a case for him or herself will have little difficulty attracting the attention of admission directors of most good colleges."[3]

One Family's Approach to Making a Good Case

Judy Gelner, author of *College Admissions: A Guide for Homeschoolers*, provides us with an excellent account of her home schooler's route to college. She writes, "I helped my son, Kendall, work his way through the college admissions tests, forms, and deadlines, all without a high school guidance office, accredited diploma, or a lot of the 'objective measurements' that most high school students present to a college. Kendall was admitted to all of the colleges to which he applied and will attend Rice University in the fall of 1988. He also applied for and received a considerable amount of financial aid."[4]

Gelner describes the goals and plans she made for her son's education as follows: "Our home school is very much an 'unschool,' a word coined by John Holt to suggest the idea that home schools do not have to be small copies of the schools we left. . . . We think that learning is far more meaningful if done at the student's initiative. We also put a lot of emphasis on doing, especially at early ages. We have lots of books around the house, so our unschool can easily provide a fairly academic background in a Montessori kind of atmosphere. . . . As learning became more natural, tests and grades became more meaningless to us. We thought less and less about working on test taking."[5]

One would think that such an unstructured approach would result in some long and windy explanations to appease the more academically oriented college admissions officers. However, the Gelners provide forthright, proud, and simple evaluations and descriptions of their home schooling experiences. For instance, on the applications that required a counselor recommendation, Judy Gelner wrote: "For the last six years Kendall has been learning at home rather than in the school setting which most of your applicants come from. So I am Kendall's counselor, teacher, the director of our school, and also his mother. I can hardly pretend to be unbiased or objective, nor do I have the kinds of comparisons to make with other students that a counselor might be able to make. But I do believe that I can supply you with information to help learn about Kendall so that you can see if his talents and characteristics match the character of your institution."[6]

For a teacher recommendation, the Gelners submitted a letter written by the father of one of Kendall's friends, who was also the coach of a team of which Kendall was a member. "I was not sure that his letter would really be considered as valid as a teacher's," writes Gelner. "Kendall was even less sure that the word of a family friend would mean anything, but I said, 'Well, you wouldn't pick a teacher who didn't like you, would you?'"[7]

Creating a high school transcript was more challenging, but this is a particularly useful document to include in a college portfolio. As an admissions officer from Colorado State University puts it, "The university is interested in the ability to handle academic work, not just following strong interests."[8] So, using a list of the schoolwork that each college under consideration expected of its applicants, Judy and Kendall thought about ways to describe his learning so it would fit into the framework of typical admissions requirements. The Gelners also provided, as required, a list of the subjects they were planning to cover in the "spring semester of the senior year."

To introduce the transcript, Judy Gelner drafted the following cover letter:

EXPLANATION OF CREDITS FOR KENDALL GELNER

Trust is at the heart of our home schooling experience. The parent learns to trust the child in his unique way of learning and growing, and the child learns to trust the parent and the help and insight he or she has to offer. Each person learns to trust his own instincts and insight.

Now we are asking you to trust us. We are giving you a form saying that we have covered all the courses which you require of incoming students. We do believe that we have covered at least as much as, if not more than, the required course work. But besides the SAT and the Achievement Test scores, we do not have other objective evidence to prove what we have accomplished.

The decision to follow a "no grade" path for Kendall's high school years was made with the knowledge that there was some risk involved. But the decision was deliberate and made after careful consideration of how he could best learn at that stage in his life. We agree wholeheartedly with John Holt that, "In the long run, love and joy are more enduring sources of discipline and commitment than any amount of bribe or threat. . . ." We think that the first part of a person's life should be spent finding what it is that brings that joy and love and then a person will be ready for the kind of discipline that you hope to find when students enter college.

We have studied by reading, discussing, and doing. Learning is usually best accomplished with a tier approach. A subject is approached in a very general and interesting way. Then we usually leave it and come back to it again and again. . . .

It is hard to define such learning in terms of semesters and credit hours, though we do have textbooks and consult curriculum guides as well as friends in school to tell us if we are accomplishing all we want or need to. Grades are beside the point. We work at something until we get it and then move on.

In all subjects what is needed most is the ability to listen, read, think, respond, and put that response into some form of communication that others can understand. The rigorous courses that you like to see students take provide that kind of experience. We have provided it, too.[9]

The Gelners also investigated financial-aid procedures and other admissions protocol for nontraditional learners, all of which appears in *College Admissions*. Anyone considering college for their home schooled children will find this book an excellent place to begin. However, it is only one family's story. Other home schoolers who opt for higher education have different schedules, ways, and means of getting there.

Another Family's Story

Ishmael Wallace was home schooled since second grade. Because music seemed to be the only course he enjoyed in public school, the Wallaces incorporated piano lessons into their home school plan. Ishmael spent as much time as he wanted playing the piano. As a result of his devotion to music and his family's careful nurturing of his increasingly evident musical talent, he was granted a full scholarship to music school. But the application process was not easy.

Ishmael decided that since his local school district was not going to give him a diploma, he would take the SAT when he was fifteen and then apply to two music schools: Mannes in New York and Curtis in Philadelphia. "Ishmael had never taken a standardized test before he took his college entrance exams," says his mother, Nancy Wallace,

MICHAEL WEISBROT

"and I think it was an advantage. He missed out on all the competitiveness and anxiety that the SAT causes most high school students.
He wasn't scared of it because he didn't really know how intimidating
the test can be for someone his age."[10]

For the record, Ishmael scored in the 700s on the verbal portion but
only in the 400s in math. His mother considers his math score not a
reflection of their home schooling—since Ishmael's younger sister
does much better in math, using the same teachers—but rather a
reflection of Ishmael's personality and learning style. "He could never
do much addition and subtraction without a calculator," she says,
"but that hasn't stopped him from using math in his life. Right now
he's working on a composition for three pianos that needs to be
twenty-one minutes long. He knows precisely how many bars of
music he needs to write for each piano in order to fill that time."[11]

Due to Ishmael's lopsided SAT scores and lack of a traditional high
school transcript, Mannes refused to consider Ishmael until he got a
high school diploma. Since he wanted to attend this school, specifically to study with Peter Serkin, Ishmael and Nancy started to navi-
gate the process of obtaining a high school diploma through the

General Equivalency Diploma (GED) exam. However, the local school district said that Ishmael could not take the exam until he turned nineteen! Further investigation revealed that pregnant girls under nineteen were allowed to take the GED course and exam in this school district. So, after protesting the double standard, Ishmael was allowed entrance to the program.

Before he was scheduled to take the exam, however, he had auditions for both schools. Curtis, which provided a full scholarship for all students accepted, admitted him immediately after his audition, with no mention of his lack of diploma. Likewise, Mannes completely dropped the diploma issue and accepted him based on his audition. Ishmael felt more welcomed at Curtis and is studying there now.

Nancy offers this observation: "It seemed that the less prestigious a school was that we looked into, the more rigid its entrance requirements. The bigger schools had much more liberal entrance policies than the littler ones. They seem much more interested in the unique student than the standardized student."[12] Her opinion is borne out by research showing that home schoolers are not wanted in smaller liberal arts institutions "due to fears related to accreditation, funding, and other factors concerning possible questions of institutional integrity."[13]

Stories of academic peevishness are not uncommon. Micki and David Colfax mention that a Johns Hopkins interviewer told their son Grant that he would have to apply as a *foreign* student. They also related a story about a junior college dean who "informed a home schooling parent that he would not, on principle, admit any student who did not have a diploma."[14]

Other Preparatory Options

The Wallaces, Gelners, and Colfaxes followed relatively unstructured home schooling curricula prior to their children's acceptance to Curtis, Rice, and Harvard. Many other home schooling parents may lack sufficient confidence to follow a totally self-designed curriculum. And some parents prefer to accumulate a more traditional "paper trail" of their work. Fortunately, plenty of options are open to these college-bound home schoolers.

One possibility is to enroll in a correspondence school. These schools typically provide elementary and high school transcripts for the work completed.[15] Another possibility is to enroll in an out-of-state school that will establish your home as a satellite school for the educational program. Upon completion of the curriculum (which you can either design with them or receive from them), these schools provide appropriate transcripts and accredited diplomas. Several fully accredited private schools offer these types of programs.[16]

Some home schooling families are lucky enough to have the cooperation of their local school district. Several of these home schools have established themselves as independent study programs affiliated with the local public school and receive the school's diploma.[17] Passing a high school equivalency exam will also net you a diploma, and the GED is the most well-known method of this sort.[18]

Another strategy for home schoolers who do not receive high school diplomas but desire to go to a particular college involves a bit of circuitousness. You can enroll in a community college that has an open admissions policy, do your best for a semester or two, and then matriculate to the college you really want to attend.

Joyce Kinmont, a home schooling mother from Utah, describes a discussion she had about this approach with a high school counselor. They were talking about a student who had a great high school record, flunked out of college during his first term, applied to Brigham Young University (BYU), and—in spite of his high school record— was not admitted. Kinmont writes, "I asked the counselor. . .what would have happened if things had been the other way around—if the boy's high school record had been poor but he had done really well in his first term at a small college and then applied to BYU. The counselor said, 'They would have welcomed him with open arms! The college record supersedes the high school record.'"[19]

Home Schooling Success
Over the last ten years, home schooling has produced some remarkable success stories regarding college admissions. One young lady graduated from her family's home school at fifteen and was accepted at the University of Texas-San Antonio at sixteen.[20] Thomas Ingersoll was accepted at Michigan State University, Boston University, Antioch College, and Wesleyan University at seventeen.[21] Daniel Lewis enrolled in a Fort Wayne, Indiana, Bible college Greek course at thirteen.[22] Alexandra Swann began an independent study program at Brigham Young University at twelve, completed it with honors at

fourteen, and began working toward her master's degree from California State University at Dominguez Hill at fifteen.[23]

Many more success stories exist. But what is even more interesting is that college admittance is not the acid test for success for most home schoolers. Indeed, some families de-emphasize college as a means of entry into the world of worthwhile adult work. For them, course grades and rank in class upon graduation do not matter as much as their children's ability to both ask good questions and find useful answers throughout their lives.

The Colfaxes put it this way: "Our goal in home schooling has always been to educate our children—to facilitate the development of intellect and character—and not merely to prepare them for college or a career. . . . Our program reflected, in what one home schooler called its 'practical bookishness,' our academic and ranch experiences, and well served our boys when it came time to apply to colleges. Had we been home schoolers who had been, say, boat builders or musicians, it would have been different in at least some respects—and almost certainly less conventionally college preparatory. Perhaps Grant would have by now become a master boat builder and Drew a sophomore at Juilliard."[24]

Getting into college is far from impossible for home schoolers. What it requires most is *determination* to learn how to take standardized tests and *ingenuity* to make a case for oneself. The lack of traditional schooling does not show a lack of education, and most places of higher learning are willing to accept this fact.

Notes

1. David and Micki Colfax, *Homeschooling for Excellence* (New York: Warner Books, 1988), 95-99.

2. Leslie F. Barneby, "American University Admission Requirements for Home Schooled Applicants," *Dissertation Abstracts International* 47, no. 3 (1986): 798A.

3. Colfax, *Homeschooling for Excellence*, 99.

4. Judy Gelner, *College Admissions: A Guide for Homeschoolers* (Sedalia, Colo.: Poppyseed Press, 1988), 1.

5. Ibid., 5.

6. Ibid., 78.

7. Ibid., 80.

8. *Growing Without Schooling* 46 (1 Aug. 1986): 4.

9. Gelner, see note *College Admissions*, 4, 83-84.

10. Nancy Wallace, telephone conversation with author, 15 Dec. 1988.

11. Ibid.

12. Ibid.

13. Barneby, "American University Admission Requirements."

14. Colfax, *Homeschooling for Excellence*, 99.

15. *Peterson's Independent Study Catalog* (Princeton: Peterson's Guides, 1986) lists hundreds of correspondence high school, college, and graduate school programs; *Bear's Guide to Non-Traditional Degrees* (Berkeley: Ten Speed Press, 1988) focuses on correspondence college and graduate programs; and *Alternatives in Education* by Mark and Helen Hegener (Tonasket, Wash.: Home Education Press, 1987) includes a useful chapter, "Alternative Higher Education," outlining several unique schools and programs.

16. Helpful private schools include the following: Clonlara, Home-Based Education Program, 1289 Jewett Street, Ann Arbor, MI 48104; Santa Fe Community School, P.O. Box 2241, Santa Fe, NM 87504; and School of Home Learning, P.O. Box 92, Escondido, CA 92025.

17. *Growing Without Schooling* 67 lists twelve friendly school districts, a number that represents only those wishing to be listed. Other school districts willing to aid home schooling families prefer to remain anonymous. To inquire about cooperative school districts in your area, write to Holt Associates, 2269 Massachusetts Ave., Cambridge, MA 02140.

18. Every state offers a high school equivalency exam. For details, contact your state department of education.

19. *Growing Without Schooling* 45 (1 June 1985): 5.

20. *Growing Without Schooling* 42 (1 Dec. 1984): 1.

21. *Growing Without Schooling* 47 (1 Oct. 1985): 10.

22. *Growing Without Schooling* 49 (1 Feb. 1986): 13.

23. *Growing Without Schooling* 50 (1 Apr. 1986): 3.

24. Colfax, *Homeschooling for Excellence*, 88, 91.

Is Home Schooling for Everyone?

Joan Armon

My stomach felt tight and queasy, my hands were sweating, and my heart was beating wildly. I held my children's small hands firmly as I led them through the heavy doors. It seemed that all eyes were on us as we entered the office. The secretary seemed exceedingly polite. The man in the next office appeared uncomfortable as he greeted us. I felt hot and fought to overcome a sense of dread as I filled in the admission forms.

Yet underneath this tangle of fear there was a calmness. In my innermost self I felt peaceful, knowing I was taking the next step in our family's evolution. It wasn't easy, though, to admit that part of our evolutionary process included allowing our children to attend a public school.

This process began even before our children were born. As we left the school, I remembered that my husband and I had often discussed what sort of education we wanted for the children we hoped to have. After much thought, reading, and discussion during the years before and after our two children came to us, our ideas regarding the children's education centered on several basic beliefs. We believed that children should be encouraged to value themselves, their fellow beings, the earth and her creatures; develop their special talents through use of the whole brain (intuition and intellect); and question, explore, create, synthesize and transcend limits.

We began the education of our children by giving special care to their early years. As Joseph Chilton Pearce stated in *Magical Child* (Dutton, 1977), "To nurture the magical child is a full-time responsibility." We knew this to be so, for the magical child is one who is allowed to learn by following his or her inner wisdom rather than the outer world's anxieties and often unnatural demands. We did not want the magical knowing within our children to be destroyed, so we spent many hours providing them with opportunities for exploration, questioning, and experimentation amidst much affection and humor.

We haven't been perfect parents, sometimes giving too much challenge or not enough, or being overanxious about their learning, or being too strict or too lax. But we have worked together within an agreed-upon philosophy, based primarily on seeing ourselves as supportive, loving resources and catalysts to their unfolding.

When our oldest child reached preschool age, she attended a Waldorf school, an educational system founded by Rudolf Steiner in Germany at the turn of the century. Our belief in the importance of integrating the intellectual, emotional, physical, and spiritual growth of a child was reinforced there. The emphasis on the creative, imaginative powers rather than the intellectual processes of young children was refreshing, as was the specific philosophical agreement shared by the teachers.

A disadvantage was the lack of tolerance for those not espousing Steiner's anthroposophical tenets. The lack of acceptance of modern technology, for example, seemed dangerously narrow. We felt that rather than demanding that our children shun such things as television or machines, it would be wiser to help them learn to balance their inner needs with use of the existing technologies of our culture. We wanted to offer them a middle way of shared decision-making in regard to conscientious use of what we decided to be sometimes useful communications mediums. We have since come to realize that perhaps tolerance varies from school to school within the Waldorf system, and we feel that, if affordable, it is on the whole an excellent educational alternative.

Following relocation to an area where the only schooling available was public school, we educated our children at home, believing that in public school they would be locked into timetables not their own and treated indifferently, with no regard for their individual talents— that their creativity and wonder would be suppressed, their reverence for life and things of the spirit crushed. The opportunities for a flexible learning environment at home were exciting. Advantage could be taken of situations and questions to seize the "teachable moment." A logical integration of math, language arts, science, and art was possible in many real-life learning experiences. There was no concern with competition or grade-level performance. We knew exactly what our children were learning, and were able to imbue that learning with our life philosophy.

But the isolation was insurmountable. Although our children were very independent and responsible within our home, they became surprisingly dependent and introverted outside our home. Such reaction may not be typical of other home schooled children, but we noticed it in our formerly outgoing daughter and son.

Since my husband worked full-time outside our home, the responsibility of seeking and creating educational experiences for our children fell almost solely on me. The network of adults and children engaged in home schooling that I sought was nonexistent in the community, except for several families whose children were already in school and who were sympathetic but unwilling or unable to undertake the demands of home schooling, or families who had infants and said they would educate their children at home some day, but who had no idea of what was really involved. I had read in John Holt's newsletter about a group of families in Canada who shared the educational responsibilities of their children. The kids would spend a week at one home studying several subjects in depth, then move on to another home for a week or two. That sort of interaction sounded ideal.

The research findings of Swiss psychologist Jean Piaget were familiar to me and often came to mind. After years of observing the behavior of children, he concluded that essential learning at cognitive and emotional levels occurs through peer interaction. Observant parents and teachers know this to be so. I actually felt that our children were regressing in some ways in these areas. It became more evident each day that contact on a regular basis with other children and adults was essential not only for our children, but also for me. I felt a need for support and sharing with other adults in my situation. I also believed it was important that our children learn from several adults with different methods, talents, and viewpoints.

As our children grew older, I felt their needs were not being met. It was easy for the three of us to get on each other's nerves over little things. I had to work hard at maintaining harmony among us and at dividing my time evenly between domestic chores and educational activities, both academic and physical.

I felt despair over our petty arguments but most of all over my daughter's emerging independence and increasingly hostile refusals to accept my assistance in regard to learning tasks. I tried a variety of approaches. I sat next to her and helped her with her work, or I suggested things for her to do while I did my chores. I took both children as many places as I could—to help with the family shopping or to do their own shopping; to visit old folks or anyone else we could find at home; to visit the library, coffee shop, park, river, or museums and grandparents in the city three hours away—yet all along I kept wondering, "Am I doing enough to meet our children's educational needs?"

Our best days were those on which we didn't attempt any academics—when I did a minimal amount of my chores with their help, then read to them and played with them. I hoped that their need to read, write, and solve math problems would emerge. It did so only sporadically. Did that mean that the culture expected too much or something wholly inappropriate of children, I wondered? The lack of "time on task" in reading, math, and handwriting bothered me, although I reminded myself that allowing education based on our children's inner developmental needs was, after all, a major reason we had chosen home schooling. I came to feel, on the one hand, that practice on a daily basis was important; on the other hand, I began to question what was really essential for our children to know. I did not want to handicap them by not teaching them what they needed to know, but neither did I want to submit them to unnecessary learning inappropriate to their holistic needs.

I often heard from our children, "What can we do?" My first reaction was usually to suggest several choices available to them, but I wondered inwardly if they shouldn't be at the point of greater independence and self motivation. In the evenings I wrestled with the questions "Am I meeting any of their needs?" and "Why are we all so unhappy?" I admitted to myself that we were hungry for contact with people. I wondered if Piaget's findings about the role of peer interaction in relation to a child's learning were more important than I had realized.

Perhaps there are some families for whom home schooling is workable: either a family whose children are very sensitive and need shelter from the world; one whose children are exceptionally bright and self-motivated and for whom a school schedule would impede a driving need to learn; or one whose children can join a network of other families sharing similar beliefs and goals. Our children clearly did not choose to learn from me, and we discussed the matter as a family for

MARILYN NOLT

weeks. Each of us explained our thoughts and feelings, and we finally agreed together that we would try school for a year, then decide what was best.

I felt despair at sending our children to public school. Hence the dread described earlier upon registering them at school. When I learned from our daughter that she was being sent to remedial reading, I felt sick and guilty—but only for a short time. I reminded myself that it was unfair and unnecessary to expect our kids to fit exactly into any arbitrarily designed learning environment and that we had chosen to educate our children at home specifically so that they could learn according to their own inner needs. That was and is an honorable, valid quest. I realized that the matter of when and how to offer learning tasks for optimal assimilation and accommodation by each student was a hot issue in education (and remains a major issue among educators today).

Those first weeks were difficult. After several months, however, my despair dissipated as the children came home tired but exuberant about friends they had made. I could not agree with John Holt's claim that children are corrupted by socializing with their peers; this was a pessimistic view, I thought. The few disruptive or mean students with whom our kids have had contact have sparked discussions at home and been the source of our children's concern and empathy. I have also come to disagree with other of Holt's claims about education and children's needs. His ideas sound good, but has he ever been home with children day after day, year after year, to experience what he advocates?

After most of the day apart, we were glad to see each other. Our children were full of stories about each day; they observed and analyzed the words and actions of their classmates and teachers, and they had a chance to compare their belief systems with those of others. I was impressed with their evaluations and the fact that their experiences seemed to strengthen their beliefs and our relationship.

Both children are now among the top students in their classes, proof to themselves that they could fit in. I once felt that I didn't want them to fit in with the average American way of life, but I've come to value the dictum "to be in the world but not of it." I've also come to see the importance of peer friendships balanced with continual questioning of tradition and of values held by others. Our children have learned that our philosophy and some aspects of our lifestyle differ from that of most of their classmates, but they also have learned that such things are a personal matter.

Although I feel that, for now, we have found a balanced way of meeting our children's needs, their current educational experience is not without disadvantages. Time spent on learning tasks is important to a degree, but it's easily overdone in school, resulting in boredom and lack of challenge. While strict scheduling allows time to be spent regularly on learning tasks, it also leads to the isolation of subject matter and skills within each subject. It is often difficult for students to sense the overall picture and to understand why they must learn what is presented to them or how it relates to their lives. There are few activities calling for deeper levels of thinking; instead, most schoolwork demands only minimal thinking processes. Finally, competition among students is sometimes overemphasized, resulting in a stress-filled environment where, as recent research has shown, thought, innovation, risk taking, and self-confidence are paralyzed.

With such disadvantages in mind, we've found that our children need us more than ever. We feel it is important to be sensitive to their emerging talents and to provide materials, time, and guidance to develop them. We conscientiously offer them opportunities for divergent, creative thought through discussions, games, reading, or projects.

Certainly the job of the school is a difficult one, and this is compounded by the numbers of children involved. In working with teachers (and as a teacher myself this past year), I've found many of them to be warm, loving people. I've seen how important it is for a teaching staff to establish common goals and a philosophy of learning, not only in theory but also in practice. I've also been surprised at the number of concerned parents I've met who have been critical of the schools. I felt that many criticisms have been petty, revolving around disagreements between teachers and students. Few parents have questioned school officials regarding educational policies or goals. Surely, parents in agreement about what is necessary for educational excellence would be a powerful force in determining, along with teachers and administrators, the direction of a school. The burden of a school is a tremendous one that should be shared by all of the adults in the community.

RESOURCES

The following is not intended to be a comprehensive list of materials and services of use to home schoolers but rather a selective resource guide for those parents who wish to help shape their children's learning experience. For reasons of space, many fine books, organizations, and materials mentioned elsewhere in this book are not included here.

Books

Albert, Linda. *Coping with Kids and School.* New York: E. P. Dutton, 1984.
Helps answer questions about what happens to your children in school, how to take an active part in their education, and what to do when problems arise. Resource organizations for parents are included.

Armstrong, Thomas. *In Their Own Way: Discovering and Encouraging Your Child's Personal Learning Style.* Los Angeles: Jeremy P. Tarcher, Inc., 1987.
Guide for parents and teachers to help understand "underachieving" children's needs and capabilities. Focuses on seven different learning modalities: linguistic, spatial, kinesthetic (bodily), logical-mathematical, musical, interpersonal, and intrapersonal.

Cusick, Lois. *Waldorf Parenting Handbook.* Spring Valley, N.Y.: St. George Publications, 1984.
Developed to meet the needs of young parents and teachers interested in Waldorf psychology and curriculum. Examines Rudolf Steiner's ideas as they apply to growing children and their educational surroundings.

Hegener, Mark and Helen. *Alternatives in Education: Family Choices in Learning.* Tonasket, Wash.: Home Education Press, 1987.
An excellent overview of alternative education, with an emphasis on home schooling. Comprehensive information on alternative higher education is also given. A practical guide that will put the most apprehensive parent at ease. Chapter titles include "Alternative Education," "Home Schooling," and "Correspondence Schools and Programs."

Holt, John. *Escape from Childhood.* Cambridge: Holt Associates 1984.
—. *Freedom and Beyond.* Cambridge: Holt Associates, 1984.
—. *How Children Fail.* Rev. ed. New York: Dell, 1982.
—. *How Children Learn.* Rev. ed. New York: Dell, 1986.
—. *Never Too Late.* Cambridge: Holt Associates, 1984.
—. *Teach Your Own: New and Hopeful Path for Parents and Educators.* New York: Dell, 1986.
—. *Learning All the Time.* Menlo Park: Addison-Wesley, 1989.
Books by educator and home schooling advocate John Holt which contain his philosophies on children and home schooling.

Hubbs, Don. *Home Education Resource Guide.* Tempe: Bluebird Publishing, 1989.
Filled with resources on such topics as legal information, textbooks, workbooks, educational software, newsletters, and home school support groups and organizations.

Montessori, Maria. *The Discovery of the Child.* New York: Ballantine Books, 1980.
A good introduction to the philosophy and teaching methods of this eminent educator. Areas of instruction covered are reading, writing, speech, music, and art.
—. *The Secret of Childhood.* New York: Ballantine Books, 1981.
Offers insight into the Montessori method of learning. Here, Maria Montessori describes the child warmly and with the exactness of the scientist. She also discusses materials and techniques needed to release the learning potential in children.

Pagnoni, Mario. *The Complete Home Educator: A Comprehensive Guide to Modern Home-Teaching*. Burdett, N.Y.: Larson Publications, 1984.
Contains information in support of home schooling, plus information about the use of the computer as a learning tool. Some sample chapters are "Why Home-School?," "What the Law Says," "Getting Acquainted with Computers," and "Educational Software." Foreword by John Holt.

Pride, Mary. *The Big Book of Home Learning*. Westchester, Ill.: Crossway Books, 1986.
—. *The Next Book of Home Learning*. Westchester, Ill.: Crossway Books, 1987.
Well worth any money invested, as the returns are plentiful. Mary Pride has done her homework and presents exhaustive lists of organizations, magazines, school suppliers, and other materials of use to home schoolers, as well as legal information and concise summaries of various educational philosophies. Written in a clear, warm, chatty style.

Priesnitz, Wendy. *School Free*. Unionville, Ont.: Village Books, 1987.
A highly acclaimed how-to book for home-based educators which includes information on legalities and policies for all Canadian provinces; how to guide your children's learning; deciding on assessment (to test or not to test); the uses of computers in home-based learning; how to deal with objections from other people; and providing socialization opportunities.

Querido, Rene M. *Creativity in Education: The Waldorf Approach*. San Francisco: H. S. Dakin Company, 1984.
Seven lectures given at the San Francisco Waldorf School. Querido describes an educational approach that has as its goal the balanced development of the whole child: hand and heart as well as mind.

Reed, Donn. *The Home-School Challenge*. New Brunswick: Brook Farm Books, 1985.
Offers views on how and why home schooling has become popular. Home school father Donn Reed gives practical and supportive

information on home schooling, using amusing anecdotes of his
and his children's experiences. Some chapter titles are "Why We
Teach at Home," "But I Don't Know How to Teach," "What
Materials Do We Need?," and "The Subjects We Teach, and Why,
and How."

—. *The First Home-School Catalogue.* 2d ed., rev. New Brunswick:
Brook Farm Books, 1986.
Overflowing with practical, engaging ideas for learning at home.
Presents many categories that parents perhaps would have over-
looked. Some of the many topics covered are adolescence, beginning to read, books, dictionaries, facts, magazines, organizations,
and resources and teaching aids.

Wade, Theodore E., Jr., et al. *The Home School Manual.* Auburn,
Calif.: Gazelle Publications, 1986.
Presents helpful guidelines for teaching at home, as well as reasons
for doing so. All subjects are thoroughly discussed. Some chapter
titles are "The Home School Alternative," "Teaching Several
Children," "Teaching Reading," "Teaching Math," and "Teaching
Science."

Wallace, Nancy. *Better Than School.* Burdett, N.Y.: Larson Publications, Inc., 1983. Available from Holt Associates, 2269 Massachusetts Ave., Cambridge, MA 02140.
Day-to-day account of observations and activities of a home
schooling family, written in an accessible style any parent can
relate to. Some of the topics covered are: "A Day in Our Life,"
"The First Six Months," "School at Home," and "The Spring
Ritual: Testing Evaluations, Home-Schooling Applications."

Magazines and Newsletters
Creative Learning Magazine, P.O. Box 37568, San Antonio, TX
78237-0568.
Offers activity and learning ideas around a monthly theme.

Growing Without Schooling, 2269 Massachusetts Ave., Cambridge, MA
02140.
Bimonthly newsletter, started by John Holt in 1977, that brings
together home schooling families from all over the country. Each

issue includes articles by home schoolers about what works and what does not work for them, a sharing of concerns; updates on the legal status of home schooling for each state, plus a directory of home school families.

Home Education Magazine, P.O. Box 218, Tonasket, WA 98855.
Bimonthly magazine for home school families. Features articles that address the concerns of parents who want to be directly involved in the education of their children. Regular departments include a two-page resource section, a children's page, letters from readers, news from around the states, and an in-depth look at curricula and resource materials.

Home School Gazette, P.O. Box 359, Burtonville, MD 20866
National newspaper published by and for home schoolers. Its purpose is to "motivate children to write and teach them how to develop their writing skills." Each news and feature story, photograph, drawing, cartoon, review, update, and editorial is created by home school children between the ages of four and eighteen. In addition, each issue contains writing tips by Home School Gazette's publisher, Ron Brackin.

The Teaching Home, 12311 NE Brazee, Portland, OR 97230; (503) 253-9633.
Shares information and provides support for Christian home schooling families and organizations. Readers share their experiences, and national leaders and writers regularly contribute columns or features. Up-to-date information on state laws and resources.

Unschoolers Network, 2 Smith Street, Farmingdale, NJ 07727.
Nine months of the year subscribers receive a one- to two-page resource and announcement bulletin; three months of the year, they receive a twenty- to twenty-four page home schooling compendium with news, resources, ideas, articles, book reviews, and letters from readers. This organization also provides useful booklets, books and casette tapes, and videotapes.

Curricula
Calvert School, Tuscany Road, Baltimore, MD 21210; (301) 243-6030.
A structured, textbook-oriented, traditional course of study. Calvert's emphasis is on developing creative thought and communication as well as basic skills. Courses of study include art (painting, sculpture, and architecture), social studies, history (which includes mythology), geography, handwriting, science, math, and language arts. Free brochure with detailed outline of subjects and topics is available.

Clonlara School, Home Based Education Program, 1289 Jewett, Ann Arbor, MI 48104.
Home Based Education Program (HBEP) provides home schooling families the following: family tuition rate; a curriculum for each student; math and communications skills guidebooks; a newsletter, "The Learning Edge," published five times a year (free to HBEP enrollees and available to others for $12 a year); contacts; time schedule; monthly record reports; interest survey; pen pals; records; standardized testing; diploma; guidance; and information on regulations.

Home Study International, 6940 Carroll Ave., Takoma Park, MD 20912; (202) 722-6570 (general information), (202) 722-6579 (enrollment information).
Offers a standard, structured program for home schooling. Established in 1909 as a service to Seventh-Day Adventists, this organization has grown into a major supplier of home study programs. Subjects include art and music, Bible (optional), health/science, language, math, physical education (grades 3-6), reading, social studies, spelling, and handwriting. Monthly payment plans are available. Grades K-12.

Educational Supply Catalogs
Addison-Wesley Publishing Co., 2725 Sand Hill Road, Menlo Park, CA, 94025; (800) 447-2226.
Infant/toddler; grades preschool-2: early-childhood education covering language development and reading readiness, early mathematics, early science, music, art/social development, and

language. Thirty-day return. Grades K-8: student and teacher books on mathematics, science, reading, computer education, social studies, foreign languages, and general resources. Many of the books are available in bilingual editions. Thirty day return.

Creative Publications, 5005 West 110th St., Oak Lawn, IL 60453; (800) 624-0822; (800) 435-5843 (Illinois).
Grades K-12: innovative books, posters, games, and "hands-on" materials for mathematics, language arts, and science. Thirty-day full refund or exchange.

Educators Publishing Service, Inc., 75 Moulton Street, Cambridge, MA 02238-9101; (800) 225-5750; (617) 547-6706 (Massachusetts). Grades K-12: this company offers both teacher's manuals and student workbooks. Subjects covered are vocabulary, phonics, reading, spelling, handwriting and typing, literature, grammar, composition, math, and foreign languages. They also supply college entrance reviews. A separate language and learning disabilities catalog is available. Only specific titles can be examined for a thirty-day period. No other returns may be made without written authorization.

ETR Associates, *Network Publications*, P.O. Box 1830, Santa Cruz, CA 95061-1830; (800) 321-4407.
Educational resources in family living, human sexuality, HIV/AIDS prevention, reproductive health, and drug abuse prevention.

Good Apple, 1204 Buchanan St., P.O. Box 299, Carthage, IL 62321-0299; (800) 435-7234, (217) 357-3981 (Illinois and foreign). Grades preschool-9: teaching materials covering timely teacher resources, math, reading, writing, language arts, arts and crafts, teacher helpers, social studies, science and health, and self-concept.

John Holt's Book and Music Store, Holt Associates, Inc., 2269, Massachusetts Ave., Cambridge, MA 02140; (617) 864-3100.
A catalog of books and videotapes. Categories include alternatives to college, children and learning, gadgets, history and geog-

raphy, learning disabilities, math, play, puzzles, and tests. All of John Holt's books are available through this company. Fifteen-day return.

Learning at Home, P.O. Box 270, Honaunau, HI 96726; (808) 328-9669.
Grades 1-6 plus a resource guide for grades 7-12: provides teaching materials that enhance the learning experience rather than offering specifics of instruction. Subjects covered are the three Rs, plus literature and poetry, social studies, art, science, and computers. This catalog also has materials for test preparation. Fifteen days given for returns and exchanges. Items returned must be in salable condition.

McGraw-Hill, 1200 Northwest 63rd Street, P.O. Box 25308, Oklahoma City, OK 73125; (800) 654-8608; (405) 840-1444 (Oklahoma).
Grades K-8: subjects offered are reading, language arts, math, social studies, early childhood, bilingual/bicultural/ESL, science/health and safety, foreign language, and home economics. Computer software available.
Grades 7-adult: titles under language arts include "Themes in Science Fiction," "American English Today," and "Writing: From Inner World to Outer World." Foreign languages include Spanish, French, German, and Italian. Social studies titles include "American Government" and "Our Constitution and What It Means." Under science, health, and safety, titles include "The Stress of Life" and "Sportsmanlike Driving." Titles under home economics include "Nutrition Almanac," "Parenting and Teaching Young Children," and "Your Marriage and Family Living."

Merrill Publishing Company, P.O. Box 508, Columbus, OH 43216; (800) 848-1567; (614) 890-1111 (Ohio).
Grades K-12: covers language arts, math, science and health, and social studies. Books, videotapes, and computer software available.

Modern Curriculum Press, 13900 Prospect Rd., Cleveland, OH 44136; (800) 321-3106.

Grades preschool-8: subjects include phonics and spelling, integrated language arts, literature and writing, thinking and reading skills, reference, math, science, social studies, and testing.

Scott, Foresman and Company, 1900 East Lake Ave., Glenview, IL 60025; (800) 554-4411.
Grades K-8: offers guides to reading and literature, language arts, math, social studies, science, health and physical education, teacher resources, English as a second language, bilingual materials for Spanish-speaking students, foreign language, preschool and kindergarten materials, and educational software.

Silver Burdett & Ginn, Customer Service Center, 4343 Equity Dr., P.O. Box 2649, Columbus, OH 43216.
Grades K-9: subjects covered include reading, language arts, math, science, social studies, music, and bilingual instruction.

U.S. Government Books, Superintendent of Documents, U.S. Government Printing Office, Washington, D.C. 20402.
A fifty-six-page catalog of publications for sale by the Government Printing Office. Almost one thousand government publications are organized into subject categories, including careers, education, environment and weather, history, law and law enforcement, and space exploration.

Wilcox & Follett Book Company, 1000 West Washington Blvd., Chicago, IL 60607; (800) 621-4272.
Textbook and workbook catalog for elementary and high school featuring fine used textbooks and new workbooks by all major publishers. Current and older editions available.

Foreign Languages
Audio-Form, The Language Source, 96 Broad St., Guilford, CT 06437; (800) 243-1234 (9:00 a.m.-6:00 p.m. EST); 1-453-9794 (Connecticut residents).
Do-it-yourself audiocassette tapes for basic, intermediate, and advanced learners. Language programs for almost every language (Afrikaans to Zulu!). Also provided is a video for American sign language.

Latin

Bolchazy-Carducci Publishers, 1000 Brown St., Unit 101, Wauconda, IL 60084; (312) 526-4344.
    A catalog of textbooks on Latin, Greek, and classical scholarship.

Ecce Romani, Longman Inc., 95 Church St., White Plains, NY 10601.
    Latin program.

Math

Cuisenaire Co., 12 Church St., New Rochelle, NY 10805.
    Math materials, especially Cuisenaire rods.

Key Curriculum Press, P.O. Box 2304, Berkeley, CA 94702; (800) 338-7638; (415) 548-2304
    Offers low-cost math workbooks for grades 1-12. Basic math through geometry is covered. Miquon math materials are available. Computer software available for grades 2-10 on whole numbers, fractions, and decimals.

Science

NASCO, 901 Janesville Ave., P.O. Box 901, Fort Atkinson, WI 53538-0901; (800) 558-9595; (414) 563-2446.
    Offers a complete line of materials on elementary science, biology, earth science, physical science apparatus, chemistry, and more. Videocassettes and computer software available.

Learning Things Inc., P.O. Box 436, Arlington, MA 02174.
    Science materials; good abacus selection. Catalog offers great photos and information about a wide variety of inexpensive science materials.

Odyssey, Department 07070, P.O. Box 1612, Waudesha, WI 53187.
    Monthly magazine about outer space, space exploration, and astronomy. For ages 8-14.

Things of Science, 1950 Landings Blvd., Suite 202, Sarasota, FL 34231.
    Each month members receive a kit filled with all the materials needed to conduct interesting and educational science experi-

ments. A booklet containing background information and detailed, easy-to-follow instructions explains why experiment results occur as they do; the basic scientific principles and facts are illustrated. Ages 9-14.

Social Studies
Cobblestone Publishing, Inc., 20 Grove St. , Peterborough, NH 03458.
Produces three magazines designed for ages eight to fifteen. *Faces* takes young readers to far-off lands to experience the lives and cultures of people. *Cobblestone* presents American history through a lively mix of stories, games, contests, maps, cartoons, songs, poems, recipes, and more. *Classical Calliope* introduces a child to the classical heritage of our civilization.

Computer Software
American Educational Computer, Suite 505, 7506 N. Broadway Ext., Oklahoma City, OK 73116.
Educational and special-interest computer software and video products. Subjects include reading, spelling, math, history, science, geography, and foreign language. Grades K-12.

Scholastic Inc., 2931 East McCarty St., P.O. Box 7502, Jefferson City, MO 65102; (800) 541-5513; (800) 392-2179 (Missouri).
Educational computer software. Subjects include: early learning, language arts, math, social studies, and science. Grades K-12.

Legal Organizations
Home School Legal Defense Association, Paeonian Springs, VA 22129; (703) 882-3838
Provides low-cost method of obtaining quality legal defense should the need arise. Basic cost of membership is $100 per year, per family. Membership benefits include complete legal representation in any court proceeding at no additional charge beyond the membership fee and a newsletter covering legal issues and other matters of concern to home schooling parents.

Organizations
Canadian Alliance of Home Schoolers, 195 Markville Road, Union-
    ville, Ontario L3R, 4V8, Canada; (416) 470-7930.
    A ten-year-old national clearinghouse of legal and practical infor-
    mation which offers support and advocacy for Canadian home
    schoolers.

Holt Associates, 2269 Massachusetts Ave., Cambridge, MA 02140;
    (617) 864-3100.
    A clearinghouse for information on home education and the
    ideas of the late writer/educator John Holt. Publishes magazine
    Growing Without Schooling; also offers a mail-order book and
    music catalog.

The Moore Foundation, Box 1, Camas, WA 98607; (206) 835-2736.
    Founded by education pioneers Raymond and Dorothy Moore. A
    not-for-profit health, education, and welfare foundation dedi-
    cated to restoring the family. Leading researchers in home-based
    education.

National Homeschool Association (NHA), Box 167, Rodeo, NM
    88056.
    A nonprofit, grass-roots organization, started in November 1988,
    that is dedicated to strengthening the home schooling movement
    by providing services to home schoolers and anyone interested in
    home schooling. Services offered by NHA include a quarterly
    newsletter, networking service, a resource referral service, and a
    single parent network. Membership is required.

CONTRIBUTORS

Ashley Montagu, the prominent anthropologist and social biologist, has taught at many universities, including Harvard, Rutgers, and Princeton. He is the author of numerous books and articles.

Peggy O'Mara is the editor and publisher of *Mothering* magazine. She is also a poet and a writer. Her children are Lally, Finnie, Bram, and Nora.

Andy LePage is a foster parent, consultant to public schools at the Florida Center for Self-Esteem, and author of *Transforming Education: The New 3 Rs*. He lives in Tampa, Florida. To order *Transforming Education: The New 3Rs*, send $14.95 plus $2.00 shipping to Oakmore House, 14782 West Village Dr., Suite 399, Tampa, FL 33624.
"How We Learn" first appeared in *Mothering* 49 (Fall 1988).

Herbert Kohl lives in Point Arena, California. His children are Tonia, Erica, and Joshua. He is both a talented educator and a prolific writer. Among his more important books are *36 Children* (1967); *Reading: How To* (1970, currently out of print); *Growing Minds* (1985); and *A Book of Puzzlements*, vols. 1, 2 (1986). His most recent book is *The Question Is College* (Times Books).
"A Decent Learning Situation" first appeared in *Mothering* 49 (Fall 1988).

Ed Clark is an educational and organization consultant who lives in Warrenville, Illinois. He has a varied background as clergyman, therapist, and college administrator and educator. He and his wife,

Margaret, have four grown children and three grandchildren.

"Nature and Nurture" originally appeared as "Nature or Nurture?" in *Mothering* 47 (Spring 1988).

Thomas Armstrong, Ph.D., is a psychologist, learning specialist, lecturer, consultant, and author of *The Radiant Child* and *In Their Own Way*.

"Utopian Schools in The Here and Now" first appeared in *Mothering* 52 (Summer 1989).

Raymond and Dorothy Moore are pioneers in home-based education and in documenting the needs of children in families and homes. Their *Home School Burnout* (Brentwood, Tenn.: Wolgemuth and Hyatt, 1988) is a blue book on home schooling. It follows a series of carefully researched books, including *Home Grown Kids, Home Spun Schools, Home Style Teaching,* and *Home Made Health* (from Word Books); *Home Built Health* (from Thos. Nelson); *Better Late Than Early* and *School Can Wait*. For information on the last two books, or extensive data on home education, send an SASE to: The Moore Foundation, Box 1, Camas, WA 98607.

"Home-Grown Kids" is an expanded, updated version of an essay of the same name that appeared in *Mothering* 21 (Fall 1981).

Ron Miller is the editor of *Holistic Education Review*. He has worked as a Montessori teacher and a camp counselor with children of various ages and has extensively studied the history of "holistic" education in American culture. *Holistic Education Review*, a quarterly journal that brings together the entire range of person-centered approaches in education, is available at $16 per year. Write to P.O. Box 1476, Greenfield, MA 01302 for a free sample copy.

"The History of Alternative Education" first appeared in *Mothering* 50 (Winter 1989).

Michael S. Shepherd, Ed.D., has taught in a bilingual educational program for the past seven years. He and his wife, Dana, operate Home Education Services to assist parents in home tutoring, curriculum planning, and information gathering. They live in Dallas, Texas, with their daughter, Lindsey Leigh.

"Homeschooling: A Legal View" first appeared in *Mothering* 47

(Spring 1988). It was adapted with permission from chapter 5 of his dissertation, "The Home Schooling Movement: An Emerging Conflict in American Education." Copies of the entire text are available at $20 each from Home Education Services, 728 S. Winnetka Ave., Dallas, TX 75208.

Susanne Miller is associate editor for *Mothering* magazine. She and her husband, Neil, live with their two children, Jeremiah and Damiana, in Santa Fe, New Mexico.

Ross Campbell is a teacher. He lives with his family, Marianne Aaal, Aragorn, and Linnea, in Sweden.

"Home Schooling: State by State" is an updated version of the article by the same name that appeared in *Mothering* 47 (Spring 1988).

Dr. Myron Lieberman is the author of *Privatization and Educational Choice*, a Cato Institute book (New York: St. Martin's Press, 1989).

Geeta Dardick, writer and photographer, specializes in nonfiction articles on business, products, parenting, farming, travel, disability, sports, and health. Her many writing credits include *Reader's Digest, California Magazine, Mother Earth News, Woman's Day*, and *Parenting*. She is also the author of *Home Butchering and Meat Preservation* (Blue Summit, Pa.: Tab Books, 1986), which was a main selection for the How-To Book Club and an alternative selection for Outdoor Life Book Club.

"Home Study and the Public Schools" is an updated version of "Independent Study and the Public Schools," which first appeared in *Mothering* 36 (Summer 1985).

Patrick Farenga is president of Holt Associates and managing editor of *Growing Without Schooling*. Pat and his wife, Day, have two daughters, Lauren and Allison.

"Home Schoolers and College" first appeared in *Mothering* 53 (Fall 1989).

Aaron Falbel is a member of the Learning and Epistemology Group at the Massachusetts Institute of Technology. His main area of research is the social context of learning. He has recently completed an in-depth case study of a small alternative school in Copenhagen, Denmark, entitled "Friskolen 70: An Ethnographically Informed Inquiry into the Social Context of Learning."

Margaret Yatsevitch Phinney is an elementary school teacher, a reading consultant, and a reading-resource specialist who regularly gives literacy development workshops and in-service training for parents, teachers, and administrators. Margaret's son Alexi attends Williams College, and her husband, Robert, is a sculptor. She and her family live in Massachusetts.

"Whole Reading" first appeared in *Mothering* 42 (Winter 1987), and "Invented Spelling" in *Mothering* 43 (Spring 1987).

Anne Running Tabbut lives in Elk Mound, Wisconsin, with her children, Julia and Andrew. She taught students with learning disabilities in public elementary schools for five years before becoming a parent. For the past ten years, she has worked as a free-lance copy-editor and writer.

"Reading: A Learning Experience That's Fun" first appeared in *Mothering* 20 (Summer 1981).

John McMahon lives in Santa Fe, New Mexico.

"Teaching Your Kids to Read" first appeared in *Mothering* 18 (Winter 1981).

Jacque Williamson enjoys educational consulting as well as mothering and home schooling Nathan, Ryan, and Rachel. Her husband, Fred, is a self-employed woodworker. They live in the foothills of Crozet, Virginia.

"Easing Children into Writing" first appeared in *Mothering* 37 (Fall 1985).

Amy Malick is the mother of Sara, Matt, and Andy. Amy's husband, Larry, is a lawyer. They live in Durango, Colorado. Formerly a high school teacher of English and journalism, Amy is now news editor of the *Durango Herald*.

"Andy Writes a Poem" originally appeared in *Mothering* 43 (Spring 1987).

Elizabeth Wild currently teaches English and social studies in an alternative school for pregnant teenagers. In addition, she is the author of a children's novel, *Along Came a Black Bird* (Lippincott, 1988). She lives with her husband and three children in Fairport, New York.

"Science In The Home" first appeared in *Mothering* 33 (Fall 1984).

Claudia Bumgarner Kirby is the mother of Quinn. She and her husband, Brad, own and operate Birdsong, a used book and record shop in Albuquerque, New Mexico. She is also an artist and calligrapher and creator of "Please Packs," activity cards for young children.

"Nurturing Art" first appeared in *Mothering* 24 (Summer 1982).

Patricia Savage, mother of five, lives in New Hampshire, where she practices her craft writing journal entries, letters, and a monthly column called "Between Friends."

"In Love With Learning" first appeared in *Mothering* 25 (Fall 1982).

Kate Kerman lives with her family at The Meeting School, Thomas Road, Rindge, NH 03461. Ada is in her fourth year at the Quaker boarding high school, which is attended by a number of home schoolers. Hannah and Jesse continue to learn at home and in the community. Kate teaches, does admissions work, and is a houseparent of six teenagers with her husband, Ed.

"Home Schooling: Day by Day" first appeared in *Mothering* 23 (Spring 1982).

Nancy Wallace, author of *Better Than School* (available from Holt Associates, 2269 Massachusetts Ave., Cambridge, MA 02140), lives in Ithaca, New York. Vita looks forward to the day when she can attend art school. Ishmael lives in Philadelphia, where he studies composition and piano at the Curtis Institute of Music. Nancy's new book, *Child's Work*, will become available from Holt Associates in spring 1990.

"Home Schooling's Unique Structure" first appeared in *Mothering* 36 (Summer 1985).

J. David Colfax, a free-lance writer, is a former professor of sociology. He and his wife, Micki, a former English teacher and education researcher, have home schooled their four sons Grant, Drew, Reed, and Garth for the past 16 years on a remote mountain homestead in northern California. David and Micki are the authors of *Homeschooling for Excellence* (Warner Books, 1988), available for $8.95.

"Beyond the Classroom" was previously published in *Mothering* 41 (Fall 1986).

Heidi Priesnitz was 14 when she wrote "First Day of School at Thirteen," which first appeared in *Mothering* 42 (Winter 1987). She now studies history and English, and she is still involved in theater. Heidi published her own children's newspaper, *Kid's Stuff*, for five years. She lives with her family in Ontario, Canada, and plans to take a year off after high school to work and travel.

Penny Barker is the mother of Britton, Maggie, Dan, Ben, and Jonah. She and her husband, Richard, are British-trained Montessori teachers who have home educated all five of their children on a farm in rural Ohio. Since 1975, they have co-directed The Country School, an experiential program in family farmstead living for children six through twelve. Penny is associate editor of *Home Education Magazine*.

"The Home Schooled Teenager Grows Up" first appeared in *Mothering* 40 (Summer 1986).

Joan Armon currently lives with her husband and two teenage children near Denver. She was one of four teachers in the Vail area who proposed and implemented an alternative integrated curriculum program within the public school, a program that subsequently won a national award. After completing a master's degree in education at Stanford, she has now returned to classroom teaching to examine how the integration of home, school, and community can promote education at deeper levels.

Joan and her husband continue to believe that a public school education is only one facet of their children's education. They seek to enrich their home learning environment through such activities as nightly family read-aloud sessions of the classics, tutoring a Laotian refugee family, nature observation and camping, community college classes, and projects such as boat building, gardening, and ethnic cooking.

"Is Home Schooling For Everyone?" first appeared in *Mothering* 24 (Summer 1982).

INDEX

Other Books from John Muir Publications

Asia Through the Back Door, Rick Steves and John Gottberg (65-48-3) 336 pp. $15.95

Buddhist America: Centers, Retreats, Practices, Don Morreale (28-94-X) 400 pp. $12.95

Bus Touring: Charter Vacations, U.S.A., Stuart Warren with Douglas Bloch (28-95-8) 168 pp. $9.95

Catholic America: Self-Renewal Centers and Retreats, Patricia Christian-Meyer (65-20-3) 325 pp. $13.95

Complete Guide to Bed & Breakfasts, Inns & Guesthouses, Pamela Lanier (65-43-2) 512 pp. $15.95

Costa Rica: A Natural Destination, Ree Sheck (65-51-3) 280 pp. $15.95

Elderhostels: The Students' Choice, Mildred Hyman (65-28-9) 224 pp. $12.95

Europe 101: History & Art for the Traveler, Rick Steves and Gene Openshaw (28-78-8) 372 pp. $12.95

Europe Through the Back Door, Rick Steves (65-42-4) 432 pp. $16.95

Floating Vacations: River, Lake, and Ocean Adventures, Michael White (65-32-7) 256 pp. $17.95

Gypsying After 40: A Guide to Adventure and Self-Discovery, Bob Harris (28-71-0) 264 pp. $12.95

The Heart of Jerusalem, Arlynn Nellhaus (28-79-6) 312 pp. $12.95

Indian America: A Traveler's Companion, Eagle/Walking Turtle (65-29-7) 424 pp. $16.95

Mona Winks: Self-Guided Tours of Europe's Top Museums, Rick Steves (28-85-0) 450 pp. $14.95

The On and Off the Road Cookbook, Carl Franz (28-27-3) 272 pp. $8.50

The People's Guide to Mexico, Carl Franz (28-99-0) 608 pp. $15.95

The People's Guide to RV Camping in Mexico, Carl Franz with Steve Rogers (28-91-5) 256 pp. $13.95

Preconception: A Woman's Guide to Preparing for Pregnancy and Parenthood, Brenda Aikey-Keller (65-44-0) 236 pp. $14.95

Ranch Vacations: The Complete Guide to Guest and Resort, Fly-Fishing, and Cross-Country Skiing Ranches, Eugene Kilgore (65-30-0) 392 pp. $18.95

The Shopper's Guide to Mexico, Steve Rogers and Tina Rosa (28-90-7) 224 pp. $9.95

Ski Tech's Guide to Equipment, Skiwear, and Accessories, edited by Bill Tanler (65-45-9) 144 pp. $11.95

Ski Tech's Guide to Maintenance and Repair, edited by Bill Tanler (65-46-7) 144 pp. $11.95

A Traveler's Guide to Asian Culture, Kevin Chambers (65-14-9) 224 pp. $13.95

Traveler's Guide to Healing Centers and Retreats in North America, Martine Rudee and Jonathan Blease (65-15-7) 240 pp. $11.95

Undiscovered Islands of the Caribbean, Burl Willes (28-80-X) 216 pp. $12.95

22 Days Around the World by R. Rapoport and B. Willes (65-31-9)
22 Days in Alaska by Pamela Lanier (28-68-0)
22 Days in the American Southwest by R. Harris (28-88-5)
22 Days in Asia by R. Rapoport and B. Willes (65-17-3)
22 Days in Australia by John Gottberg (65-40-8)
22 Days in California by Roger Rapoport (28-93-1)
22 Days in China by Gaylon Duke and Zenia Victor (28-72-9)
22 Days in Dixie by Richard Polese (65-18-1)
22 Days in Europe by Rick Steves (65-63-7)
22 Days in Florida by Richard Harris (65-27-0)
22 Days in France by Rick Steves (65-07-6)
22 Days in Germany, Austria & Switzerland by Rick Steves (65-39-4)
22 Days in Great Britain by Rick Steves (65-38-6)
22 Days in Hawaii by Arnold Schuchter (65-50-5)
22 Days in India by Anurag Mathur (28-87-7)
22 Days in Japan by David Old (28-73-7)
22 Days in Mexico by S. Rogers and T. Rosa (65-41-6)
22 Days in New England by Anne Wright (28-96-6)
22 Days in New Zealand by Arnold Schuchter (28-86-9)
22 Days in Norway, Denmark & Sweden by R. Steves (28-83-4)
22 Days in the Pacific Northwest by R. Harris (28-97-4)
22 Days in Spain & Portugal by Rick Steves (65-06-8)
22 Days in the West Indies by C. & S. Morreale (28-74-5)

All 22 Days titles are 128 to 152 pages and $7.95 each, except *22 Days Around the World* and *22 Days in Europe*, which are 192 pages and $9.95.

Kidding Around Atlanta, Anne Pedersen (65-35-1) 64 pp. $9.95
Kidding Around Boston, Helen Byers (65-36-X) 64 pp. $9.95
Kidding Around the Hawaiian Islands, Sarah Lovett (65-37-8) 64 pp. $9.95
Kidding Around London, Sarah Lovett (65-24-6) 64 pp. $9.95
Kidding Around Los Angeles, Judy Cash (65-34-3) 64 pp. $9.95
Kidding Around New York City, Sarah Lovett (65-33-5) 64 pp. $9.95
Kidding Around San Francisco, Rosemary Zibart (65-23-8) 64 pp. $9.95
Kidding Around Washington, D.C., Anne Pedersen (65-25-4) 64 pp. $9.95

The Greaseless Guide to Car Care Confidence: Take the Terror Out of Talking to Your Mechanic, Mary Jackson (65-19-X) 224 pp. $14.95
How to Keep Your VW Alive (65-12-2) 424 pp. $19.95
How to Keep Your Subaru Alive (65-11-4) 480 pp. $19.95
How to Keep Your Toyota Pickup Alive (28-89-3) 392 pp. $19.95
How to Keep Your Datsun/Nissan Alive (28-65-6) 544 pp. $19.95
Off-Road Emergency Repair & Survival, James Ristow (65-26-2) 160 pp. $9.95

Address all orders and inquiries to:
John Muir Publications
P.O. Box 613
Santa Fe, NM 87504
(505) 982-4078
(505) 988-1680 FAX